W9-AEM-524

A Legal Guide for

LESBIAN AND GAY COUPLES

by Attorneys
Hayden Curry & Denis Clifford

Edited by Attorney Robin Leonard

Nolo Press • 950 Parker St., Berkeley, CA 94710

IMPORTANT

Nolo Press is committed to keeping its books up-to-date. Each new printing, whether or not it is called a new edition, has been completely revised to reflect the latest law changes. This book was printed and updated on the last date indicated below. Before you rely on information in it, you might wish to call Nolo Press, (415) 549-1976 to check whether a later printing or edition has been issued.

PRINTING HISTORY

Difference between new *editions* and *printings:*

New *printing* means there have been some minor changes, but usually not enough so that people will need to trade in or discard an earlier printing of the same edition. Obviously, this is a judgment call and any change, no matter how minor, might affect you.

New *edition* means one or more major—or a number of minor—law changes since the previous edition.

First Edition	1980
Second Edition	April 1984
Third Edition	February 1985
Fourth Edition	January 1986
Second Printing	November 1986
Fifth Edition	January 1989
Editor	Robin Leonard
Illustrations	Linda Allison
Production	Stephanie Harolde
	Michael Sigal
Book Design	Toni Ihara
	Amy Ihara

Please read this: We have done our best to give you useful and accurate information concerning legal realities of lesbian and gay couples. But please be aware that laws and procedures are constantly changing, and that you have a responsibility to double check the information you read here before relying on it. Of necessity, neither Nolo Press nor the authors make any guarantees concerning the information in this publication or any use to which it is put.

ISBN 0-87337-077-5

Library of Congress Card Catalog No.: 80-18278

Copyright © 1985, 1984, 1985, 1986, 1988 by Hayden Curry and Denis Clifford

ACKNOWLEDGEMENTS

We thank all those friends, new and old, who worked with us on this book; their assistance has been truly invaluable and working with them was fun. Special thanks to Robin Leonard for all her help updating, revising and editing this edition, Ann Heron for her interest and assistance, and Jake Warner for his continued editing contribution. Thanks also to those who read and criticized the original manuscript: Linda Gryczan; Gloria Bosque; Michael Fuchs; Linda Graham; Joseph Nieberding; Sue Saperstein; Kim Storch; Michael Thistel; Jim Duerr; Floyd S. Irvin; Patrick Ferruccio; Keith Kelgman; Donna J. Hitchens; Linda Guthrie; Zona Sage; Terri Lyons; Mary Morgan; Phyllis Lyon; Kay Clifford (Mom); Pamela Gray; and Roberta Achtenberg. And a special note of thanks to Sayre Van Young for preparing the Index.

And we thank all those who gave assistance and/or advice: Rev. Jim N. Dykes; Candi Jensen and the staff at Harry Britt's office; Pat Norman; Elizabeth W. Calaway; Donald Knutson and the staff of Gay Rights Advocates; Susie Williams; Jay Berlin; Taj Tellalian; Marynella Woods; N.S.P.; Tom; Mervin Cherrin; Robert E. Lyon; Matthew; Carol Seider; Sandy Weiker; Christie Rigg; Ronald Lee; John Schmidt; Dennis Jaeger; and the staff of the National Gay and Lesbian Task Force.

Finally, our continued appreciation to all our friends at Nolo Press: Toni Ihara, Stephanie Harolde, Barbara Hodovan, Linda Allison, John O'Donnell, Claudia Goodman-Hough, Steve Elias, Catherine Jermany, Jack Devaney, Amy Ihara, Kate Thill, Mary Randolph, Barbara Kate Repa, Albin Renauer, David Cole, Jackie Clark, Leili Eghbal, Sue Fox, Lulu Cornell, Janet Bergen, Karen Chambers, Monica Kindraka, Ken Cober and Michael Sigal.

ABOUT THE AUTHORS

Hayden Curry and Denis Clifford are partners in the Oakland, California, law firm of Clifford, Curry and Cherrin. We first met in 1967, in a special training program for recent law school graduates going into poverty law, and later worked together for several years in a neighborhood legal services office in East Oakland.

We feel this book has evolved from our earlier work with the civil rights movement and poverty law. One of the strongest conclusions we drew from our years of bringing "test cases" for the rights of poor people was that the established (or establishment) legal system was cumbersome, and generally unsympathetic to minorities. We came to believe that preventative law—people creating their own legal arrangements and avoiding courts and lawyers—was both eminently sensible and long overdue.

It's ironic, but true, that while laboring in South Florida for the rights of the economically oppressed and racial minorities, Hayden was simultaneously suppressing his own awareness of himself as an oppressed minority—a gay man. It was necessary for him to reach the healthier and more supportive climate on northern California before he could begin the process of publicly coming to terms with his identity, and be able to work overtly for his own minority group. Denis has been an observer and supporter of Hayden's coming-out process (and he hasn't exactly been standing still the last twenty-some years either).

After leaving legal services, we set up our private law practice, which has served many lesbian and gay clients. Our belief that litigation and courts should be the last resort for problem-solving was reaffirmed by our clients' experiences; we began helping them devise ways to solve their problems outside traditional (and expensive) legal remedies.

Writing this book has been a shared experience. We've both learned a lot. We don't believe people are confined to understanding only those who have the same sexual identity as they do. One of the beauties of being free is that people can learn, as we have, that our differences can bring us closer. We hope this book will do that for many lesbian/gay couples, and it was in this spirit of optimism that we worked and wrote together.

FOREWORD

There are at least some 20 million lesbians and gay men living in the United States today. These men and women represent a community that is as diverse as American society. There are gay people in every economic class, racial group, religious organization, and occupation. There are only two things all lesbians and gay men have in common. The first is that solely on the basis of their sexual identity and who they chose to love, they are feared and despised by many people in our society. An inevitable result of these intense negative feelings has been the development of numerous stereotypes about lesbians and gay men—for example, that all gay people are promiscuous, molest children, engage in sexual behavior in public, are psychologically maladjusted, and are untrustworthy. The second commonality is that for centuries these false assumptions have been the underpinnings of institutionalized discrimination against lesbians and gays.

The ugly heritage of all this is still with us, as I, and any activist attorney representing lesbians or gays, knows all too well. I was recently reminded of the depth and the inanity of this prejudice in the course of an employment discrimination case. My client had applied for a deputy sheriff position in a Northern California county, and had scored extremely well on various application tests. In the course of taking a required lie-detector test, she was asked if she had sexual relations with "people of the same sex." She answered yes. Asked when the most recent incident occurred, she responded candidly, "Last night." The Sheriff's Department immediately disqualified her as an applicant for the sole (and admitted) "reason" of her sexual orientation. I subsequently filed suit to compel the department to evaluate her application independently of any reference to her sexual preference. What bearing could that have on her job? During an administrative hearing, a psychiatrist (flown up by the Sheriff's Department from Los Angeles) testified that when gay people are under stress they act out sexually and, therefore, if my client came under stress while working in the county jail, she might molest the prisoners. The psychiatrist also testified that my client was a self-destructive personality, and that he knew that because she had admitted to being a lesbian during her lie-detector test. The psychiatrist stated that a "healthy" person would have lied. By the way, this "expert" had never met my client. Even the hearing officer was amazed by this "expert" testimony, and my client won the hearing.

Obviously, there is much that still needs to be done to remove the absurd and vicious prejudices against lesbian and gay people from our laws and institutions. It's a struggle that involves thousands and thousands of committed people, and many different arenas. One major task is to educate the public to the realities of lesbian and gay life, and to seek changes in the laws that oppress gay people. Legal changes alone are not enough. Unless we change the cultural prejudices and stereotypes that underlie oppressive laws, the real changes we seek won't be achieved. But while we all try to change the system, it's equally important to provide assistance and information that will help lesbian and gay people with the world as it now exists. One of the most dramatic changes in gay life in recent years has been the increased number of lesbian and gay couples openly living together as loving couples. This is one area in which solid legal information has long been needed, and an important reason why I am pleased to participate in the publication of this book.

For example, many gay women and men are parents. All too often they find themselves prevented from or limited in spending time with their children solely because of their sexual orientation. Even though more and more gay parents are successful in their court fights to retain custody or visitation with their children, it is often with conditions that would not be imposed on a heterosexual parent. For example, in a recent case, a lesbian mother was granted the right to visit with her children, but only in the presence of another adult, and only if her lover was not in the same county. There was never any evidence presented in the case that the mother had ever behaved in an improper way either toward the children or in front of the children. The judge just assumed that, since the mother was a lesbian, terrible things would happen if she were allowed to visit the children either alone or with her lover. What can gay parents do for themselves to avoid this kind of court trouble? Do they have to leave everything up to their lawyer? The answer is that there are practical steps gay parents can take regarding child custody, but only if they are informed of what their legal rights and choices are before they can act effectively.

There are also other areas in which lesbian and gay couples face possible discrimination but can take steps to minimize the impact of such discrimination on their lives. As this provocative and informative book will describe, a lesbian or gay couple can create their own living-together contract, agree on the purchase of jointly owned property, make arrangements regarding children, plan together for the eventuality of death, etc. In sum, the book provides lesbian and gay couples with essential information that they need to make intelligent decisions about many of the legal matters that affect their lives. Of course, as authors Curry and Clifford remind us, lesbian and gay people must continue to work for legal reforms that will provide recognition and respect for their lives and relationships.

Although it isn't possible in this short space to make a complete agenda of needed changes, there are certainly some areas that deserve mention. For example, same sex marriages are not legally recognized in any state. A great number of governmental, legal, and economic benefits, as well as the support of social services agencies, is dependent upon marriage. Unlike heterosexual couples, lesbians and gay men do not have the choice of taking advantage of these benefits through marriage. In addition to being denied tangible opportunities or services, lesbian and gay family units are deprived of the acceptance and support that more traditional families take for granted. Adoptions are, at best, very difficult. In case of a death, one member of the couple is not entitled to the other's social security or pension payments. Further, lesbian and gay families also find themselves excluded from family insurance policies; the ability to file joint tax returns; joint credit; inheriting from each other, unless there is a will; publicly subsidized housing;

and the services provided by many public agencies. It is time that these areas of discrimination be eliminated from a society that considers itself dedicated to freedom.

Donna J. Hitchens, J.D.
(Former) Director of the Lesbian Rights Project
San Francisco, California

TABLE OF CONTENTS

INTRODUCTION

1 LESBIAN AND GAY COUPLES AND THE LAW

A. Introduction   1:1
B. How to Use This Book   1:3

2 GAY AND TOGETHER: DO YOU REALLY NEED A CONTRACT?

A. Introduction 2:1
B. What is a Living-Together Contract?   2:3
C. The Law Applicable to Living-Together Contracts   2:4
D. Sexuality and Living-Together Contracts   2:7

3 CONTRACTS

A. When Should You Have a Living-Together Contract?   3:1
B. Write Your Contract Down   3:2
C. Can You Really Write Your Contract Yourselves?   3:2
D. Coming to an Agreement   3:3
E. Models for Contracts   3:4
F. What Property Should You Include In Your Contract? 3:6
G. Sample Living-Together Contracts   3:8
H. Arbitration and Mediation   3:24
I. Cooling-off Clauses   3:26
J. Modifications   3:27

4 LIVING TOGETHER AND THE WORLD: PRACTICAL MATTERS

A. Renting a Home—Discrimination   4:2
B. Renting Together   4:5
C. Moving Into Your Lover's   4:5
D. Roommates: The Legal Relationship of One Tenant to the Other   4:8
E. Domestic Partnerships   4:11
F. Cash and Credit   4:14
G. Insurance   4:20

5   Buying a Home, and Other Real Estate Ventures

    A. The American Dream, Updated   5:1

    B. Finding a House   5:3

    C. How Much Can You   5:5

    D. Your Home as Investment   5:8

    E. Proceeding With Your Purchase   5:8

    F. Taking Title to Your New Home   5:12

    G. Contracts for People Buying or Owning Homes Together   5:15

6   Marriage, Children and Divorce

    A. Some Experiences   6:1

    B. Divorce—A Good Divorce Can Be as Precious as a Good Marriage   6:3

    C. Child Custody   6:12

    D. Visiting Your Child   6:24

    E. Supporting Your Child   6:26

    F. Child Support When Visitation   6:28

    G. After the Divorce   6:29

7   So You Want to Become a Parent?

    A. A Few Preliminary Steps   7:2

    B. Having Your Own Child   7:4

    C. Adopting a Child   7:18

    D. Becoming a Foster Parent   7:24

    E. Guardianships   7:30

    F. Co-Parenting Arrangements   7:36

8   Medical Emergencies

    A. Introduction   8:1

    B. Authority Over Property   8:4

    C. Authority for Medical Decisions   8:9

    D. Self-Deliverance and the Right to a Natural Death   8:24

    E. Estate Planning Note   8:27

    F. Burial and Body Disposition   8:27

9   *LOOKING (WAY) AHEAD: ESTATE PLANNING*

     A.   Introduction   9:1
     B.   Reflections on the Death of a Mate   9:3
     C.   Wills   9:4
     D.   Financial Estate Planning   9:21

10   *POTPOURRI*

     A.   Changing Your Name to Suit Your Style   10:1
     B.   Immigration: Can My Foreign Lover Come Visit or Live with Me?   10:3
     C.   Welfare—Will Living with Your Lover Mean a Cut-Off?   10:6

11   *GOING SEPARATE WAYS*

     A.   Introduction   11:1
     B.   Another Plug for a Living-Together Contract   11:3
     C.   Mediation and Arbitration   11:12

12   *LAWYERS AND DOING YOUR OWN RESEARCH*

     A.   Having a Lawyer Review Your Work   12:1
     B.   Fighting in Court   12:2
     C.   Bringing Political Cases   12:3
     D.   Doing Your Own Research   12:4
     E.   Lesbian and Gay Legal Referrals   12:6

APPENDIX

INDEX

RECYCLE YOUR OUT-OF-DATE BOOKS & GET 25% OFF YOUR NEXT PURCHASE!

Using an old edition can be dangerous if information in it is wrong. Unfortunately, laws and legal procedures change often. To help you keep up to date we extend this offer. If you cut out and deliver to us the title portion of the cover of any old Nolo book we'll give you a 25% discount off the retail price of any new Nolo book. For example, if you have a copy of TENANT'S RIGHTS, 4th edition and want to trade it for the latest CALIFORNIA MARRIAGE AND DIVORCE LAW, send us the TENANT'S RIGHTS cover and a check for the current price of MARRIAGE & DIVORCE, less a 25% discount. Information on current prices and editions is listed in the NOLO NEWS (see above box). Generally speaking, any book more than two years old is of questionable value. Books more than four or five years old are a menace.

OUT OF DATE = DANGEROUS

This offer is to individuals only.

gay/lesbian 1/89

INTRODUCTION

This book is designed to help lesbian and gay couples understand the laws that affect them and to take charge of the legal aspects of their lives. Much of the material covered can also be very useful for lesbians and gays who aren't in a couple.

Many of the legal consequences of "coupling" are immediately apparent, but many others don't surface until times of stress—misunderstandings, separation or death. Married couples' relationships are defined by law; lesbian and gay couples, as we know, can't legally marry. This discrimination can mean, among other things, higher estate tax rates and insurance payments, the unavailability of marriage discount prices or memberships, and the inability to adopt, but it also allows lesbian and gay couples the freedom to create their own legal relationship.

This is an optimistic book. Our purpose is to explain your legal alternatives and show you how to use them to contribute to a harmonious and productive life together. We feel strongly that discussing and planning the financial, practical and legal aspects of a relationship leads to greater understanding and trust. It's possible to use the law in a positive, conflict-avoiding way. Unfortunately, however, there's also a less happy theme to this book—failure to work out your legal relationship with each other can lead to surprising, and dire, consequences. We've heard too many horror stories not to warn you.

This is also a practical book. We supply legal documents in the form of sample living-together agreements, durable powers of attorney, wills, co-parenting agreements, etc. so you can design and prepare your own documents. Our focus is on the nitty-gritty of daily life; we spend little time discussing broader political concerns, such as the essential struggle of lesbians and gays to remove prejudice from the laws and culture of America. One of the happiest results of this struggle is that it is now matter of fact that thousands and thousands of lesbians and gay men live together as couples in pursuit of life, liberty and happiness. This doesn't mean that the political work is over—it obviously isn't—but that our focus is on the personal and not the political.

Certainly you'll find evidence of our anger at, and frustration with, a society that has made being lesbian or gay so difficult. The AIDS crisis has lead to increased oppression and the increased need for prudence. It has been necessary to use fictitious names for some of the examples in this book. And the information we provide is especially essential if you haven't told your family, friends or the world about your relationship and sexual orientation.

A Personal Statement by the Authors

We've been close personal friends for over two decades. Hayden is gay and has lived with his lover for many years. Denis is straight. We mention this because people are curious and we want to get it out and out of the way. For those of you who are interested, we speak a little more about who we are—and our friendship—in the About the Authors section at the beginning of this book.

Because this book is designed for lesbians as well as gay men, we felt a special responsibility to seek out the advice, experience and resources of the lesbian community, especially the lesbian legal community. We didn't want to presume knowledge of their experiences. Obviously, there are many similar experiences in being a lesbian and being a gay man (calling a lesbian a "Dyke" and calling a gay man a "Faggot" hurts in much the same way). The law, too, treats the two communities as one. But aside from the anatomical, there are many differences between lesbians and gay men. One major difference is economic. As Phyllis Lyon, a lesbian activist in San Francisco, pointed out to us, gay men, on the average, make considerably more money than lesbians, who, as women, make between 65 and 70 cents (nationwide) for every $1.00 men make. Where appropriate, we discuss other important differences in the text. We want to thank the many lesbian women who helped us to assemble these materials. They provided information and encouragement, assisted with defining issues and problems, and helped scrutinize the manuscript from its initial draft to the finished product. And beyond all that, we made new friends.

Some Words About Words

Wouldn't it be simple if there was a genie who created words for such realities as "a man who loves men" or "a woman who loves women" or "comrades through life who share sexual intimacies" that meant exactly what we wished them to mean, neither more nor less? These words would be free of latent sexual prejudice and orientation, and their meaning and political acceptability wouldn't erode over time. Unfortunately, the opposite has been more the case, as words have been part of the perpetuation of homophobia. "Faggot," for instance, is derived from the French word for the bundles of sticks used to burn homosexuals at the stake, and its use should serve as a reminder of that oppression. As Truman Capote said, "A fag is a homosexual gentleman who has left the room."

Words free of ugly overtones, which accurately (to say nothing of poetically) describe the realities we discuss in this book aren't easy to find. What *do* you call the person you live with? "Life partner" sounds legalistic and cumbersome. "Co-vivant" does have a delightful French ring to it, but seems more than slightly pretentious. "Living in bedlock without benefit of wedlock" is silly, but at least it rhymes. How about "consort," "spouse equivalent" or "URAW," a Welfare Department term for a person living with an "unrelated adult woman" (URAM, for men).

"Lover" is the word we use. It's accurate and succinct. We also use the words "lesbian" and "gay" because those are the words used most often in our own particular culture (San Francisco Bay Area) by women and men to identify themselves. As for general pronouns, sometimes we use "she," sometimes "he," and sometimes the awkward "he or she." We know that creating and using words untainted by the prejudices of the past and reflective of pride and self-worth is important, so we've tried to be sensitive to the power and implication of words. But finally, words are just that—words; they won't break our bones, and we're all free to use the ones we like best. When Christopher Isherwood was asked what he liked to be called, he answered, "I don't really like the word 'gay' for it makes us seem like silly ninnies. I rather like the karate chop sound of 'faggot.' The word 'homosexual' is too much of mouthful. Frankly, when alone and with friends, I say 'queer.'"

Help Us Out

We expect that gay and lesbian lives, and the laws applicable to those lives, will continue to change, grow and evolve. In this regard, we wish to thank the people who've commented or sent us letters giving us their views and experiences on living together. Please continue to help us prepare future editions; send your comments—experiences you've had that could be useful to others; problems you've solved (or haven't); suggestions for subjects you feel need to be covered; or a viewpoint you feel is missing. Write us at Nolo Press, 950 Parker St., Berkeley, CA 94710.

The 1988 Edition

As we revised and updated this book in early 1988, we contemplated the changes in the lesbian and gay community over the last nine years. Hayden has a great many more wrinkles than he had nine years ago; he got them the old-fashioned way, he earned them. And Denis has worry lines too. Although, we must say, growing older seems like a rather fine alternative these days.

The tragedy of AIDS continues. In February, we buried our good friend Dan Bradley. Dan's story is similar to many of ours. When we worked with him in legal services in the late 60's and early 70's we didn't know the torments he was going through discovering his homosexuality. By the late 70's, when the cultural and political climate had become positive, Dan, in true Bradley fashion, burst out of his closet with an announcement in the New York Times—"High Government Official Announces He is Gay." In the early and hopeful 80's, Dan became a national gay rights leader. But his true heroism came after he was diagnosed with AIDS. Rather than retreat into his illness, he used the small energy he had to fight for the rights of people with AIDS and ARC. Now Hayden has made Dan's quilt for the Names Project; Hayden's mother did the needlepointing.

We've lost many wonderful friends and many more are ill. The political right has used AIDS to fan hatred and discrimination against us. Much of our time is spent caring for our brothers, and our political energies are sapped by health care and survival issues.

There's another side to this tragedy. We've matured as a group. We've coalesced as a community. We're vastly proud of the compassion we, men and women, have shown each other, and the organizations we've built.

We've set up programs to care for our community: volunteers become buddies to care for people with AIDS, whether to clean their apartments or take them to the hospital; friends and groups organize meal rotations or give out free food; volunteers care for pets and eventually find new homes for the dogs and cats of those who die; visiting parents and families are given housing when they come to visit; many parents of someone who has died are adopted by lovers and friends of that person. And we've created our own memorial: The Names Project encourages the friends of someone who died due to the virus to stitch a 3' x 6' quilt for that person. The individual quilts are woven together; as anyone who's seen it knows, each patch is a beautiful and powerful expression of love and grief. Quilts contain favorite teddy bears, black chiffon dresses or jogging t-shirts, with sentiments ranging from "Dear brother, our parents wouldn't let me put your name on this, but I love you" to "Thank you for sharing your time here with me."

The lesbian community has shown deep concern, caring and commitment. They've taught gay men a lot about taking care of themselves. And the lesbian community has emerged powerfully: lesbians are running for political office and having babies. One synagogue in San Francisco with a special outreach to the gay and lesbian community boasts nearly 40 children members. A glorious generation is on its way, children that are exceptionally wanted and loved. We know of at least one memorial scholarship set up for the children of lesbian and gay parents. And we pray to whatever gods we believe in that this scourge of a virus will pass and that these children will grow up in healthy environments. We already know they're growing up in loving ones.

We've proven ourselves a proud, caring and dedicated clan. We're exhausted. We're sad. We'll do what's needed of us.

Berkeley, California
H.C.
D.C.

-1-

LESBIAN AND GAY
COUPLES AND THE LAW

A. INTRODUCTION

Most lesbian and gay people we know are wary of "the law," even if they're
lawyers themselves, and for good reason. For eons, the law has been a force for
oppression. The litany of codified homophobia includes sodomy laws, loitering
laws, specific exclusion from the military, prohibitions against child custody, etc.
In addition, the law has permitted—and in some cases even encouraged—many
other types of oppression, such as job and housing discrimination, and police
entrapment. Obviously, a legal system that makes people criminals because of
sexual orientation doesn't engender trust.

The U.S. Supreme Court decision in *Bowers v. Hardwick*, 478 U.S. 186 (1986),
upholding the constitutionality of applying the Georgia sodomy statute to gay
men, was explicitly made on "moral" grounds. So the heritage of mistrust for the
legal system remains appropriate. True, things have changed somewhat in recent
years, at least in most urban parts of America (see the charts at the end of
Chapter 2), but the legal system continues to discriminate against lesbians and
gays. Although our legal system generally does a good job of protecting certain
freedoms, like freedom of speech, even here the law's homophobia takes over. In
1987, the U.S. Supreme Court ruled that the Congress and the U.S. Olympic
Committee can control the use of the word "Olympics." They did this by denying

the San Francisco Arts and Athletics, Inc. the use of the phrase "The Gay Olympics" to describe their every-four-year international athletic competition (*San Francisco Arts & Athletics, Inc. v. United States Olympic Committee*, 107 S.Ct. 2971 (1987)).

Other consequences of the law's homophobia affects lesbian and gay couples more intimately than Supreme Court decisions on sodomy or language: lesbian and gay couples cannot legally marry, no matter how deep their love and how firm their commitment, and are thus denied the numerous legal rights that come with marriage.

These rights include the rights to:

- file joint income tax returns
- claim dependency deductions
- claim estate and gift tax benefits
- recover damages based on injury to your lover
- enter hospitals, jails and other places restricted to "immediate family"
- live in neighborhoods zoned "family only"
- obtain health insurance, dental insurance, bereavement leave and other employment benefits
- obtain unemployment benefits if you quit your job to move with your lover to a new location because he or she has obtained a new job
- automatically make medical decisions in the event your lover is injured or incapacitated (otherwise, parents, adult children or siblings are given the right)
- automatically inherit your lover's property in the event he or she dies without a will (otherwise, it goes to parents, children and siblings)

We, too, are mistrustful of our legal system—and its homophobia is just one reason. The law tends to be cumbersome, time-consuming, expensive and incredibly picky. As you'll see throughout this book, we urge you to avoid courts and litigation if at all possible. But avoiding lawsuits doesn't mean you can avoid the legal system altogether. The fact that lesbian and gay couples are no longer in the closet and live together openly, necessarily brings them into contact with the meshes of the law. This is especially true if the couple, or one or both individually, have children or significant amounts of money or property. We're often asked such questions as, "Is it possible for a court to remove my child from my home because I live with my lover?" "If I die, can my lover inherit my car and my house?" "Can a hospital legally prevent me from visiting my lover in intensive care?"

We answer these specific questions later in the book. What we can tell you generally, however, is that the opportunities for legal hassles to intrude into a couple's life are endless, and the best way to avoid entanglements with the law is to take matters into your own hands. In this book, we give you the information necessary to create legal documents to give yourselves many of the rights which accompany marriage. Although we can't show you a document which will allow you to file a joint income tax return (they don't exist), we can show you how to make a will leaving your property to your lover.

B. HOW TO USE THIS BOOK

Each chapter in this book covers an area of major concern to a lesbian or gay couple. The chapters that all lesbian and gay couples should read and consider are:

- Chapters 2 and 3, both of which discuss living together and contain sample living together contracts;
- Chapter 8, which shows how to prepare a durable power of attorney, an essential document which authorizes your lover to make medical decisions for you if you become incapacitated, and to visit you in the hospital if you're placed in intensive care;
- Chapter 9, which helps you draft a basic will.

Check the Table of Contents to see the range of materials covered. Because you may not be interested in every chapter (buying a house or raising children may be the furthest thing from your mind), use the Table of Contents as a "road map" to get quickly to the subjects of interest to you. Once you understand the rules pertaining to your relationship, and what you want, it's time for paperwork—the preparation of the written documents. We've provided sample forms to use or adapt to meet your specific needs.[1]

Durable powers of attorney and wills must be written down—the law will simply ignore any argument that an "oral" will or power of attorney exists. Living-together contracts don't have to be written—but we strongly advise that they are. It's not that we think most people are untrustworthy, but memories tend to grow dim over time and two honest, sincere people can have radically different recollections of the same set of facts. Not only does writing down your understanding prevent a bitter battle of dim memories, it also helps ensure that you've come to a genuine understanding in the first place.

---

[1]Throughout this book, we provide basic, simple examples of documents. More detailed examples are found in Nolo books on specific subjects, such as *Nolo's Simple Will Book* and *The Power of Attorney Book.*

Many of the subjects we cover—including living-together contracts, powers of attorney, having children and prior families—are areas in which the law is changing. Also, state laws can vary considerably, and what is legal in Washington may not be in Alabama. Obviously, we can't guarantee that everything you read will be up to the minute when you read it. Fortunately, for most concerns of gay and lesbian couples, the solutions are sufficiently pragmatic as to be applicable with changing laws and in different states. Where laws vary significantly, however, and where the differences can cause problems, we refer you to sources to obtain specific, up-to-date information. Overall, however, this book provides you with what you need.

Of course, in many areas of the law, gays and lesbians aren't free to create their own legal rules. If you are confronted with criminal prosecution, job discrimination or a violation of your right of privacy, you will probably need to see a lawyer. Obviously, much of the need for protection from this type of unfair treatment could be eliminated by enacting anti-discrimination ordinances and repealing laws regulating sex between consenting adults. We're all for these reforms (and assume that you are, too), but we cover what you can do for yourself—not what society should do, nor how you can legally fight discrimination (we discuss this in Chapter 12).

We've heard people say that talking about law and contracts is unromantic and that it's absurd to mix such mundane concerns with love. "Does being in love really require that we talk to a lawyer before we move in together?" we were recently asked. No, but it makes sense to understand the rules that affect your lives. We don't believe that learning your legal rights need be negative. Part of the romance of being a couple is sharing your daily lives, which usually includes a home (owned or rented), money and possessions. Remember, too, that unless a lesbian or gay couple makes an agreement about their property (hers/his; mine; and ours), someone else may end up making it for them. Any dispute over property could be dragged into a messy, confusing and expensive court proceeding. More importantly, thoroughly examining and discussing the financial and practical realities of being a couple usually leads to greater understanding and trust, not less. It is possible to use law in a positive, conflict-avoiding way.

-2-

GAY AND TOGETHER: DO YOU REALLY NEED A CONTRACT?

A. INTRODUCTION

Until fairly recently, a gay couple who lived together normally did so circumspectly. To go public was to risk overt legal oppression. In addition, the couple's property rights were usually in legal limbo. If there was a dispute, neither person was likely to venture to court, when doing so might result in the couple's being jailed for "immoral conduct," "infamous crimes against nature," or some other felony invented by puritanical minds to punish anyone whose sexual behavior or preference differed from their own rigid views. The risk of exposing one's sexual identity commonly outweighed any benefits a lawsuit might bring.

There are some advantages to living outside the law—outlaws have traditionally been seen as heroes since well before the days of Robin Hood. But legend aside, having no effective legal rights can be disastrous. Years ago, before living-together contracts had been accepted by the courts, we handled a case involving two gay men who separated after years of living together. Phillip, our client, was quite wealthy; Emile wasn't. Emile's lawyer was stymied when she sought to draft what would have been a simple divorce action had a traditional couple been involved. But because there hadn't been a marriage, she couldn't file for a divorce, nor request compensation for Emile's domestic services and several years of carpentry work on Phillip's house. As there had never been a written contract, no simple "breach of contract" action was possible. She couldn't base a case on the ground of an "implied contract," because sodomy was still a crime, and a court would probably hold any implied contract illegal because it was based on illegal sex. In her zeal to represent Emile, and in her frustration with the legal system, the attorney filed two legal actions—one seeking damages for rape, and the other for replevin (an ancient English common law remedy), to recover part of the property.

Phillip, a successful business person, said that he could deal with the social blackmail of being charged with rape (which we all thought was preposterous), but asked us "What the hell! Am I supposed to list 'replevin' on credit applications that ask for all pending lawsuits?" Eventually, after considerable preliminary litigation, we were able to get both people to recognize that traditional legal remedies were inadequate to deal with the reality of their break-up, and that they had to create their own equitable compromise outside the legal system. Finally, they did.

Married people—whatever other problems they have—don't face these sort of problems. Marriage is a contractual relationship, and saying "I do" commits one to a well-established set of rules governing the couple's property rights. Although these rules are rarely, if ever, adequately explained to people before they reach the altar, they are at least available should divorce occur. One reason there's been a movement in the gay and lesbian community to allow marriages for same-sex couples has been to get the property rights that go along with the married status.

Recent years have seen changes in the property rights of unmarried couples. Led by legal decisions involving unmarried heterosexual couples, courts have begun to hold that non-married couples generally have the right to create whatever kind of living-together contracts they want when it comes to financial and property concerns; as a result, many written agreements for property ownership, income sharing, compensation for domestic services, etc. are considered legally binding in court. But far more important than setting out property rights, the existence of the agreement helps you avoid litigation (defined by Ambrose Bierce as "a machine which you go into as a pig and come out as a sausage"). The danger, trauma and expense of litigation are more likely to be visited on those who haven't defined their understanding in an agreement than those who've taken the time to make one.

Warning! As we discuss in Section D below, courts in different states aren't required to follow consistent legal rules in the regulation of people's domestic lives. Many states have already ruled that contracts between members of gay and lesbian couples will be enforced. Two states (Georgia and Illinois) outlaw contracts between any unmarried couples, and others have yet to consider the question. In some states, oral copulation and sodomy are still illegal, and a conservative judge might refuse to enforce a living-together contract on the theory that the contract is based on "sin." Even in states which have legalized sodomy, any contract which even hints of sex will be thrown out of court. A California appellate court refused to uphold a gay living-together contract, declaring that it explicitly referred to rendering services as a lover in exchange for property, and was therefore an agreement for prostitution.[1] In most states, however, courts will enforce properly drafted living-together contracts between gays or lesbians.

B. WHAT IS A LIVING-TOGETHER CONTRACT?

A contract is no more than an agreement to do (or not to do) something. It contains promises made by one person in exchange for another's promises. A living-together contract can be comprehensive, covering every aspect of your relationship, or it can be specific, covering only the brown-shingle house you just bought next to the rose garden. These contracts needn't be the fine-print monsters

---

[1]*Jones v. Estate of Daly*, 122 C.3d 500, 176 Cal.Rptr. 130 (1981). But see also *Whorton v. Dillingham*, 202 Cal. App. 3d 447 (1988), where the court ruled that the inference to sex (using the term lover) could be cut off and the rest of the contract enforced.

rammed down your throats when you buy insurance or a car. You can, and should, design your contract to say exactly what you (both) want, in words that you (both) understand. In fact, a simple, comprehensible and functional document using common English is much better than one loaded with "heretofores" and "pursuants." After all, when your contract is done, a major objective is for you both to understand it.

C. THE LAW APPLICABLE TO LIVING-TOGETHER CONTRACTS

The legal rules governing living-together contracts have mostly been made by courts and judges, not by legislatures. The "leading case" (that's lawyers' lingo) is *Marvin v. Marvin*, involving the late actor Lee Marvin and the woman he lived with, Michelle Marvin. Although they weren't married, she changed her last name to his. They had no written contract, and their courtroom battle involved whether there was another basis for giving Michelle rights to Lee's property. Michelle claimed, among other things, that Lee had promised to care for her for the rest of her life. The trial ultimately came down to whom the judge found more believable. Because Michelle's testimony was often contradicted by a number of reputable people, it was Lee. Nonetheless, the trial court gave Michelle $104,000 and Lee got to keep most of his money. The appellate court felt that the award was like alimony, wiped out the judge's decision, and she received nothing at all.[2]

In the *Marvin* litigation, legal principles involving the rights of unmarried couples (the part of the case important to you) were announced by the California Supreme Court.[3] The court first declared that marital property laws don't apply to couples not legally married. Then, the court recognized that unmarried couples are here to stay, and that

> *The fact that a man and a woman live together without marriage, and engage in a sexual relationship, doesn't in itself invalidate agreements between them relating to their earnings, property, or expenses. Neither is such an agreement invalid merely because the parties may have contemplated the creation and continuation of a non-marital relationship when they entered into it. Agreements between non-*

---

[2]Although the trial court decision has no value as legal precedent, it has a positive affect. It demonstrated to millions of us just how confusing and miserable things can get for couples who don't create written contracts.

[3]*Marvin v. Marvin*, 18 C.3d 660, 557 P.2d 106 (1976).

> *marital partners fail only to the extent that they rest upon a*
> *consideration of meretricious sexual services.*[4]

Okay, now we arrive at the point of interest to us. Even though Lee and Michelle were straight, the logic of *Marvin* applies equally to gay and lesbian couples. In the well-publicized court battle between Billy Jean King and her lesbian former lover, there was no dispute that *Marvin* applied. Indeed, in California and many other states that have adopted the *Marvin* reasoning, the right to contract extends to both straight and gay/lesbian couples, allowing lesbian and gay couples to avoid problems such as those faced by Emile and Phillip.

1. A Closer Look at the Marvin Case

Because *Marvin* has proved persuasive in many states, we pause here to look closer at what the case decided.

The court basically declared three things:

- Unmarried couples may make written contracts
- Unmarried couples may make oral contracts
- Where no written or oral contract exists, the court may examine the couple's life under the judicial microscope and decide whether an "implied" contract exists.

The court didn't quite stop there. It held that if a judge can't find an "implied" contract, she may presume "the parties intended to deal fairly with each other" and find one lover indebted to the other by invoking ancient formidable legal doctrines.

"Dealing fairly with each other" sounds fine, but the reality is that establishing anyone's right to any legal remedies (ancient or not) requires litigation, where it's unlikely anyone will win but lawyers. Even assuming a lesbian or gay couple had their oral or implied contract dispute heard by a fair and humane judge, what can they expect? Probably a lot of mud slinging. If you claim that your lover had an affair, she is likely to claim that you had three. If you argue that you did the cooking, he'll claim that he bought the car. If you prove that you contributed most of the income, she'll say she paid for a vacation and provided you the use of her boat. On and on it goes, while the attorneys' meters

---

[4]This is the wonderful legal term for people who make love without a marriage license. (It sounds like a great business. Can't you hear the phone receptionist, "Hello, Meretricious Sexual Services..."). If you put in your contract that it is based on the performance of sexual acts, the contact is invalid.

click away at $150 per hour. "Who needs it?" you ask. Hopefully, no one, especially not you.

Our point here is simple: Although the *Marvin* case allows written, oral and implied contracts, the latter two types are very difficult to prove. Evidence is likely to be subjective and conflicting. The determinative issue is usually who the judge believes.

Example: Patti and Katherine decide to live together. After her college graduation, Patti enters dental school. Although Katherine had intended to finish school, too, she postpones her plans and gets a job selling neon signs to support them both until Patti gets her drilling permit. Although they had various conversations about the long-term future of their relationship, nothing was written down. After four years, Patti passes her dental boards. Katherine is now ready to resume her education. What happens? Patti falls in love with a classmate and moves out. Katherine is left with the flea market furniture, the flea-ridden dog and the feeling she has been ripped off. What are her rights? Assuming that Patti and Katherine intend to treat each other fairly, what can be reconstructed from their conversations or deduced from their conduct? A reasonable assumption might be that because Katherine put Patti through dental school, Patti would reciprocate and pay Katherine's school expenses. A written agreement stating this would probably be enforced, but there's no such agreement. Would a court find an implied agreement? Could Katherine prove an oral one? Maybe. It's not certain, even though Katherine has a sympathetic case.

The *Marvin* decision is technically limited to California. Still, it has great meaning to all lesbian and gay couples in the United States. The California Supreme court is extremely influential, and many states follow its lead. In fact, many state courts have had *Marvin*-like cases come before them and have upheld the right of unmarried couples to form written agreements. So far, only Georgia and Illinois have rejected the *Marvin* reasoning and continue to find that the "immoral" nature of living together prevents the participants from forming a contract.

Oral Contract Note: Most state courts actually faced with the question of living-together contracts have enforced written ones, rejected implied ones, and fallen somewhere below the middle with oral ones. When a couple splits up and one partner says there was an oral contract, while the other emphatically denies it, a judge is unlikely to find one, unless there's other evidence (such as a witness to a discussion about the contract or specific conduct which tends to substantiate it). Paradoxically perhaps, when one partner dies and the other claims there was an oral contract entitling him or her to some property, a judge is more likely to be sympathetic to the survivor and find a contract, especially because no one (except perhaps a relative of the deceased) is there refuting it. We discuss this more in Chapter 9, Estate Planning.

2. Alimony/Palimony

Alimony exists only in divorce laws and is therefore available only to married couples. Unmarried couples can agree to alimony-like support in a contract, but absent a contract, a court can't order it. When a gay or lesbian couple separates, fairness can dictate that one person support the other for some period of time. This may occur when one person has given up a job and moved a long distance to join the other, and the new living arrangement doesn't work. Or, it may be the case if one partner has been raising the couple's child. We know of one case in which a judge enforced a written contract between two women lovers for one to pay the other support after their separation.[5]

If you want to provide for future support in your living-together contract, be explicit. How much? For how long? If you don't want to provide for support, simply state in your agreement that neither person will be obligated to support the other after separation.

D. SEXUALITY AND LIVING-TOGETHER CONTRACTS

As we stated at the beginning of the chapter, if a contract states (or even implies) that a promise was made in exchange for sexual services, the contract won't be enforced. So don't make any reference to sexuality; identify yourselves as "partners," not "lovers." The less cute you are the better.

In addition, if sodomy, oral copulation or other "crimes against nature" are illegal in your state, there's a risk that a judge might refuse to enforce a gay living-together contract. Table 1 shows the states that still outlaw sex between unmarried adults.

Can you challenge your state's sodomy law? It would be futile. In *Bowers v. Hardwick*, 478 U.S. 186 (1986), the U.S. Supreme Court upheld the constitutionality of applying the Georgia sodomy statute to gay men. For the time being, this means that the criminal laws of the states in Table 1 cannot be challenged on ground of violating the U.S. Constitution. Because this area is

---

[5]Reported in 4 Family L. Rep. 532 (1978).

changing, however, Table 1 may not be up to date when you read this book. If you live in a "Table 1" state, you may want to double check.

TABLE 1			
SEX LAWS IN THE UNITED STATES			
	Fornication Illegal	Cohabitation Illegal	Sodomy and/or Oral Copulation Between Consenting Adults Illegal
Alabama	No	No	Yes
Arizona	No	Yes	Yes
Arkansas	No	No	Yes
Florida	No	Yes	Yes
Georgia*	Yes	No	Yes
Idaho	Yes	Yes	Yes
Kansas	No	No	Yes
Kentucky	No	No	Yes
Louisiana	No	No	Yes
Maryland	No	No	Yes
Massachusetts	Yes	No	Yes
Michigan	No	Yes	Yes
Minnesota	No	No	Yes
Mississippi	Yes	Yes	Yes
Missouri	No	No	Yes
Montana	No	No	Yes
Nevada	No	No	Yes
North Carolina	Yes	Yes	Yes
Oklahoma	No	No	Yes
Rhode Island*	Yes	No	Yes
South Carolina*	Yes	No	Yes
Tennessee	No	No	Yes
Texas	No	No	Yes
Utah*	Yes	No	Yes
Virginia	Yes	Yes	Yes
Washington, D.C.	Yes	No	Yes

* In Georgia, Rhode Island, South Carolina and Utah, there's no separate statute for cohabitation, but is probably illegal under the fornication statute.

We're certainly not suggesting that you not discuss your sexual relationship when preparing your contract; a force as powerful as passion can destroy, as well as enhance, any relationship. But discussing what's sexually expected, permitted, condoned or forbidden, isn't the same as mentioning sexuality in a property contract. As we aren't therapists, we have nothing more to add about passion, except to note that it seems here to stay.

TABLE 2
STATES WHERE ALL PRIVATE SEXUAL ACTS
BETWEEN CONSENTING ADULTS ARE LEGAL

Alaska	Maine	Oregon
California	Nebraska	Pennsylvania
Colorado	New Hampshire	South Dakota
Connecticut	New Jersey	Vermont
Delaware	New Mexico	Washington
Hawaii	New York	West Virginia
Illinois	North Dakota	Wisconsin
Indiana	Ohio	Wyoming
Iowa		

-3-

CONTRACTS

A. WHEN SHOULD YOU HAVE A LIVING-TOGETHER CONTRACT?

Obviously, you don't need a contract in a brief relationship. But in a long-term and serious relationship, whether you're basking in the glow of just having "joined forces" or you've been together 20 years, it's appropriate to think about the legal consequences. If you are mixing assets or sharing expenses, it's essential that you have a written agreement. The safe rule is that the sooner you agree on how (and if) to share your property, the less confusion you'll face later. But don't despair if you've been together for years and have accumulated lots of property. It's never too late to write an agreement.

As we mentioned in Chapter 2, married people are handed a contract by the state, the provisions of which fill several heavy volumes at the local law library. Unfortunately, most married couples never take the time to understand the contract—unless they separate. So, as unfair as it is to prohibit lesbian and gay couples from marrying, there's at least one advantage: gay and lesbian couples can design agreements tailored to their needs.

Does this mean you need a contract any time you live with a lover for an extended period? Yes. Simply put, we believe you should prepare a written agreement if significant money or property is involved. But what if you're both stone-broke NINKS[1]? If there's no property, and little prospect of getting any soon, put away the pen and paper and take a nap in the sun.

B. Write Your Contract Down

We quote the French legal scholar, Beaumanoir, who wrote in *Coutumes de Beauvaisis* (1283): "For the memory of men slips and flows away, and the life of man is short, and that which isn't written is soon forgotten." Enough said, we hope.

C. Can You Really Write Your Contract Yourselves?

Yes. It isn't difficult to write a solid, legal living-together contract. This doesn't mean that it won't take some effort. But we emphasize that once you arrive at your understanding, there's nothing to fear from the contract itself. As we've stated, legally, a contract is no more than a promise (or promises) to do something, in exchange for someone else's promise (or promises) to do something. If Mary promises to repair Joan's car, and in exchange, Joan promises to do the shopping, there's a contract.

One reason people get nervous at the mere mention of contracts is that most have had contracts thrust upon them. If you want insurance coverage, a bank loan or a lease, you must accept the terms of the one-sided contract that goes with it. You can't call up a bank and ask them to reduce the interest rate on your loan. Fortunately, living-together contracts need not, and should not, be written like these standard-form albatrosses.

Once you create your contract, it's binding. It's virtually impossible to persuade a court to alter the terms of a written contract, unless the change is also in writing. Of course, a living-together contract, like any other contract, won't be enforced if one person has improperly taken advantage of the other. A good rule of thumb here is that if one partner is more savvy in financial matters than the other, and a lot of property is involved, the inexperienced person should briefly consult with a lawyer before signing.

---

[1]No Income, No Kids.

Example: Joanna is a 40-year-old real estate broker with several business interests. Francoise is a 26-year-old actress from France with no business experience and an imperfect grasp of English. They plan to live together indefinitely. Joanna will buy a house; Francoise will do extensive repairs on it. Joanna and Francoise agree that Francoise won't receive any ownership interest in the house until they live in it for three years. Until then, Francoise's labor will be credited against her rent. Francoise should have any contract carefully explained to her by a lawyer or other knowledgeable third person to make sure that she knows what she's agreeing to, and that, broadly speaking, it's fair.

D. COMING TO AN AGREEMENT

Before you can write down your understanding, you must first arrive at it. Sound simple? Perhaps, but many couples find that when they sit down to record their understanding, they don't have one! Each person has made assumptions, and they haven't been the same.

How do you start? It's up to you. There are as many styles of arriving at an agreement as there are people. You may sit down at an oak table with a typed agenda, meander through a park and talk, or pour champagne and light candles. Our only suggestion is that you each read the entire book, especially Chapters 9 and 11 (on estate planning and going separate ways, respectively) before making decisions. Both subjects may seem far away right now, but it's important that you think about them when you are writing your contract.

Come to think of it, we do have one suggestion: make your session as much fun as possible. Go slowly; cover both your hopes and fears. Don't hesitate to focus on mundane economic realities. We have found in our own lives that it's almost always better to replace vague hopes and fears with certainty, even if significant compromise is needed to achieve it.

If we were making a recipe for an agreement, we would suggest large doses of humor and generosity, mixed in equal parts with prudence, fairness, skepticism and patience, combined with the ingredients of your lives: your assets, present and future earnings, children, likely inheritances, etc. Another important ingredient is your future expectations. Do you expect your lover to leave you his half of the house at death? Does she expect you to be responsible for her kids if she becomes ill? There's one final ingredient—understanding the legal consequences of your actions. For example, if you give your lover half of the car, will you be responsible for accidents he causes? (We answer this in Chapter 4.)

E. MODELS FOR CONTRACTS

In deciding what to include in a living-together agreement, many people find it useful to consider models commonly used when people couple. We include here a brief discussion of the most common ones.

The "Marriage" Model: Marriage[2] partners' property rights are set out by state law, and generally fall into two categories: community property[3] and common law. Under both systems, property owned *prior* to marriage remains the owner's separate property. Under community property, each spouse owns one-half of all property (except gifts and inheritances to one spouse specifically) acquired *during* marriage, no matter who earns or acquires it. The idea is that marriage is a partnership.

All common law states but Mississippi have adopted the concept of "equitable distribution" at divorce. This means that property acquired during marriage is divided fairly, and the result somewhat resembles the division in a community property state. If you want this sort of merging of property in your relationship, design a contract to achieve it.

---

[2]Defined by Ambrose Bierce as "the state or condition of a community consisting of a master, a mistress and two slaves, making in all, two."

[3]The community property states are Arizona, California, Idaho, Louisiana, Nevada, New Mexico, Texas, Washington and Wisconsin.

The "Socialist" Model: You might choose a socialistic approach to resolving property questions. You pool your resources, with each contributing according to ability to do so (such as three-fourths and one-fourth), and each using the pooled resources according to needs. Unless you provide a lot of details, this can be pretty vague. For example, who gets what if you separate? Does the three-fourths and one-fourth split make sense? While you're living together, who decides the spending priorities if money's tight?

The "Business" or "Partnership" Model: You may wish to arrange the financial details of your relationship similarly to a business partnership. Each contributes her or his individual resources and abilities and each is given a percentage ownership in all property accumulated together. As you'll see, we use partnership-style agreements in many of the sample contracts in this book, especially with real estate agreements (see Chapter 5). The partnership model is well-designed to keep an accurate accounting of your joint resources.

The "Subsidized" Model: Sue, a student, moves in with Evelyn, a well-established accountant. They agree that Evelyn will support Sue until she finishes school. In this situation, Evelyn, especially, will want a written agreement in the event they split up. Sue and Evelyn will probably want to say that neither has any financial obligation to the other upon separation. This means that Sue wouldn't have to return money advanced by Evelyn for Sue's education, and Evelyn would have no future obligation to support Sue. Or, they may think it sensible that Evelyn help Sue out for a short time after separation.

The "Splitsies" Model: Here each partner agrees to be absolutely responsible for his or her own support. Like college roommates, each buys separate food, records, clothes, etc. Obviously, this model can be taken to extremes or can be worked out in a fairly easy-going, common sense, "I-paid-for-breakfast, you-pay-for-lunch" way.

The "Personal" Model: Along with economic provisions, in an ideal world you could create a "personal" agreement to include anything and everything relevant to your living situation (except sexuality), including the division of chores, where the couple will live, how vacations will be taken, and even who feeds the canary. You should understand, however, that living-together contracts are enforceable in court only to the degree that they concern financial matters. Provisions pertaining to personal conduct aren't enforceable. A judge won't tell your living companion how often she has to wash the dishes or to remember not to put cream in your coffee.

Because a judge won't enforce personal arrangements in a relationship contract, don't include them. Instead, write a separate emotional document; you may want to include thoughts like those of Mrs. Millamont in Congreve's *The*

Way of the World, who told her lover Mirabell that she would retain the following rights:

> *Liberty to pay and receive visits to and from who I please, to write and receive letters without interrogatories or wry faces... to wear what I please, and choose conversation with regard only to my taste; to have no obligation upon me to converse with wits that I don't like, because they are your acquaintances, or to be intimate with fools, because they may be your relatives.*

There's still a slight risk, though, that a disgruntled ex-lover would claim that the emotional document invalidates your living-together contract (on the ground that it was "really" based on sex).

These aren't the only models. As we've said before, you have the freedom to create any type of agreement you want. If there's a provision in one of the samples in this chapter that you don't like, make like Chico Marx in *A Night at the Opera*—"You no like-a dat clause? We atake-a it out"—and get rid of it. Of course, Chico eventually ripped out every clause—an understandable impulse, but not a wise one if you want to end up with an agreement.

F. WHAT PROPERTY SHOULD YOU INCLUDE IN YOUR CONTRACT?

In writing up your living-together agreement, you'll want to include all your property. This includes property you had before you began living together, and the property you acquire during the relationship.

Property Owned before Living Together: You each probably had some property before you got together. You can continue to own your old TV, oriental tapestry, and middle-aged cocker spaniel, while your lover holds onto her 10-year-old Datsun and the collected works of Virginia Woolf, or you can each donate items (or even all you own) to your relationship.[4] Whatever you decide, put it in writing. This may seem unnecessary, but we can tell you that when no agreement is written and property is informally mixed together, problems can develop in separating it. You may want to deal with use of valuable items as well as ownership. Who gets to use the property? Who pays for upkeep? For instance, Alan owns a boat and wants to keep it if he and Fred ever split up. Fred agrees to

---

[4]Normally there's no problem in this, but if one person gives another property worth over $10,000 a year, gift taxes are assessed. (See Chapter 9, "Estate Planning.")

help with upkeep in exchange for using it without acquiring any ownership interest. It's up to you how detailed to get.

Property Inherited or Received by Gift During the Relationship: Many people will want to keep separate the property that they inherit or receive by gift from their family or friends. Others will want to donate the property to the relationship. Again, it's up to you. Remember though, any property given to both of you is legally owned by both. If separate inherited or gift property is to stay separate, however, don't forget to cover questions of use and control, and the identity of the property.

Property Bought During the Relationship: Many people make purchases item by item, understanding that whoever makes the purchase owns the property. George buys the kitchen table and chairs, and Ham, the lamp and stereo. If they split up, each keeps the property he bought.

Purchases also can be pooled. Ham and George can jointly own everything bought during the relationship, and divide it all 50-50 if they separate. A consistent approach to property ownership may simplify things, but is required by neither law nor logic. Ham and George could choose a combination of the two methods. Some items may be separately owned, some pooled 50-50, and some shared in proportion to how much money each contributed toward the purchase price or how much labor each put into upkeep.

Expenses During the Relationship: And then there are the day-to-day costs for food, utilities, laundry, housing, etc. As prices go up, it's not always clear how the bills will be met. But even if you substitute margarine for butter, or vin ordinaire for Chateau Mouton-Rothschild, you must adopt a plan. We can't help you choose what you buy, but we can suggest how to share expenses:

- Split 50-50 (with dinner and the theater now and then as a gift).
- Each contributes to the day-to-day expenses in proportion to his or her income (to be reviewed and adjusted at regular intervals, e.g., each year or every six months). We have two friends who live this way. One is wealthy and the other isn't. The woman with the churchmouse income was going crazy (broke, anxious and very dependent) trying to keep up with the queen-of-the-hill lifestyle of her lover. Finally, the two saw that they had a serious problem and adopted a plan under which all expenses were divided 80-20. It probably saved their relationship.

G. SAMPLE LIVING-TOGETHER CONTRACTS

At the back of this book you will find two tear-out contracts: One keeps a couple's property separate; the other combines it. Read them carefully, but hold off using them until you have read the specific agreements in this chapter and the rest of the book. The contracts are designed to cover the major areas of concern to most lesbian and gay couples. They may meet your needs perfectly, but it's more likely you'll want to make some modifications to fit your circumstances. Here's how to do it.

Deletions: To remove clauses, or even few words, simply cross them out and put both of your initials by each deletion. If you find it necessary to remove a number of provisions, retype the entire contract to avoid confusion.

Additions: Additions require a little more work. You must write or type the new clause and insert it into the contract. The small space before the signature lines is for minor additions. If you don't need this space, simply cross it out with a large X. But don't cross it out too fast. After reading the living-together contracts in this chapter, you may find things you want to include in your agreement. Don't be shy. Add them. Take the time to design a contract right for you.

By the time you finish modifying one of our agreements, your changes may pretty much replace the original. Congratulations! You've created your own contract. If you're at all nervous about the legality of the new document, especially if a lot of money or property is involved, deal positively with your anxiety. Have a lawyer look at it. But be careful when dealing with attorneys.[5] Many charge outrageous prices and have little experience with the problems of lesbian and gay couples. Do some investigating before making an appointment, and get the fee in advance. Remember, you've already done the work; you're just asking the lawyer to check it. A fee of $75 to $150 should normally be adequate.

Signing the Contract: Whether you use one of our tear-out living-together contracts or design your own, photocopy the final draft so you each have a copy. You and your lover each sign and date both copies. It makes no difference who keeps which—both are "originals." Notarization is optional unless your contract involves real property. If it does, notarization is needed to record the agreement at your county property records office. Failure to notarize doesn't make your contract illegal or unenforceable. It does help prove that your signatures are not forged, in the unlikely event that anyone might question their validity in the future.

Relax: Creating a contract that touches upon the very core of your relationship is bound to be an emotional experience. If either of you begins to feel overwhelmed, stop and regroup. Some couples will design a good agreement in an hour; other couples will take a month.

Short-Form Property Contracts: The living-together agreements we provide in the Appendix are quite thorough. For those of you who don't need to have such thorough agreements, we provide, on the following two pages, two simple, one-page living-together agreements. The contracts following those two are designed to fit specific situations. Read them all carefully. You may find that all or parts of various agreements meet your needs.

CONTRACT FOR KEEPING INCOME AND

ACCUMULATIONS MOSTLY SEPARATE:

Roosevelt Jackson and Alan Stein make the following agreement:

1. They are living together now and plan to continue doing so.

2. All property owned by either Roosevelt or Alan as of the date of this agreement remains his separate property and cannot be transferred

---

[5]We discuss using lawyers more in Chapter 12.

to the other unless the transfer is done in writing.

3. The income of each person, as well as any accumulations of property from that income, belongs absolutely to the person who earns the money. Joint purchases are covered under the provisions of clause 7.

4. If Roosevelt and Alan separate, neither has a claim against the other for any money or property, for any reason, with the exception of property covered under Clause 7 below (the joint purchase clause), or unless a subsequent written agreement specifically changes this contract.

5. Roosevelt and Alan will keep separate bank accounts, credit accounts, etc., and neither is responsible for the debts of the other.

6. Living expenses, which include groceries, utilities, rent, and day-to-day household upkeep, will be shared equally. Roosevelt and Alan agree to open a joint bank account into which each agrees to contribute $500 per month to pay for living expenses.

7. Roosevelt and Alan may make joint purchases (such as a house, car or boat). The joint ownership of each specific item will be reflected on any title slip to the property. If no title slip exists, or if it's insufficient to record all the details of their agreement, Alan and Roosevelt will prepare a separate, written, joint ownership agreement. Any such agreement will apply to the specific jointly-owned property only, and won't create an implication that any other property is jointly owned.

8. This agreement sets forth Roosevelt and Alan's complete understanding concerning real and personal property ownership and takes the place of any and all prior contracts or understanding whether written or oral.

9. This agreement can be added to or changed only by a subsequent written agreement.

10. Any provision in this agreement found to be invalid shall have no effect on the validity of the remaining provisions.[6]

Dated: _____   Signature:_____
                        Roosevelt Jackson
Dated: _____   Signature:_____
                        Alan Stein

---

[6]If a particular clause of the contract is deemed by a court to be unenforceable for some reason, this clause acts to keep the rest of the contract in effect. Without this clause, it is possible that the entire contract would be considered invalid, depending on how important the unenforceable clause was to the entire agreement.

CONTRACT FOR COMBINING INCOME AND ACCUMULATIONS

Aline Jones and Mary Wiebel agree that:

1. They are living together now and plan to continue doing so.

2. All property earned or accumulated prior to Aline and Mary living together belongs absolutely to the person earning or accumulating it, and it cannot be transferred to the other unless it's done in writing.

3. All income earned by either Aline or Mary while they are living together and all property accumulated from that income belongs equally to both, and should they separate, all accumulated property will be divided equally.

4. Should either person receive real or personal property by gift or inheritance, the property belongs absolutely to the person receiving the inheritance or gift and it cannot be transferred to the other unless it's done in writing.

5. In the event that either Mary or Aline wishes to separate, all jointly-owned property under Clause 2 will be divided equally.

6. Once the jointly-owned property is divided, neither party will have any claim to any money or property from the other for any reason.

7. This agreement represents the complete understanding of Aline and Mary regarding their living together and replaces any and all prior agreements, whether written or oral, and can be added to or changed only by a subsequent written agreement.

8. Any provision in this agreement found to be invalid shall have no effect on the validity of the remaining provisions.

Dated: _____   Signature:_____
                                        Aline Jones
Dated: _____   Signature:_____
                                        Mary Wiebel

Contracts Covering Jointly-Acquired Items: The majority of couples we know adopt the basic keep-things-separate approach. Often, however, a couple wants to own some major items together. The desire to jointly own property may have to do with the poetry of love or may be dictated by economic necessity. As you have doubtless already noted, the basic keep-things-separate contract in this book provides a structure for joint ownership of some property. You prepare a separate written contract covering each jointly-owned item. The following contract accomplishes this task. After you modify it to meet your needs, sign it and staple or clip it to your basic keep-things-separate contract.

Note: If you have completed a combine-all-income-and-accumulations contract, like the one above, you don't need this joint-ownership agreement. You already provide for equal ownership.

CONTRACT COVERING A JOINT PURCHASE

Carol Takahashi and Louise Orlean agree as follows:

1. We will jointly purchase and own a carved oak table costing $1,000.

2. If we separate and both want to keep the table, we will agree on its fair market price[7] and flip a coin. The winner keeps the table after paying the loser one-half of the agreed-upon price.

3. If we decide to separate and neither wants the table, or if we both want it but can't arrive at a price we agree is fair, we will sell the table at the best available price and divide the proceeds equally.

4. Any provision in this agreement found to be invalid shall have no effect on the validity of the remaining provisions.

Dated: _____   Signature:_____
                                             Carol Takahashi
Dated: _____   Signature:_____
                                             Louise Orlean

---

[7] If you're worried about what happens if you can't agree on a fair price, include a provision for an appraisal or for arbitration. (See "Arbitration and Mediation" at the end of this chapter.)

Sometimes, only one partner can make a purchase. This commonly occurs when the purchase is paid in installments, but only one of you has good credit. But it's also common that even though only one name appears on the purchase contract, you want to jointly own the property. You can accomplish this with the following agreement:

CONTRACT COVERING A JOINT INSTALLMENT PURCHASE
WHEN ONLY ONE PERSON HAS GOOD CREDIT

James O'Brien and Brian Joyce make the following agreement:

1. James has credit with Sears to purchase a washing machine and dryer.

2. Under the contract with Sears, James agrees to pay $1,000, principal and interest, in monthly installments of $100 for ten months. The first payment is due on July 1, 19__.

3. James and Brian intend that the washer and dryer be owned equally and that each pay one-half the $1,000, by each paying one-half of each installment.

4. Each month, Brian will give James $50 toward the installment. James will then directly pay Sears the entire installment on or before the date it's due.

5. If one person fails to pay his share, the other has the right to make the entire payment and will proportionally own more of the washer-dryer set. Thus, if James ends up paying $400 and Brian $600, Brian will own three-fifths of the washer-dryer and James, two-fifths.

6. Brian and James will record all payments.

7. If James or Brian dies, the financial interest in the washer-dryer belonging to the deceased person will go to the survivor, who will be obligated to pay the entire amount still owing.[8]

8. If James and Brian separate, either may buy out the other's interest in the washer-dryer by paying one-half the fair market value, less any money still owing.

9. If James or Brian can't agree on who will buy the other out, or the amount to be paid, the washer and dryer will be sold. Each will receive one-half of the net proceeds from the sale, unless one has paid more than the other, as provided in clause 5. In that case, each will receive the percentage of the net proceeds corresponding to the percentage of the payments he's made.

10. Any provision in this agreement found to be invalid shall have no effect on the validity of the remaining provisions.

Dated: _____ Signature:_____
James O'Brien

Dated: _____ Signature:_____
Brian Joyce

Careful! Only the partner signing an installment or credit contract is legally obligated to pay, even if the couple has an agreement splitting the cost. Thus, Brian doesn't have to pay Sears if James stops. Brian has a legal contract with James, but not with Sears. Of course, the store doesn't care who pays the bill, so Brian can send the money and the store will credit James's account. In addition, if Brian moves to Guatemala, James is stuck for the whole bill.

Agreements Covering Joint Projects: Tony and Ray live together. Both are landscape gardeners and share a dream of building a greenhouse and raising orchids on a piece of land they jointly own. They know it's a big job and want to anchor their dream on a strong foundation of good business practice. They make the following agreement:

---

[8]For an expensive item, such as a car, consider adding: "This provision shall be incorporated into James's will and Brian's will."

JOINT PROJECT AGREEMENT[9]

Tony Freeling and Ray Vivaldi agree as follows:

1. They both want to build a glass and wood greenhouse to house tropical orchids.

2. Each will contribute $9,000 towards the purchase of construction materials. The money will be kept in a joint bank account and both Tony and Ray's signatures will be required on checks.

3. Each will work at least 40 hours per month on building the greenhouse.[10]

4. They will keep neat records, recording all hours worked and money spent for materials.

5. If they separate, Ray will have the opportunity to buy Tony's share for an amount equal to Tony's actual cash investment plus $15 per hour for the time he has worked on building the greenhouse.

6. At separation, if Ray decides not to buy Tony's share under the terms of clause 5, Tony will have the opportunity to buy Ray's share on the same terms.

7. If neither Ray nor Tony elect to purchase the other's share of the greenhouse, it will be sold and the proceeds equally divided.

8. If either Tony or Ray fails to work on the greenhouse 40 hours per month for three consecutive months, the other may buy out his share under the terms set out in clauses 5 and 6.

9. If either Tony or Ray dies, the other becomes sole owner of the greenhouse. If either Ray or Tony makes a will, this provision will be incorporated into that will.

10. Any provision in this agreement found to be invalid shall have no effect on the validity of the remaining provisions.

Dated: _____   Signature:_____
                                             Tony Freeling
Dated: _____   Signature:_____
                                             Ray Vivaldi

---

[9]This agreement can be modified to cover building a cabin, refurbishing a boat or any other major project. You may want to provide for some contingencies not covered here. What happens, for example, if the project costs more than originally estimated? What arrangements should be made for operating the greenhouse, once it's finished?

[10]If Tony is a professional carpenter and Ray only semiskilled, it may be fairer for Ray to contribute more money or Tony to get a greater hourly salary (see clause 5).

Here's another joint project contract. Patti and Maria's shared dream is to own and run a bakery—supporting themselves through their mutual love of scones and croissants. They know the odds are against any small business succeeding and that they'll have to work extremely hard to make their dream a reality. While they aren't paranoid, they want to protect their enterprise if they separate, or if one loses interest but the other wants to continue. Also, they face another reality—Patti has more cash to invest initially, but they eventually want to own the business equally.

ANOTHER JOINT PROJECT CONTRACT

Patti Valdez and Maria Ness agree as follows:

1. They desire and intend to jointly own and operate a bakery in San Francisco, California (at a rented location not yet ascertained).

2. Patti will contribute $75,000 and Maria $25,000 toward the working capital of the business.

3. They both will work diligently in their bakery business, and it will be the principal business endeavor of each.

4. Initially, Patti will own three-quarters of the business and Maria one-quarter. Each will receive pay of $450 a week for her work in the bakery. Any profits beyond salaries and operating expenses will be paid to Patti, until she receives $50,000 plus interest at 10% per year on the unpaid balance of the $50,000. Once Patti receives the $50,000 plus interest, the business will be co-owned by Patti and Maria equally, and all profits beyond salaries and operating expenses will be divided equally between them.

5. Should either Patti or Maria decide she no longer wishes to operate the bakery, the person wishing to continue may purchase the other's interest in the bakery as set out under Paragraph 7.

6. Should Patti and Maria separate and be unable to work together, but both wish to continue the bakery under sole ownership, they will ask someone to flip a coin; the winner will have the right to purchase the loser's interest as provided in Paragraph 7. Likewise, if Patti and Maria separate and only one person wishes to maintain the bakery, that person has the right to purchase the other's interest as provided in Paragraph 7.

7. If for any reason Patti or Maria wishes to purchase the other's interest in the business, she will pay the fair market value of the other's share. If Patti and Maria cannot agree on the fair market value, they will

submit the question of fair market value to binding arbitration to be decided by _____ [insert the name, or names, of a knowledgeable person, or people, who you both trust to determine a fair price].

8. Should either Patti or Maria die, the other becomes the sole owner of the bakery business. Patti and Maria agree they each will make a will containing this agreement.

9. Any provision in this agreement found to be invalid shall have no effect on the validity of the remaining provisions.

Dated: _____   Signature:_____
                                                    Patti Valdez

Dated: _____   Signature:_____
                                                    Maria Ness

---

Note: As you know, we don't advise seeing a lawyer for every little problem. If you and your lover are going into a business together, however, you will be investing a great deal of your time—and probably money—for a significant period of time. A formal partnership agreement is essential. *The Partnership Book* (Nolo Press) is an excellent step-by-step guide to preparing such an agreement. We also think it's sensible to have your agreement checked by a sympathetic lawyer with small business experience. However, because you will have done most of the work yourselves, the lawyer shouldn't be expensive.

Agreements Allowing One Person "Time Off": Suppose you and your lover both work outside the home and one of you wants to take a leave to be an artist, take a trip, adopt a child or just stay home. How do you work out the details so that each feels treated fairly? One way is to agree that one of you will work for a while and support you both, in exchange for getting an equal amount of time off later. Or, the person working could provide a loan to the one taking time off. Or, if the person taking time off will be raising the couple's child, no "exchange" may be needed, because both partners are equally contributing to the relationship. No matter how you arrange it, you must specify how much time equals how much money, and, if appropriate, set a method of repayment.

Below is a "time-off" agreement. Leslie and Chris are a lesbian couple who have lived together on and off for three years. Leslie is a poet and Chris an illustrator, but both have had to take ordinary part-time jobs in order to make ends meet. They recently decided to embark on a new living-together arrangement. It will allow each person time to pursue her own interests, and still take care of the homey little details, such as rent and groceries. So that each may work full time at her art, they will take turns supporting each other.

AGREEMENT ALLOWING ONE PERSON TIME OFF

Leslie Rutherford and Chris Richards agree as follows:

1. Each of us will retain whatever property we currently own as our separate property (lists are attached to this contract). All income stemming from the earnings of either of us while we live together, including income from our artistic pursuits, will be jointly owned and kept in joint bank accounts. Any property purchased with this income will be jointly owned.

2. We will each work at full-time jobs for alternating six-month periods for the duration of this agreement. Chris will work the first six-month period and then it will be Leslie's turn.

3. The person employed will be responsible for all personal and household expenses for both of us.

4. If we separate during a year—that is, before each person has supported the other for six months—the support obligation will continue for the remainder of the year in an amount roughly equal to that previously contributed.

5. If one of us wants to end the living arrangement, we agree to participate in conciliation sessions with a mutually acceptable third person. If, after a minimum of three sessions, one of us still wants to separate, we will. Each will take her separate property (property owned prior to living together), and all joint property (property acquired while living together) will be equally divided. No financial or other responsibilities will continue between us after we separate, except as set out in clause 4.

6. Any provision in this agreement found to be invalid shall have no effect on the validity of the remaining provisions.

Dated: _____   Signature:_____
                                          Leslie Rutherford
Dated: _____   Signature:_____
                                          Chris Richards

Agreements for People in School: It's common for one partner to help the other with educational expenses or support while he or she's in school. This is a situation for a written agreement. Suppose Sam supports George while he's in plumber's school. Surely Sam has some expectations as to how their lives will improve once George graduates. If George leaves Sam just after graduating, Sam's likely to feel that George owes him something. A court might well agree, but shouldn't have to address the question. Sam and George should define their expectations in a written agreement. If George leaves the relationship immediately after graduation, is Sam owed anything? If so, how much? How will it be paid?

CONTRACT FOR EDUCATIONAL SUPPORT

Sam Chung and George Fujimoto make the following agreement:
1. They are both students. Because of financial considerations, they will take turns going to school. Because Sam has already started school to learn plumbing, and because his schooling takes less time to complete than George's, he will go to school first. George will pay Sam's educational expenses and support for them both for the next 18 months. After 18 months, Sam will assume these responsibilities for two years while George finishes his accountant's training. If their relationship dissolves during the first three and one-half years, the financial responsibilities won't be affected. Specifically, if Sam and George separate during the first 18 months, George will continue to pay Sam's tuition and will pay Sam $5,000 per year for living expenses. At the end

of the 18 months, Sam will pay George's tuition, and his living expenses at $5,000 per year, for two years. Should they separate after George starts school, Sam will pay George's remaining tuition (up to two full years in accounting school) and pay him $5,000 per year for living expenses. Expenses will be paid in 12 equal monthly installments on the first day of each month.

2. All property owned by Sam or George before the date of this contract remains his separate property and can't be transferred to the other except by a written agreement.

3. During the first three and one-half years, all income and all property accumulated from that income, excluding gifts and inheritances, will be jointly owned. After the first three and one-half years, all jointly-accumulated property will be inventoried and equally divided. Thereafter, each person's earnings will remain his separate property and neither will have any rights in the present or future property of the other. If George and Sam separate before the end of three and one-half years, all property accumulated since the beginning of this agreement will be equally divided according to the fraction of the time each provided support. (For example, if Sam supports George for 18 months and George supports Sam for 12 months, Sam is entitled to three-fifths of the property.) If they separate, neither will have any continuing financial obligation to the other except as set out in Paragraph 1.

4. Any provision in this agreement found to be invalid shall have no effect on the validity of the remaining provisions.

Dated: _____   Signature:_____
                         Sam Chung
Dated: _____   Signature:_____
                         George Fujimoto

Contracts for Work Done Around the House: With some couples, one person works outside the home while the other cooks, cleans, shops and otherwise takes care of the home. This sort of labor division can pose tricky problems. How should the homemaker be compensated? Or suppose both people work outside the home, but one also makes significant improvements to the home, while the other idles in the sauna? Is it fair that the person who does the extra work should receive nothing for her or his labors? Only you can answer these questions, and no two answers will be the same. But remember one thing—these situations are likely to lead to misunderstandings unless you discuss them, and write down your agreement.

The worst thing you can do if one person works outside the house and contributes most of the cash income and the other works in the home is ignore it. Why? Because the person with the money also has the power, and relationships rarely prosper when one person has too much of anything. It's easy to compensate the person who works at home by sharing the cash income. A person who does carpentry work on a jointly-owned house, while the other goes off to Madison Avenue on the 8:10, can be compensated at an agreed-upon hourly rate, with the compensation either paid in cash by the other or added to the carpenter's equity in the house.[11] To compensate a homemaker, agree upon a weekly salary (e.g., $200 per week) or trade services (you fix the car while your lover does the laundry). We're not suggesting you write an agreement for one of you to toast the bread and the other to butter it, but it's very wise to have a clear understanding if significant time or money is involved.

Note: If one person works as a homemaker and the other has a good income, you may want to think about the homemaker's future if you split up. You can agree on a period of support payments for the homemaker, thereby creating your own alimony-like arrangement by contract.

CONTRACT TO COMPENSATE A HOMEMAKER

Sandi Potter and Carole Samworthe agree that as long as they live together:

1. Sandi will work full-time (40 hours a week) as a city planner.

2. Carole will work in the home, taking care of her daughter, Judy, and performing the domestic chores, including cleaning, laundry, cooking and yard work. Sandi will pay Carole $150 a week for her

---

[11]See Chapter 5 for contracts related to buying a house.

services. This payment will be adjusted from time to time to reflect changes in the cost of living.

3. Sandi will also provide reasonable amounts of money each month for food, clothing, shelter and recreation for the entire family as long as they live together. This payment will be adjusted from time to time to reflect changes in the cost of living. Sandi, however, assumes no obligation to support Carole or Judy upon termination of this agreement.

4. Sandi, as Carole's "employer," will make social security payments for her and will obtain medical insurance for her and Judy.

5. All property purchased or accumulated by either Carole or Sandi will be owned by the person purchasing or accumulating it. The property cannot be transferred from one person to the other except by a written agreement. The house will be provided by Sandi and will be owned solely by her.

6. Either Sandi or Carole can end this agreement by giving the other two months' written notice. If Sandi and Carole separate, Sandi will pay Carole severance pay at the rate of two months for every year the agreement has been in effect. Sandi's agreement to pay this money is part of the consideration necessary to get Carole to agree to this contract. This money will be paid in a lump sum at the time of separation. Neither Carole nor Sandi will have any other financial obligation to the other upon separation.

7. Any provision in this agreement found to be invalid shall have no effect on the validity of the remaining provisions.

Dated: _____   Signature:_____
                                         Sandi Potter
Dated: _____   Signature:_____
                                         Carole Samworthe

Agreement for Sharing Household Expenses and Chores: After a whirlwind courtship, Lynne Jacobs and Sarah Elderberry decide to live together. Lynne's an ad executive and Sarah works as a designer. They have roughly equivalent salaries and want to keep their property separate, but want to share household expenses. The choices they make in the following contract are typical of thousands of gay and lesbian couples.

SHARING HOUSEHOLD EXPENSES

Lynne Jacobs and Sarah Elderberry agree as follows:

1. They plan to live together indefinitely.

2. They will maintain separate bank accounts and separate credit accounts.

3. The earnings and property of each will be kept separate.

4. The separate property of Lynne and Sarah owned at present and acquired in the future can become joint property or the separate property of the other only by a written agreement signed by the person whose property is to be reclassified.

5. Lynne and Sarah will each be responsible for her own personal expenses. This includes clothing, medical/dental bills, and long-distance telephone calls. Household expenses, including rent, food, utilities and cleaning, will be paid jointly. Lynne and Sarah agree to keep receipts for all expenses, and to do an accounting each month. The person who spends less will pay the other whatever sum is necessary to arrive at a 50-50 split.[12]

6. Lynne, because she's a gourmet, will food shop and cook. Sarah will wash dishes and do general cleaning. They will both maintain the plants and pets.

7. Lynne and Sarah each agree to make a valid will, revocable upon the termination of this agreement, leaving all their property to the other upon death.[13]

8. Either Lynne or Sarah can end this agreement at any time. If they separate, they will equally divide jointly purchased property. Neither, however, will be obligated to support the other.

9. Any provision in this agreement found to be invalid shall have no effect on the validity of the remaining provisions.

Dated: _____   Signature:_____
                                                          Lynne Jacobs

Dated: _____   Signature:_____
                                                          Sarah Elderberry

---

[12]Lynne and Sarah could instead open a joint bank account to pay household expenses. Each person contributes a set amount at the beginning of the month and either can write checks for agreed-upon purchases.

[13]See Chapter 9, Estate Planning.

H. ARBITRATION AND MEDIATION

Sometimes, people who can't agree about a provision of a contract go to court and let a judge decide. But when disagreements occur, there are alternatives to court. We prefer mediation and, if necessary, arbitration, because they're cheaper, faster and usually less painful than litigation. Under either alternative, your dispute is resolved by following procedures you included in your contract. Your contract can call for a professional mediator or arbitrator, a trusted friend, a group of three colleagues, the minister of the local gay church, etc.[14]

Mediation is an informal meeting with you, your lover, and the person or persons who will help you reach a compromise. You discuss the situation and work together at reaching a mutually satisfactory decision. You then write out your agreement, sign it and agree to be bound by it.

Arbitration is a bit different. It, too, is informal, but you and your lover each present your version of the dispute to the person or persons you've chosen to make the decision. After the presentation, the arbitrator(s) decides how to resolve the dispute. Normally, the parties agree to be bound by the arbitrator's decision. This means that if one of you decides to sue in court, the court will enforce the arbitrator's decision, unless the arbitrator was blatantly biased or crazy. Business and labor have used arbitration for years, partly because they realized that getting a dispute settled quickly is as important as who wins and who loses. Many people feel that mediation is even more advantageous because it's non-adversarial and encourages the people with the dispute to arrive at a compromise solution.

What follows is a sample mediation/arbitration provision you can add to the agreements in this book, including the ones in the Appendix. If you don't like ours, other mediation and arbitration provisions appear in many books at your local law library.

Note: If you write an agreement and don't include an arbitration or mediation provision, any dispute that can't be solved informally may wind up in court.

---

[14]One caveat: "professional" arbitrators are very expensive, so check fees and consider whether using a non-professional person is an acceptable alternative. Another caveat: selecting a friend can put the friend in an awkward position. She may change from a friend to a former friend, if one or both of you don't like her decision. Often a person known to and respected by both partners, but a close friend of neither, is a good choice.

MEDITATION/ARBITRATION CLAUSE

Any dispute arising out of this suit shall be mediated by a third person mutually acceptable to both of us. The mediator's role shall be to help us arrive at our solution, not to impose one on us. If good faith efforts to arrive at our own solution to all issues in dispute with the help of a mediator prove to be fruitless, either of us may make a written request to the other that our dispute be arbitrated. This shall be done as follows. Either of us may:

(a) initiate arbitration by making a written demand for arbitration, defining the dispute and naming one arbitrator;

(b) within five days from receipt of this notice, the other shall name the second arbitrator;

(c) the two named arbitrators shall within ten days name a third arbitrator;

(d) within seven days an arbitration meeting will be held. Each of us may have counsel if we choose, and may present the evidence and witnesses pertinent;

(e) the arbitrators shall make their decision within five days after the hearing. Their decision shall be in writing and shall be binding upon us;

(f) if the person to whom the demand for arbitration is directed fails to respond within five days, the other must give an additional five days' written notice of his or her intent to proceed. If there is no response, the person initiating the arbitration may proceed with the arbitration before the arbitrator he or she has designated, and his/her award shall have the same force as if it had been settled by all three arbitrators.

Dated: _____   Signature:_____

Dated: _____   Signature:_____

I. COOLING-OFF CLAUSES

In your agreement, consider adding a clause to remind yourselves of your commitment should the stress of a moment threaten to drive you apart. We call these "cooling-off" clauses; although they're not enforceable in court, they're excellent expressions of intentions. One clause simply states that if one person wants to leave the relationship, he or she will take some time to cool off before grabbing the cat and the good wine glasses and heading for the hills. Imperfect souls that we are, we make a lot of hasty, irrational decisions when we're hurt or angry that we later come to regret. A cooling-off provision can break the routine and give you time to try to work things out. Noel Coward understood the value—and the limits—of this kind of agreement in "Private Lives." If either spouse called "Solomon Isaacs" during a fight, a truce would immediately begin. It worked well until one day, when the husband cried "Solomon Isaacs" and his wife broke a record over his head, shouting "Solomon Isaacs, yourself." As you can see, cooling-off clauses don't always work.

Here are some sample cooling-off clauses:

ALTERNATIVE 1

In the event either person is seriously considering ending the relationship, that person will take a vacation, finding another place to stay, whether with a friend or at a hotel, for at least three days before making a final decision. At least four more days will pass before we divide the property. In addition, we agree to attend at least one counseling session if either one of us wants it.

ALTERNATIVE 2

Either of us can request a cooling-off period for any reason, including that we are fighting. We will spend four days separately. At the end of four days, we will meet for a meal and try to discuss our difficulties rationally, and with affection for each other.

ALTERNATIVE 3

At the request of either one of us, we agree to attend a minimum of four counseling sessions with a friend or professional before making any irrevocable decisions concerning our relationship.

J.   MODIFICATIONS

Modifications of a written contract should always be in writing, since ancient, but still applicable, legal doctrines usually make oral modifications of a written contract unenforceable. In addition, the contracts in this book require that any modifications must be in writing. A modification can simply state that you agree to change your contract, and then set out the change. Date and sign all modifications. If you're making major changes, tear up the old agreement and start over.

Despite broad legal principles and contractual provisions requiring written modifications, sometimes oral modifications are enforceable in court. The precise requirements for proving oral modifications vary among states, but usually, at least the following is required:

- There must be "clear and convincing" proof of the oral modification.
- The person trying to enforce the modification (called the "promissee" in legalese) must have done all or part of what he or she agreed to do under the modification.
- The "promissee" must have relied on the other person's oral agreement to his or her detriment. For example, John and Tim agree in writing that the house they live in, plus the fixtures and improvements, are John's. John asks Tim, an engaging if naive chap, if he'll help redo the foundation and says, in front of three witnesses, that if Tim agrees to do it, John will give Tim a one-fifth interest in the house. Tim thinks this is fair and does the work. John never changes the deed. Three years later they separate. A court is likely to order John to give Tim his one-fifth share.

-4-

LIVING TOGETHER AND THE WORLD: PRACTICAL MATTERS

When you and your lover decide to live together, you're probably acting on romantic impulses. Unfortunately, in our over-complicated society, practical problems inevitably tag along in the wake of romance. Most of these problems aren't legal and don't involve lawyers. All the barristers in the world can't help you when you and your lover discuss whether or not to be monogamous, what to play on the stereo and what to hang on the living room wall. Many day-to-day hassles, however, are connected with law. Some, such as employment discrimination and criminal prosecutions for soliciting, aren't addressed here because they aren't specifically related to living as a lesbian or gay couple. In this chapter, we focus on the legal situations—house or apartment rentals, money and credit, insurance, etc.—facing gay and lesbian couples. Our goal is to be specific enough to be helpful without being overly technical. If you want more information on a subject, check the Resources and Bibliography in the Appendix.

Although lesbian and gay couples lose the practical benefits and protections of marriage, there are some advantages to being the same sex and not married. For example, unlike married couples where both people work, lesbian and gay couples aren't discriminated against by income tax regulations. In addition, reasonably discrete gay couples often face less trouble when traveling than do unmarried straight couples; few hotels or resorts worry about two people of the same sex sharing a room. For the same reason, lesbian and gay couples sometimes find it easier than unmarried straight couples to rent a home in many parts of the country. Of course, there are disadvantages. For one, family plans offered by the travel industry aren't normally available to lesbian and gay couples.[1]

Tragically, lesbian and gay couples have few legal protections. At present, no federal laws prohibit discrimination against lesbian and gay people or couples in areas such as employment, housing, credit or insurance. These protections exist in a few states and localities, but often the places that pass anti-discrimination ordinances are places that largely accepted lesbian and gay people before the laws were passed. We mean no criticism of anti-discrimination ordinances when we say that in cities such as Madison and San Francisco these laws are more symbolic of lesbian and gay political acceptance than they are the wedges to bring about change. We support and applaud lesbian and gay political activists while, at the same time, we've written a book about living, not fighting political struggles. It is important to remember, however, that because of the many pioneering political battles, lesbian and gay couples can live openly in many parts of the world.

A. Renting a Home—Discrimination

If a private landlord discriminates against you, there's not much you can do about it. Lesbian and gay couples have little legal protection against housing discrimination except in the few localities that have passed anti-discrimination ordinances.[2] This raises the question of whether to inform a prospective landlord that you're gay. It's far from automatic that a landlord will discriminate against you because of your sexual orientation. There are all sorts of landlords. Some "love their gay boys because they do know how to keep an apartment." Most are concerned with money and responsible tenants, not your private life. But it's not the landlord's business, and nothing legally requires you to volunteer the information. This is a tactical, not a legal, decision. If the landlord lives downstairs and is almost sure to figure it out, it may make sense to be candid. If the landlord lives halfway across the country, why bother? If the landlord discovers your relationship, however, and decides to evict you, there's usually little you can do, unless you have a lease.

---

[1]Many large cities, however, have lesbian or gay operated travel agencies. Also, many gay or lesbian resorts, hotels, etc. are available if you want to vacation completely at ease. We discuss travel problems, especially of foreigners entering the United States, in Chapter 10.

[2]Also, theoretical prohibitions against discrimination against gays exist in public housing and federally funded housing, like housing for the elderly. And a California court ruled that housing discrimination against gays violates the state civil rights law (*Hubert v. Williams*, 133 Cal. App. 3d 1 (1982)).

If you rent under a month-to-month rental agreement, your landlord simply gives you a 30-day notice to get out. It can be for any reason or no reason at all, and you have no protection.[3] You're in much better shape if you have a lease, where a landlord must rely on a violation of one of the lease clauses (e.g., pay your rent on time, don't damage the apartment) to evict you before the lease ends. We've never seen a lease clause saying "you cannot live here if you are—or become—queer." But most leases prohibit illegal activity on the premises, and a landlord might threaten to evict you in a state where sodomy is illegal. In conservative parts of the country, local judges (who decide if the landlord can evict you) and sheriffs (who do the physical evicting), may, too, be hostile to gays and require the landlord to present little proof that you're gay. But in the urban areas of those states where gay sex is illegal, this sort of eviction would be extremely difficult. Why? Because to prove that illegal activities transpired on the property, the landlord would have to present evidence, not just vague suspicions. In most cases, if you keep your mouth shut, such proof would be impossible to get.

Note: Some leases and written rental agreements contain illegal provisions, such as one giving the landlord the right to evict you immediately, with no court action, if you are late with your rent. Before signing your lease or rental agreement, read it carefully; if something rubs you the wrong way, ask that it be crossed out. Watch especially for clauses prohibiting "immoral behavior" or "association with undesirable people." In the 25 states with no laws regulating the sexual behavior of consenting adults, the first clause has no meaning anyway, but in the other states, it can be a problem if the landlord uses it to evict you. If your landlord agrees, cross out the offending language and have your landlord add his or her initials.

A friend experienced a nasty situation several years ago. He describes it as follows:

"One night, my landlady, who lived downstairs, telephoned and shouted, 'It's illegal, you two living together. Get out or I will call the cops.' To be honest, even though I was a lawyer, the call was so incredibly jarring and frightening that my first response was to do just that—to get out. But after talking it over with my lover, we decided that we had to stay and fight. And then, after staying long enough to establish the fact that we weren't being driven out, we realized that we wanted to move. Right or wrong, legal or illegal, wasn't the question. We simply didn't want to live above someone who was hostile to us. We learned one

---

[3] A growing number of cities, such as Los Angeles and San Francisco, have passed rent control ordinances requiring "just cause for eviction," even for month-to-month tenancies. These ordinances offer considerable protection because being gay or lesbian is not one of the "just causes."

valuable lesson from the experience though: never rent from someone who lives in the same building, unless you know she's okay."

If your landlord evicts or otherwise harasses you because you're gay, find out if any local ordinance prohibits discrimination. If so, you may want to fight, which means either getting a lawyer to help you or representing yourself. Either way, you'll have to file a written response to the eviction papers and raise the defense that you're being illegally discriminated against. Keep in mind, however, that you may still have a problem, even with an ordinance prohibiting sexual orientation discrimination in housing. Many landlords are smart enough to state a non-discriminatory (phony) reason for evicting you.

If no local ordinance prohibits housing discrimination against gays or lesbians or requires "just cause for eviction," you are, essentially, at the mercy of your landlord. If you already have a lease, you're protected for the remainder of the lease term, but after that, you're in the same position you'd be in if without a lease. Your landlord can tell you to leave after giving you proper notice (usually 30 days) under the laws of your state.

Important: We can't address every possible landlord-tenant situation here. There are many books on the subject, including Nolo's *Tenants' Rights* (California edition). Also, tenants' rights projects operate in many cities. If you have a serious problem and you can't get help or information any other way, consider a one-time consultation with a lawyer. Get the fee in advance. It shouldn't be a lot. (See Chapter 12.)

B. RENTING TOGETHER

Let's assume you find that wonderful little affordable house next to the park and you and your lover happily sign a lease, or reach a rental agreement with your landlord. Are you each obligated to pay one-half of the rent? No. You've each made a contract obligating you to pay all rent and be financially responsible for all damage done.

Example: John and Alfonso agree to verbal month-to-month tenancy in a brown-shingle bungalow. After three months, John becomes unhappy with the relationship. One day, he refuses to pay his share of the rent and attacks the house. The result is two broken windows, a badly-dented radiator and a refrigerator without a door. Not surprisingly, Alfonso asks John to move out, which he does. Alfonso also asks John to pay for the damage and for his half of the rent. John laughs. If John doesn't pay, Alfonso is legally responsible for all rent and damage, and the landlord can sue him if he doesn't pay. Alfonso can sue John for reimbursement, but whether Alfonso will ever collect largely depends on whether John has assets.

Example: Louise and Arlene sign a one-year lease. After six months of amicably living together, Arlene quits her job and leaves. The parting isn't so amicable after Arlene informs Louise that she knows Louise is responsible and will take care of the rent. Louise is liable for it all for the next six months. Louise, however, does have a partial out. If she doesn't want to stay, she can try to find someone to take over the remainder of the lease. Most areas of the country suffer from a rental housing shortage and this is relatively easy to do. Even if the lease prohibits subletting and the landlord insists on enforcing it, Louise can legally move out with no financial obligation as long as she finds a suitable new tenant who will pay at least the same rent. This is because the law requires the landlord to do whatever possible to re-rent the apartment ("mitigate damages," in legalese), and not just sit back and insist on the lease payments.

C. MOVING INTO YOUR LOVER'S RENTED HOME

It is often easier psychologically for two people moving in together to obtain a new place. It's common, however, for one partner to move in with the other. What are the obligations when one of you moves into a house or apartment rented by the other? Is the move legal? Is the original tenant required to tell the landlord that someone has moved in?

Legally, you must notify your landlord that you have a new roommate only if a written lease or rental agreement requires it or limits the number of people who can occupy the unit. But even with no requirement, it's normally wise to notify. The landlord will almost surely figure it out, and it's especially important to avoid looking sneaky if you have a month-to-month tenancy (as opposed to a lease) where the landlord can evict for any reason. Whether you tell the landlord that you're lovers or merely roommates is entirely up to you. Usually, the landlord will want more rent for the additional person. Unless the amount is exorbitant, you're probably wise to accept the increase. Even if your lease or rental agreement requires notice to the landlord of a new tenant, all that usually results is an increase in rent.

If your lease doesn't cover someone else moving in, you can probably bargain with your landlord if your lover moves in. For your landlord to get you out before the lease expires, he would have to establish that you have violated one or more lease terms. Even if your lease prohibits someone else from moving in, once your landlord accepts rent knowing that you live with someone, many courts will refuse to let him enforce the lease prohibition. If your lease simply states that the premises shall not be used for "immoral or illegal purpose," it is highly unlikely your landlord can terminate the lease simply because you live with someone, unless your state has a sodomy law; even then, the landlord's case would be difficult to prove.

1. Is There a Legal Relationship Between the New Tenant and the Landlord?

Assume Renee moves into Jane's apartment. Does Renee have a legal relationship with Jane's landlord? If so, what is it? More specifically, does Renee have a legal duty to pay rent if Jane fails to? If Jane moves out, does Renee have the right to stay? If Jane damages the formica or lets her dog scratch the wall, does Renee have a legal obligation to pay the landlord for the damages?

There are no simple answer to these questions. It depends on how long Renee has lived in Jane's place, coupled with lots of other factors. If Renee just spends a few nights, she'd have no obligation to pay rent and no rights as a tenant. The same would be true during the first weeks of her tenancy, if Renee moved in. Remember, Jane, not Renee, entered into a contract with the landlord. But just as Renee has no legal obligations at this early stage, she has no rights either. If Jane moves out, Renee can't stay unless the landlord consents.

There are factors, however, that transform Renee into a tenant, and give her all the legal rights and responsibilities that go with tenant status. Renee becomes a tenant by:

- Getting the landlord to prepare a new lease that includes both Jane and Renee as tenants.

- Talking to the landlord and agreeing orally to a tenant-landlord relationship. Be careful of two things, however. An oral agreement is difficult to prove—if the landlord reneges, you may have a hard time proving you made an agreement. At the same time, an oral agreement can be easily implied from a casual conversation. Suppose Renee meets the landlord in the laundry room, introduces herself, explains that she's moved into Jane's apartment and agrees to pay rent. The landlord says "okay." A valid agreement's been formed. Renee can be evicted only in a formal court action, but is liable for all rent and damage to the apartment. So, if you're not sure you want to become a tenant, be careful of casual conversation with the landlord.

- Paying rent directly to the landlord or property manager. If this is done, especially if done repeatedly, an "implied contract," as it is known in legalese, is formed. Nothing formal has been said or written down, but the conduct of both Renee and the landlord clearly creates a landlord-tenant relationship.

2. Moving On

It's been known to happen that one partner wants to move on, while the other wants to stay. If this is in the wind, be clear about rights and responsibilities before the move takes place. Suppose Jane wants to move, in order to take advantage of a job offer in another state. What should she do? First, she should notify her landlord in writing of her intention. If she has a month-to-month tenancy, 30-days notice is sufficient. If she has a lease, she should give the landlord as much notice as possible. Remember, the landlord has a duty to re-rent the place as quickly as possible. If Renee wants to stay and her credit checks out, she'd be the logical person to take over the lease.[4] If the landlord refuses to rent to Renee, Jane's obligation for the rest of the lease is over. The landlord had a chance to re-rent the place (to Renee) and turned it down. Now it's his responsibility to find another tenant.

---

[4]Renee, in fact, may already be a tenant if she's paid rent or spoken with the landlord.

D. ROOMMATES: THE LEGAL RELATIONSHIP OF ONE TENANT TO THE OTHER

This is an important section. Although many tenants have problems with their landlords, the truth is that people sharing a home get into more hassles with one another than they do with their landlord. One reason is because we deal with landlords at arm's length and take steps to protect ourselves; we aren't usually businesslike with those we love. But whatever the reason, we've learned that paying reasonable attention to business details helps to preserve romance.

Renting a Home Together: It's wonderful for a couple to move into new quarters together. The new apartment or house represents a fresh start, with no ghosts of past relationships or already-established territorial rights. There's no need to say, "Well, I guess I can move my clothes out of *my* hall closet to give *you* more room" or "I painted the bathroom red, white and blue stripes, and I'm not about to repaint it soft yellow." Remember—whatever relationship you establish with your landlord, the crux of living together will be the understandings you two work out. Don't underestimate the need to be clear. Renting a place to live isn't only a large monetary investment, but it also provides you with a special haven of relaxation and refuge. Obviously, it's worth a little effort to ensure that you both will feel secure and protected.

Start with a complete understanding—who pays what portion of the rent, who gets the place if you split up, etc. Once you decide, write it down. It can be part of an overall living-together contract or a separate agreement. Either way is fine. The important thing is to not ignore it.

Note: Nothing you agree to is binding on your landlord unless he's made a party to the agreement. But this wouldn't make sense; the main purpose of the agreement is to record your understandings in the event a dispute later arises.

Here is an agreement covering moving into a newly (jointly) rented living space:

RENTING TOGETHER CONTRACT

Audrey Rabinowitz and Candice Dunk have just rented Apartment 6B at 1500 Avenue B, New York, New York and agree as follows:

1. We each agree to pay one-half of the rent and one-half of the gas, electricity, water and fixed monthly telephone charge. We'll keep a book next to the telephone to record our long-distance calls; each person will pay for her calls. Our rent will always be paid on time and the utility bills will be paid within ten days of receipt.

2. If either wants to leave, she must give the other, and the landlord, at least 30 days' written notice. The person moving agrees to pay her rent (before she moves) for the entire 30-day period, even if she leaves sooner.

3. We intend to live as a couple and neither of us wants a large number of house guests. Therefore, no third person will be invited to stay overnight without the permission of both of us.

4. If it happens that we want to end our living arrangement, but that we each want to remain at this address, a third party will flip a coin to decide who remains. The loser of the coin flip will move out within 30 days and will pay all her obligations for rent, utilities and any damage to the apartment.[5]

Dated: _____   Signature: _____
                                   Audrey Rabinowitz

Dated: _____   Signature: _____
                                   Candice Dunk

Moving into a Home Already Rented by One of You: If one partner moves into an apartment or house already rented by the other, turning it into a shared home requires a great deal of sensitivity and openness, especially by the person who was there first. Sometimes, a party to rechristen the home your shared home provides a valuable symbolic "rite of passage."

However you manage the exciting emotional change, it's a good idea to write down your economic and legal understandings. If you fall in bad times, a

---

[5]Some people adopt an approach more rational than flipping a coin. They have an objective third person decide, based on proximity to work, needs of any children, relative financial status or other factors. This approach can work well, but don't pick a close friend, who's likely to end up a friend of only one of you.

question like, "whose apartment is this—legally?" can come up and cause pain and paranoia. Write down your understanding when you begin living together; it forces you to clarify the issues. Here is a sample agreement that may prove helpful:

MOVING IN CONTRACT

Roger Rappan and Peter Majors agree as follows:

1. Roger will move into the apartment that Peter has been renting at 111 Prairie Street, Chicago, Illinois, on August 1, 19__ and will pay Peter one-half of the $500 monthly rent on the first of each month. Because Peter has been renting under a lease, he will continue to pay the landlord on the first of each month for the remainder of the lease term (six months).

2. Roger and Peter will each pay one-half of the electric, gas, water, garbage and monthly telephone service charge. Peter will collect the payments, because the accounts are in his name.

3. For the first six months, Peter retains the first right to stay in the apartment should he and Roger decide to separate. If either person decides that Roger should move out during this period, he shall give (or be given) 30 days written notice and shall be responsible for his share of the rent and utilities during the 30 days.

4. After the initial six-month period, if Peter and Roger decide to continue living together, they shall jointly lease the apartment and change half of the utilities into Roger's name. From this point forward, they have equal rights to stay in the apartment,[6] should they break up. If both want to retain the apartment, but either or both wants to end the relationship, a third party will flip a coin to determine who gets to stay.

Dated: _____   Signature: _____
                                         Roger Rappan
Dated: _____   Signature: _____
                                         Peter Majors

---

[6]Obviously, this is only one way to handle it. Peter could always hold onto the first right to keep the apartment, or alternatively, he could share this right with Roger from the start.

Note: What do you do if you never made a written living-together agreement and you get into a serious dispute? All you can do is make the best effort to compromise, remembering that, in most good compromises, each person believes he gave at least 60%.

Here are a few suggestions when both people want to stay, but not with each other, and nothing has been written down.

- If one person occupied first, pays the rent *and* is the only one who signed the lease or rental agreement, the law gives her a superior claim to the apartment. But the law also requires that the other be given reasonable notice to find another place (at least 30 days).
- If both partners have a strong relationship with the landlord (both pay rent or both signed a lease or rental agreement), they probably have equal rights to stay. This is true even if one occupied first. Flip a coin or have a third person mediate or arbitrate to settle the dispute. Avoid court action if you can.

E. DOMESTIC PARTNERSHIPS

In the last few years, some courts and governments have begun to acknowledge that large numbers of unmarried couples—both heterosexual and homosexual—live together, and that the partners depend on each other for emotional and monetary support in much the same way that traditionally married couples do.

Legal recognition of unmarried families has been extremely slow, but the fact of recognition is important. We discuss some of the legal consequences of recognition in the hope that the lesbian and gay community can build and strengthen the rights of unmarried couples. Some apply solely to unmarried non-gay couples, but most apply to both gay and straight families, sometimes called "domestic partnerships."

1. Private Organizations

Many institutions, such as museums, health clubs and public television stations, which used to offer membership discounts to spouses, are now offering them to "any two people," "two friends" or "a household," regardless of marital status or sexuality.

Employers, too, are recognizing that unmarried couples exist, and that the employee deserves benefits which had previously been reserved for married employees. Some employers extend bereavement leave to any employee who is part of a couple. Some airlines which offer discounted flights to employees and their spouses, now permit employees to take along a "friend." Unfortunately, no laws require employers to extend benefits, and therefore, there's nothing you can legally do if they aren't offered.[7]

2. Health Insurance

Many people obtain health insurance through employment; far more do not, and either have no insurance or purchase it on their own. Group health plans (usually available only to employers) are frequently less expensive and/or provide better coverage than individual plans. In addition, group plans rarely require medical examinations before covering employees. Insurance companies also offer individual or group "family" plans. If you search very hard, you might find an insurance company that offers coverage to a lover, or to children of a lover. Consumers United Co-op America Insurance Company in Washington, D.C. has allowed employees to cover their lovers.

---

[7]The Lesbian Rights Project, 1370 Mission St., 4th Floor, San Francisco, CA 94103 publishes "Recognizing Lesbian and Gay Families: Strategies for Extending Employment Benefit Coverage" which provides ideas for employees on how to negotiate with unions, employers and others in order to obtain employment benefits for gay couples.

3. Domestic Partnership Laws

The Berkeley, California Unified School District and the City of Berkeley were the first public employers to adopt policies seeking group medical insurance with companies willing to insure an employee's "domestic partner," as well as an employee's immediate family (traditionally, the spouse and kids). The "domestic partner" may be a lesbian, gay or straight partner.

Unfortunately, because insurance companies cry "outrageous expense" at covering non-marital partners, and because of AIDS, domestic partnership laws may have little practical impact. To date, no health insurance carrier for Berkeley or its School Board has been willing to extend coverage to "domestic partners" except in dental insurance. As long as insurance companies are wary or unwilling to extend coverage, domestic partnership legislation will do no practical good.

One interesting question with "domestic partnerships" is what qualifies someone as a "domestic partner." What steps must be taken to identify the partner? How long need the couple be together? How do you change or terminate a partnership? A vetoed San Francisco bill defined domestic partners as:

> *not related by blood; neither was married nor were they related by marriage; they share the common necessaries of life; they declare that they are each other's principal domestic partner; and neither has, within the first six months, declared that he or she has a different domestic partner.*

The bill would have allowed the partners to register with the county.

4. Governments Benefits

A gay man in California was awarded unemployment insurance from the state when he left his job to care for his lover who was dying of AIDS. Married partners have for years received benefits if they quit their jobs to care for terminally ill spouses. In extending the benefits to gay couples, the Unemployment Appeals Board declared that gay relationships are often as serious, loving and committed as marriages.

In another California case, a gay man was awarded Workers' Compensation death benefits when his lover, a county district attorney, committed suicide because of job-related stress. The Workers' Compensation Appeals Board found that the lover was dependent on the employee for support, and said that the homosexual relationship of the two men shouldn't preclude the lover's rights to benefits.

These cases, however, are not the norm. Most unmarried partners are denied unemployment, workers compensation and other benefits when seeking those benefits in situations usually reserved for married people.

F. CASH AND CREDIT

"Getting and spending, we lay waste our powers."—William Wordsworth

As most of us eventually learn, often to our chagrin or regret, money is funny stuff and can do strange things to people. While most of us aspire to rise above crass money concerns, it doesn't require a big dose of realism to see that any couple must clearly state who pays for the rent, car installments or groceries. If one partner feels she is being monetarily exploited, she is almost guaranteed to be resentful, and perhaps even enraged. A written agreement is essential; but remember, it's no substitute for trust and communication. Contracts won't enable two people to continue loving one another or prevent them from splitting up, but if times get hard, a written agreement can do wonders to reduce paranoia and confusion and help people deal with one another fairly.

1. Debts

Because you live with someone doesn't mean your financial lives need become one. Indeed, as long as you keep your property and debts separate, you'll have no financial obligation if your lover lives beyond his financial means. This means your paycheck cannot be garnished and your property cannot be taken to satisfy your lover's overdue bills. If your lover declares bankruptcy, your property cannot be taken, *as long as you have kept it separate.*

Common Sense Note: Just as it doesn't make sense to crawl in bed with someone who has the flu, it isn't wise to put your money in a joint bank account, in joint ownership of a car or in other joint investments with anyone who has a bad case of spendthriftitis. If your lover owes money, her creditors can cause you difficulties if you've mixed your money and property. Indeed, when living with someone with debt problems, sign a contract keeping everything separate (such as the first "Living-Together Agreement" in the Appendix) to avoid possible confusion.

2. Joint Bank Accounts

Sometimes couples maintain joint bank accounts for limited purposes, such as household expenses or a distinct project (e.g., renovating a house together). Joint bank accounts are sensible if you limit their purpose and keep adequate records. That said, let us add that we do know lesbian and gay couples who have peacefully maintained joint bank accounts for years. But still, a joint account is a risk; each person has the right to spend all the money in it, unless you require both signatures on checks and withdrawals. Another problem is record-keeping. It's hard to know how much money is in an account if you both write checks. If your joint account is for a specific purpose (e.g., a vacation), identify it as such. Some banks allow you to name the account (e.g., "The Anderson-Henry Vacation Account"). And don't forget—if you have a joint account, you're both responsible for all checks drawn on it—even if your lover violates your trust, empties the account and puts the money on the nose of a slow pony.

If you decide to open a joint account, obtaining one won't be a problem. Financial institutions are happy to have your money under any name or names. You'll have to decide how many signatures will be necessary to write a check or make a withdrawal. It's easier to require only one signature, but it's riskier, too.

Note on Power of Attorney: A power of attorney gives someone else the authority to act for you. Giving your lover (or a friend) a power of attorney to sign checks or handle other financial matters can be useful when you travel for an extended period or are seriously ill. We discuss powers of attorney in Chapter 8.

3. Plastic

Joint charge accounts are risky. If you want to be generous, be generous with cash, not credit. Sometimes lesbian and gay couples, however, have a psychological need to act married, and so they acquire lots of joint cards. Well, as our mothers used to say, "You can't say I didn't warn you."

It isn't too difficult to put two names on a credit card, as long as one of you establishes sufficient income, savings, etc., to cover all potential charges. Some stores refuse to open joint credit accounts to up-front lesbian or gay couples, but this sort of prejudice can usually be circumvented by presenting yourself as business partners. In urban areas, more and more—but not all—stores seem willing to open joint credit accounts for gay and lesbian couples. Why shouldn't they? It means more people are responsible for a debt. Thus, if Renee and Jane have a joint credit card, and Renee allows her brother Flaubert to charge $2,500 on it, Renee and Jane are both legally obligated to pay the bill, even if Jane didn't know about it, or knew about it and opposed it. Similarly, if Jane retaliates by leaving Renee and going on a buying binge, Renee is legally responsible for all the charges Jane makes.

Important: When a couple breaks up, they should immediately close all joint accounts. All too often, one person feels depressed during the break-up and tries to pamper himself or herself with "retail therapy." Don't just allot the accounts so that each of you keeps some of them. You're both still liable for all accounts—and you could get stuck paying his or her "therapy" bill.

4. Credit and Credit Agencies

A store or financial institution isn't obligated to lend money or give credit to anyone who applies for it. In times of high interest and tight money, lenders can, and do, get pretty picky. In times of economic stability, stores and banks lend to people considered good financial risks, and refuse to lend to bad risk applicants. We haven't encountered many recent stories of discrimination against individual lesbians or gays in credit. At least in major urban areas, ability to pay seems to be the criterion used—not sexual identity.

But suppose you believe you were discriminated against in requesting credit. Is there anything you can do about it? Maybe. Congress passed a law prohibiting creditors from discriminating on account of race, color, religion, national origin, sex, marital status or age, or because all or part of a person's income derives from public assistance.[8] There are no reported cases involving alleged discrimination against lesbians or gays under this law. It's possible that courts would interpret this law, as courts have with other anti-discrimination laws, not to include sexual orientation in the ban on "sex" discrimination. Even if "sex" were to include sexual orientation, proving a case would be difficult.

Other rights all persons have under the Equal Credit Opportunity Act include:

- A creditor may not ignore income from a part-time job.
- A creditor may require disclosure of alimony and child-support payments made, but not payments received, unless the received payments help establish income.
- A creditor cannot require use of a married name, and must allow credit to be issued in either a given name or a combined surname.
- A creditor may not ignore income from child-support or alimony payments in determining creditworthiness, but may consider how likely they are to be paid.
- A creditor cannot terminate an account or require a reapplication if the borrower's name or marital status changes unless there's evidence of unwillingness or inability to pay a bill. If the creditor denies an applicant credit, the creditor must state the reason for the denial.
- Married or previously married women whose credit accounts were in their husbands' names can request that independent credit histories be developed from the marital credit histories.

Checking Your Credit: If you've lived together for a long period of time, or have had joint credit cards or bank accounts, it's possible that your credit histories have become intertwined, or even erroneously attributed to each other. This is usually not to your advantage, especially if one of you has bad credit. What can you do, aside from getting angry when your credit application is denied? Simple. Check your credit rating.

Credit bureaus are companies that specialize in keeping computerized credit histories (and lots of other information) on almost everyone. When a bank, department store, landlord or collection agency wants information about a person, they can get it by paying a small fee to a credit bureau. It is perfectly legal for credit bureaus to keep all sorts of information about you in a credit file (work history, military history, residences, roommates, etc.). Thus, if you've been up front with the world, a credit bureau may have your sexual orientation on record.

---

[8]This is called the "Equal Credit Opportunity Act," 15 U.S.C. §1691. The act provides for penalties of up to $10,000 for an individual plus any money the individual lost as a consequence of being discriminated against. Penalties for large groups of people suing together (class actions suits) can mount to $500,000.

Fortunately, the Fair Credit Reporting Act gives you the right to examine your credit file. If the file contains false or outdated information, the credit bureau is required to correct it, or, if it disputes your claim that it's false or outdated, to include your version of the dispute in your file. For detailed information on your rights, see *Billpayers' Rights,* Warner and Elias (Nolo Press).

Reminder: Credit histories can follow you—and sometimes haunt you—for a long time. Before you open a joint account, beware that if your lover runs up large bills and doesn't pay them, or pays late, these facts can stay in your credit history for seven years.

5. Buying a Car Together

Many couples share one car, especially if they live in an area in which mass transit makes owning two cars unnecessary. If you purchase an automobile jointly, prepare an agreement reflecting your joint ownership, and properly complete the ownership documents. Even if only one of you obtains the loan to finance the car, you can both be legal owners if that's what you want.

Vehicle ownership is reflected on a "title" slip issued by your state motor vehicles department. The type of "title" you have (we discuss them in detail below) affects what happens to the deceased person's share when he dies. In addition to the title slip, you should draft an agreement stating who gets the car if you split up. Also, if one of you owns more of the car than the other, record your ownership portions in writing.

When you register your car with the state, you must indicate the owner(s). If you intend joint ownership, register it in both names. If you want the car to belong to only one of you, register it in that person's name. Just make sure you agree before you make the purchase who will own it, use it and pay for it.

In most states, there are three possible ways to jointly own and register a motor vehicle:

- *The "or" form:* This is usually expressed as "Renee Parker *or* Jane Axelrod." In many states, if the "or" form is used and one owner dies, ownership and registration is transferred to the survivor without going through a court probate proceeding. The "or" form, however, normally permits either owner to sell the car without the permission, or even knowledge, of the other.

- *The "and" form:* This is normally written as "Renee Parker *and* Jane Axelrod." The "and" form requires both owners' signature if the car is sold or given away. In many states, if one owner dies, her one-half passes by her will, or if she didn't write a will, to her "next of kin" (usually children, parents or siblings). If she wants her lover to inherit her share, she must have a will so stating (see Chapter 9).

- *The "Joint Tenants" form:* This is usually written as "Renee Parker and Jane Axelrod as joint tenants" (or JTRS). Joint tenancy requires both signatures to sell or give the car away. And, if one person dies, ownership and registration passes automatically to the survivor. In many states, however, banks, finance companies or other lenders won't allow the car buyers to put title in joint tenancy until the loan is completely paid off.

Note: This information is general. Different states have different procedures. Check with your state department of motor vehicles for details.

Being the registered owner of a car carries with it possible liability. In most states, a registered owner is financially responsible for any accident caused by his car, even if someone else is driving. The owner (or his insurance company) can pursue the driver for the money paid to the injured person, but the owner is liable even if the driver takes the first boat to Tahiti. The reason for this is simple and sound: It encourages car owners to carry insurance, and to carefully select who can drive their cars. As a practical matter, it means that you don't let just anyone (even your lover) drive your car unless you have ample insurance.

We strongly urge every car owner to carry auto insurance. The automobile is the only lethal weapon most people use regularly. The statistical risk of an accident is all too high, and, if an accident occurs, there's a good chance that the damage will be serious. If you don't carry insurance, you may be economically wiped out, and even worse, an injured person may go without compensation because of your irresponsibility.

G. INSURANCE

Ambrose Bierce observed that insurance is "an ingenious modern game of chance in which the player is permitted to enjoy the comfortable conviction that he is beating the man who keeps the table." Like Bierce, we're no great fans of insurance. Sure, insurance is sometimes necessary or prudent, but it often seems that some giant corporation[9] makes a lot of money by pandering to, or creating, people's fears.

Aside from our mistrust of large organizations—not to mention the TV ads full of cavalry charges, abandoned railroad stations and folksy neighbors—we're frankly bothered by that contemporary killjoy, the idea that you shouldn't breathe unless you're insured against all possible disasters. Every time a fence closes off a field, an owner blocks off a swimming hole or some other accommodation closes down because people can't afford insurance and won't proceed without it, we all lose. You've heard it at least a dozen times. "Our insurance company says we won't be covered if we let you..." Or "We're very sorry, but our lawyer won't let us take the risk." It seems like every week an ice-skating rink or child care center closes because it couldn't get or afford insurance.

But aren't there times when you do need insurance? Suppose your home burns down, a child runs in front of your car, someone steals your color TV with its two video game attachments, you suffer an injury and can't work or a nuclear reactor has a core melt-down? Certainly, those so inclined will have lots of fun imagining possible needs for insurance. And as we've said, we believe everyone should have automobile (liability) insurance. Also, we believe you should have health insurance. We don't have space to discuss most other types of insurance here, but we do believe that most Americans are over-insured much of the time. Here, our concern is the problems lesbian and gay couples face in getting insurance. We will let you decide whether you need insurance in the first place. There are gay and lesbian insurance agents in all urban areas. If you have a problem, try to find one and talk it over with him or her.

---

[9]Some insurance companies—Equitable, State Farm, Metropolitan Life—are owned by their policyholders and normally sell insurance through their employees. We regard the policyholder-owned insurance companies as a fascinating example that organizations come to exist on their own. These companies don't maintain the capitalist fiction of most United States corporations, that they exist to make profits for the stockholders. These insurance companies just exist—with no one really owning them and only managers running them.

1. Life Insurance

Most lesbian and gay people we know don't have life insurance, and, except for special circumstances (such as one or both minor children), we don't see any reason for them to get it. Of course, many people get life insurance at little or no cost to them as part of their employee benefits, but otherwise, life insurance makes sense only if:

- You have dependent children and there's insufficient support (remember to consider any social security they'll receive) for them if you die without insurance.
- Life insurance is included in your overall "estate plan," especially where you want your lover (especially if he or she is financially dependent on you) to receive a lump sum if you die (see Chapter 9).

If you are given life insurance as an employment benefit or purchase a policy for yourself, and you want your lover to receive the proceeds if you die, it's perfectly legal to name your lover as the beneficiary. You cannot, however, buy a policy on your lover's life and name yourself as the beneficiary. Insurance companies don't believe that non-married partners have an "insurable interest" in each other, and limit buying insurance on another person to married spouses or business partners.

2. Renter's (or Homeowner's Personal Property) Insurance

Lesbian and gay couples should be able to buy joint renter's insurance (against theft, fire destruction, etc.). Although we know a gay couple who were refused joint homeowner's insurance, most couples we know find it. The couple denied insurance was told by the company that it didn't insure gay couples because if the couple broke up and one person moved out, taking the other's possessions, the remaining person could claim "theft" of his or her missing property. (That is indeed what the insurance agent said—we checked.) Of course, the idea that this is more likely to happen with gay couples than with straight couples, married or not, is nonsense, but so is all discrimination lesbian and gay couples face in their daily lives.

Our friends wound up with two policies (one each), but most people we know have shopped around and obtained one policy. Insurance companies, for the most part, insure property—not people—and are willing to issue one policy for a given address. They don't care who lives in the place nor what the relationship is. If you do have to buy two policies, it's usually more expensive than covering everything with one policy. (But on the whole, renter's insurance is pretty cheap.) In addition, we've been told by a gay insurance agent that if you buy two policies, use the same insurance companies. Two giant companies asked to settle a claim may try to shift responsibility to the other, rather than write you a check and let you replace the lost, stolen or damaged property.

3. Automobile Insurance

Jointly purchasing automobile insurance can be a problem for a lesbian or gay couple, but not to the extent it was a few years ago. Before issuing a policy, many companies want a complete list of the people who live in the house. Do they have cars of their own? What are the license numbers? The insurance company will run a check with the motor vehicles department to ensure that people with bad driving records aren't likely to be driving your car. And the more your living situation seems communal, with people coming and going, the less likely the company is to write insurance.

Lesbian or gay lovers who each own a car should have no trouble getting separate insurance. If you want joint insurance, insurers won't insure your cars jointly as if you were married, but rather, most will write you each a separate policy, and name the other as secondary driver. Of course, this costs more, which is probably one main reason the companies refuse to change it. If you really want one policy, change your title slips (you have to call the motor vehicles department), putting ownership of both cars in one person. The insurance will list the owner as the primary driver, and the other as a secondary driver. Of course, you'll need a separate written agreement stating clearly who really owns which car.

If you jointly own just one car, you still may have trouble getting one insurance policy. Your best bet is to find a sympathetic insurance salesperson, and explore all the angles and then compare prices.

Time out for a story: We have four friends (two lesbian couples), Selina and Barbara, and Rhonda and Laurie. Selina and Barbara bought a Honda, took title in the "or" form, and sought to get insurance together. They called company X and were told that unmarried couples couldn't get insurance together. Company Y wrote them a policy. Rhonda and Laurie bought a Toyota, also taking the "or" form. They, too, called company X and were happily written a policy. Moral: Be persistent—insurance salespersons and agents can differ tremendously, even with the same company.

4. Health Insurance

Unless you qualify for state health care, we feel it's a great mistake not to have health insurance. Of course, you want insurance before any illness occurs. Some insurance companies will cover you after you suffer an ailment, for example a back problem, but will exclude any coverage for the back. As they put it, they exclude "pre-existing conditions."

Many lesbian and gay leaders feel that insurance companies are attempting to avoid insuring gay men because of the high medical expenses for people with AIDS. One fear is that companies will use a positive result on an HIV test as proof that AIDS was a pre-existing condition, and then refuse to pay the costs of treatment for AIDS-related illnesses. We are among those who recommend that gay men get the HIV and T4 cell test. If your doctor does the tests, however, the results will be in your medical records and can be supplied to the insurance company. Therefore, we recommend you get tested at a clinic which guarantees confidentiality or, better yet, anonymity, not only of the result but of the fact that you took the test. At present, California, New York, Massachusetts and Washington, D.C. have laws prohibiting insurance companies from requiring applicants to take an HIV test.[10] Legislation is pending in other states.

We discussed other aspects of health insurance in Section E(2) of this chapter.

5. Disability Insurance

Disability insurance pays you a certain sum of money (depending on how much insurance you have) each month while you are unable to work. To determine if you need disability insurance, and if so, find out if you're covered by other plans and, if so, how much they'll pay if you're disabled. You may be covered by workers' compensation, which pays you if you are injured on the job. Or, you may have a state disability plan through your job, which pays you if you can't work. In addition, anyone who has had Social Security deducted from his or her pay may qualify for social security disability (SSD). AIDS and many AIDS-related conditions qualify one for SSD.

Even if you're covered by state or federal disability plans, the maximum benefits payable in the event of disability may be inadequate. If so, private disability insurance can help. Most insurance agents will be delighted to tell you more about disability insurance than you ever thought you'd want to know.

---

[10]In New York and Massachusetts, this regulation applies to health insurers but not life insurers.

-5-

Buying a Home, and Other
Real Estate Ventures

A. The American Dream, Updated

To Freud, a home symbolized motherhood. For E.M. Forster, in *Howard's End*, it was a sign of stability and the best of the old order. Others have likened a home to a "castle" and valued it as a haven of peace and refuge. One way or another, home ownership has long been an important part of our culture. Indeed, it's probably fair to say that if you dream of purchasing a home, you dream along with much of America. Unfortunately, however, this dream has fast become a nightmare for many people as inflation, real estate speculation and the falling productivity of corporate capitalism threatens to produce a situation where only the affluent can afford a home. Still, the dream of home ownership remains vital, and is realized by many people willing to sacrifice in other areas.

Beyond the emotional urges, there are many practical reasons to find and own a home—a hedge against inflation and rent raises, avoiding the powerlessness of being a tenant, tax deductibility of mortgage interest and many other financial advantages. In addition, owning a home offers a lesbian or gay couple some privacy from the sometimes hostile intrusions of the world.

At the same time, there can be drawbacks to owning a home. The first time the boiler explodes, you may pine for the days when you could just call your landlord. You might recall Thoreau, who noted that most people didn't own their houses; their houses owned them. Still, despite the drawbacks, it *is* your home. It can be fun to tear down walls, plant your own trees, paint an ivy decoration across the dining room walls or even fix the boiler. Most Americans agree with Mark Twain, who advised to "Buy land. They aren't making any more of it."

Over the past few years, many lesbians and gay men have followed Twain's advice. Of sociological note, many bought in the "inner city." The much-proclaimed "decay" (even "death") of many American cities suddenly disappeared, not because of urban renewal, but because thousands of people wanted to buy homes in the city. Many bought in poor, rundown neighborhoods, and the homes were (or proved to be) a bargain. Old, dilapidated buildings—brownstones, lofts, Victorians—were painted, renovated and restored as the middle class left the suburbs. Planners call this "gentrification" and it's expected to continue. Many American cities are beginning to have the population characteristics of Paris and other European urban areas, the affluent in the central, inner-city areas, and the poor crowded out to the fringes.

Like any social movement, the renaissance of our inner cities is complicated. Many poor people have been and will be displaced by escalating rents and housing costs. Understandably, there's been a lot of anger in low-income communities, and this has sometimes taken the form of hostility directed at gays. Because money talks, the displacement of poor people from their old urban neighborhoods will probably continue. We regard this as a serious problem and feel it imperative that some means of communication between the gay and low-income communities be established (or strengthened). Unfortunately, we don't have any ready solution, but we feel that lesbians and gays must do more than dream of a society that provides decent housing for everyone.

The process of buying and fixing up a home together can be a wonderful foundation for a relationship, both spiritually and economically. Of course, owning your home can be damn scary too. The longest part of this chapter suggests ways to handle the practical aspects of buying your home. No getting around it—buying a home involves money, and it's wise to make an agreement concerning ownership. We also recognize a prevalent trend for friends (not just lovers) to purchase property together. Therefore, we include a number of contracts on how to buy together—with a lover, friend or "investment group." But before you can pin down your agreement, you have to find the house, arrange for financing and understand the ways in which you can hold title to the property. Let's begin with these first steps.

B. FINDING A HOUSE

We haven't any magic advice on how to find that home you've been dreaming about. Some folks love fixing a place up and others hate it. Some crave a view, while others can live with almost no light. Everyone wants a bargain. Good luck!

Lesbian and gay couples usually have no special problems in finding a house to buy, though financing can be problematic in some areas. (See the next section.) Of course, some realtors and sellers are uncomfortable representing or selling to lesbian or gay couples, so, if you're in an urban area, you may want to use a gay realtor. Remember, in some states, you'll be committing a technical crime by cohabiting, though we've never heard of any enforcement of laws against oral copulation or sodomy for buying and living in a home together. In short, the god Mammon is stronger than the god Discrimination.

Some communities (or neighborhoods) have adopted zoning ordinances prohibiting unrelated people from living together. Most of these laws are aimed at barring groups,[1] though a few prohibit even two unrelated adults from living together. These laws have been used to harass lesbians and gays who lived together, just as they have been used to discriminate against heterosexual couples

---

[1]The United States Supreme Court upheld the constitutionality of a law prohibiting more than two unrelated adults from living together, against the charge that the law discriminated against unrelated people. *Village of Belle Terre v. Boraas*, 416 U.S. 1 (1974).

or groups. Before you buy, make sure the town—or neighborhood—isn't zoned only for people related by "blood, marriage or adoption."[2]

The most common way to find a home is to use an agent or realtor. Buying real estate involves understanding what—to the uninitiated—seems like strange rules and jargon; often people feel it's easier to let someone knowledgeable do the work. But you aren't required to use a realtor, nor are you obligated to work with just one. At the start it's wise to shop around. Eventually, you may find it preferable to select one realtor and work with only him. The advantage of this is that you gain the status of a valued customer and, at least in theory, get a chance at the "hottest" deals (the ones the realtor would otherwise save for his close relatives). If a dozen agents are looking for you, chances are none of them are looking very hard. And, using more than one agent can lead to problems. If a realtor shows you a home, he has a right to a commission if you buy it, even if you buy it through a different realtor. Both realtors may want commissions; at the very least, they'll both be furious with you.

In most states, realtors will assist you with all aspects of the purchase. In addition to finding homes, they should give you advice on prices, school districts, transportation, demographics and economic trends in the area (are property values going up or down). A realtor should also help you find the experts you need—e.g., a termite inspector, a roofer or a soil engineer—and assist with arranging financing and the closing.

A real estate agent's commission is a percentage of the price of the home, and is traditionally paid by the seller.[3] Because the realtor isn't being paid on an hourly basis, take your time and ask all the questions you want. A common commission is six percent, but it's supposedly negotiable; courts have declared it an illegal restraint of trade for all members of a business to set one commission rate. Thus, you'll find commission competition in some urban areas, and a seller may locate someone who'll do a good job and charge less. After all, six percent can be a large chunk of money (for a $150,000 house, it's $9,000). Because the seller pays the commission, however, the buyer won't save much unless the seller's willing to pass along some of the savings.

---

[2]Certain neighborhoods in Denver, Colorado and White Plains, N.Y. restrict each household to people related by "blood, marriage or adoption." Unmarried heterosexuals have been forced to move out—or marry—a choice lesbian and gay couples don't have. Several states, however, including New Jersey and California, prohibit local communities from discriminating against groups or unrelated people in housing.

[3]Because the seller traditionally pays the agent's fee, in most states the agent is legally the agent of the seller. If you're worried about this conflict of interest, you can hire an attorney to look over the papers, or even hire a "Buyer's Broker" who you pay to look for you.

A small but significant number of people sell their homes without using a realtor. You don't violate any laws looking for homes sold "by owner" at the same time that you're working with a realtor.[4] You can find homes sold "by owners" by checking newspaper ads or driving around and looking for "for sale by owner" signs. There are several paperback books explaining the ins and outs of buying or selling a home yourself.[5]

Legally, realtors who share in the commission paid by the seller, represent the seller. In most states this is true even if the realtor has actively showed the buyer many houses and has never met the seller. When it comes to the actual negotiations and bargaining over your buying a house, however, quite a gap can develop between this legal truth and the marketplace reality. A realtor doesn't get a commission until a sale is consummated; it's therefore in her interest to consummate the deal. This may not be in your interest at all. There is an overriding point here: the realtor most lawyers work with has no legal or practical duty to act in a way as to maximize the buyer's interest.

In some states, such as Florida and New York, lawyers have gained a monopoly over some aspects of real estate transactions, particularly the "closing" of a sale. In these states, realtors cannot conduct closings, or even give their clients advice about them, as that would be "practicing law without a license." What this means is that you have to waste time and money and hire a lawyer, or do it yourself. If you think this is bad (and it is), in Ireland it's worse—you normally can't rent an apartment without using a lawyer. If you're in a state such as Florida or New York, you can learn to do your own closing. Your local law library will have the necessary information.

C. HOW MUCH CAN YOU AFFORD TO PAY?[6]

If you've thought about buying a home, no doubt you've wondered what you can afford to pay, and whether it's even possible to purchase one. Traditionally, lenders will loan you money only if your total monthly housing costs (mortgage, insurance and taxes) don't exceed 28% of your monthly gross

---

[4]Most realtors aren't fond of this practice, but you have the right unless you signed a contract explicitly prohibiting you from doing so.

[5]In California, see Devine, *For Sale by Owner* (Nolo Press).

[6]This section gives a brief introduction to the subject of home financing. For more information see *The Common Sense Mortgage*, Miller (Harper & Row), available through Nolo Press.

income. They then make sure that no more than 36% of your gross monthly income is spent on housing costs and other long term debts (like car payments or student loans). We're not so conservative. If you're thinking of buying a house, *and* if you believe your income will increase over the next few years and that the value of the home will go up, it's reasonable to scrimp and save in other areas in order to put a larger percentage of your income into a home.

Table 5.1 shows monthly mortgage payments on a $70,000 mortgage at different interest rates. To figure out the total monthly cost, add payments on any second mortgage, taxes, fire and other insurance, utilities and an estimate for repairs. (Five percent of the monthly mortgage amount is a rough figure if the house is in pretty good shape.)

TABLE 5.1
MONTHLY PAYMENTS ON A $70,000 MORTGAGE

Interest rate(%)	15-year period($)	30-year period($)
7	625.69	464.81
8	668.96	513.64
8.5	689.32	538.24
9	709.99	563.24
9.5	730.96	588.60
10	752.22	614.31
10.5	773.78	640.32
11	795.62	666.63
11.5	817.73	693.21
12	840.12	720.03
12.5	862.77	747.09
13	885.67	774.34
14	932.22	829.42

In the late 1970s, many lenders were caught with low fixed-rate mortgages when interest rates soared. To protect themselves in the future, they devised adjustable rate mortgages (ARMS) permitting themselves to raise (or, in theory, lower) the interest rate during the pay-back period; the interest rate raises or lowers depending on the general interest rates. An adjustable rate loan usually starts lower than a fixed rate loan, and is almost always assumable by a new buyer; fixed rate loans usually aren't assumable. Choosing between a fixed rate loan and an ARM involves deciding:

- whether you believe assuming an adjustable rate loan would attract a buyer if you decide to sell your house

- whether your crystal ball predicts interest rates will soar, decline or remain stable
- how long you will own the home (adjustable rates are almost always lower for the first few years)

TABLE 2

EXAMPLE OF PAYMENTS ON A $70,000 MORTGAGE WITH ONE
ADJUSTABLE RATE MORTGAGE OF 11.5%[7] BEGINNING INTEREST RATE

(Teaser rate)	Payment
7.5%	$489.45
7th month real rate	
9%	$563.24
Top possible rate	
14%	$829.41

Note: Convertible ARMS are also available. This means for a very small premium you can get an ARM that is convertible to a fixed rate mortgage at your option. Details of this type of mortgage vary greatly and you will have to check them out with local lenders.

15-YEAR MORTGAGES

Many lenders allow you to choose either a 15-year or a 30-year mortgage. The 15-year mortgage is highly touted as saving you thousands of dollars over the 30-year because, for an increase in the monthly payment, you can pay off your mortgage in half the time. The higher monthly payment, however, is often substantial, and is usually reason enough that you don't choose this option. But even if you choose the 30-year option, you can always pay a little extra each month (or whenever you have an extra chunk of money) on the loan to be applied against the principal. In this way, you have the flexibility of paying the mortgage off earlier without committing yourself to the higher 15-year payments.

---

[7]Obviously if interest rates are lower or higher, ARMS will be available for an initial rate that reflects this.

D. YOUR HOME AS INVESTMENT AND TAX SHELTER

Now the good news! There are many financial benefits to owning a home, especially in times of rapid inflation. Not only will home ownership provide you with a place to live, but with any luck your investment will go up in value. In addition, Congress has concluded that Americans should be encouraged to own homes and has written tax laws to create significant tax advantages for homeowners. These rules allow you to deduct from your income for tax purposes all interest you pay on your mortgage, and all your property taxes. By comparison, renters get no such deduction, even if, as is usual, their rent helps pay the landlord's taxes and mortgage interest payments.

Homeowners qualify for another tax advantage. (Now you know why tax accountants say that people with good incomes can't afford not to own real estate.) If you sell your home and use the proceeds to buy another within 24 months, you're allowed to postpone paying taxes on the profit made in the first sale until you sell your second home. And, if you sell the second and buy a third, you get the same postponement. This means you can keep buying up more expensive properties and postpone paying taxes on your accumulated profits while you're doing it. Or to say it another way, you can use money you would have had to pay taxes on for a larger investment.

There's also a tax rule that helps older folks whose homes have skyrocketed in value. It works like this. Any time after you reach age 55, you can sell your home without paying taxes on the first $125,000 profit. You can do it only once. As with all rules we discuss here, however, be sure to check the current status of the tax laws before acting.

E. PROCEEDING WITH YOUR PURCHASE

Once you find the house you want to buy, there are a few details to take care of before you actually buy it.

1. Inspections

Any contract to purchase a home should allow you time to make all necessary inspections.[8] These routinely include termite, electrical and plumbing, and a roof inspection. In addition, you may want a soil engineer to check the foundation, or a general contractor to do a full inspection. Your purchase contract should be contingent upon these experts reporting that the house either is in good condition or can be repaired for a reasonable price.

2. Financing That White Picket Fence

After you've conducted the inspections and reached a firm agreement on price and terms, you will have to come up with money. Usually, your obligation to buy is contingent on your finding financing for a specific amount at a specific interest rate. Obviously you don't want to sign a contract to purchase a home, and then not be able to find a loan you can afford.

Few of us can pay all cash for a house. We borrow money from a bank,[9] family member, the seller or a loan shark, and accept whatever conditions the lenders impose. Most often, you'll borrow from a bank. In exchange, the bank will require you to sign a note promising to repay the money plus a healthy

---

[8]A buyer often pays for inspections, but it is possible to negotiate with the seller and have her pay a portion.
[9]We use the word "bank" to refer generically to any lending institution—a savings and loan association, a mortgage company, an insurance company, etc.

interest. Your promise to pay, standing alone, however, won't be sufficient security for the bank; it will also require you to sign a document giving it the power to foreclose (i.e., repossess) the house if you default on your payments. This document is normally called a mortgage, or a deed of trust.

Discrimination Against Lesbian and Gay Couples: In the past, many lenders refused to loan to lesbian and gay couples. For the most part, this has changed. Banks usually look to both persons' incomes. Also, any bank will lend money to two people if it believes they're (just) business partners. Obviously, we believe banks should accept the fact that stable lesbian and gay couples are here to stay, and should evaluate loan applications accordingly. (Support your local gay banker!) This would mean that the banker would have to judge whether each partner could afford the mortgage payments if the couple split up. In an era when a marriage certificate is little guarantee that a couple will stay together, it's a judgment bankers must make every time they lend to married couples.

If a bank refuses to lend you money based on your joint income and assets, there's little you can do about it. You may be being discriminated against, but it *ain't* illegal. Find another lender. The sad truth is that you may have to present yourselves as business partners. If you still can't find a lender willing to take into account both of your incomes, you'll be limited to a home that one only of you can afford. We haven't heard of a recent instance of a lending institution refusing a loan to one half of a lesbian or gay couple, though it must have happened in the bad old days. Certainly your private life is no valid concern of a banker if you alone are borrowing money.

The Financing: Traditionally, a lender will loan 80% or 90% of their appraisal of a home's value. They usually require either a 10% or a 20% down payment[10] to ensure resale of the home and recoupment of their investment if you default on the mortgage. Remember, your contract to buy should state that it's contingent upon your finding satisfactory financing—usually at least 80%-90% of the sales price—at an affordable interest rate, for a set number of years. This allows you legally to get out of the contract (or renegotiate it) if a lender won't lend you enough money or at an interest rate you can afford.

It's often worthwhile to be creative in your financing. Ask the seller if he has a loan which can be "assumed." An assumable loan may be at a lower interest rate than those currently available, and could save you "points," the nasty charge

---

[10]If you qualify for a loan through the Federal Housing Authority, Veteran's Administration, a state-aided Veteran's loan or an inner city loan, the down payment and often interest rates are lower.

you must pay the lender for the privilege of obtaining a loan.[11] Also, ask the seller if he's willing to finance any portion of the purchase. (In real estate jargon, this is called "carrying the paper.") Sometimes a seller doesn't need all his money at once, especially if he's not planning to buy another home. He might be willing to take the money from you in payments, at an interest rate higher than what he could get elsewhere. His loan to you is very secure because you'll give him a mortgage on the house, and he can foreclose if you don't pay.

Assume that you're infatuated with a home selling for $180,000. Your savings, borrowing from parents and friends and a loan on your car total $36,000. You need $144,000 more (plus $9,000 for closing costs). The seller has owned the home for a few years and has a $90,000 mortgage at 9% interest. Here are several possible methods of financing your purchase:[12]

Plan A

Offer to purchase the home for $180,000 cash as follows:

- $36,000 down payment
- $114,000 at current bank interest rates; 10% interest will cost you $1,263.70 per month

Plan B

Pay the sales price of $180,000 as follows:

- $36,000 down payment
- $90,000 by assuming the seller's old mortgage at 9%; payments are $724.16 per month
- $54,000 loan from the seller; offer monthly payments of $514 including interest at 11%, with a final (balloon) payment for the remaining balance due in seven years. (The monthly interest payment rate and the time of the balloon payment are negotiable.)

Total monthly payments equal $1,238.16.

Plan C

To make it more attractive to the seller, offer $2,000 above the sales price.

Pay the sales price of $182,000 as follows:

---

[11]One "point" equals one percent of the loan. If you're assessed two points on a $150,000 loan, that will cost you $3,000 ($150,000 x .02).

[12]All rates are figured on a 30-year repayment schedule.

- $36,000 cash down
- $90,000 by assuming the seller's old mortgage at 9% with payments of $724.16 per month
- $56,000 loan from seller; monthly payments are $533.30 per month, including interest at 11%, with a final (balloon) payment due in seven years.

Total monthly payments equal $1,257.46.

To summarize: The sales price is only one consideration in any home purchase. The amount of down payment, interest rates, length of repayment, etc., can be at least as important.

3. Escrow and Closing Costs

In buying and selling a house, paperwork and money must eventually change hands. The practice is for the buyer and seller each to deliver their money, house deeds, etc., to a third person, called the "escrow holder" (usually a title company). The escrow holder hangs on to everything until all inspections are complete, the papers are signed and financing is arranged. Then, "escrow closes," the deed is recorded with the county, the buyer receives the deed establishing that she's now the owner of the house and the seller gets the money. It's usually not until you're near closing the entire deal that you learn about "closing costs."

Closing costs are all those costs that have to be paid at the time the escrow closes. The buyer's closing costs often include recording fees, termite inspections, next year's taxes, the bank charges (including a month's prepaid interest, "points," and often a "loan origination fee"[13]), title search and title insurance costs and attorney's fees. Closing costs always mount up, often nearing several thousand dollars. Be sure to get an early estimate of these.

F. TAKING TITLE TO YOUR NEW HOME

When you buy your home, you have to decide how you want the recorded deed to read, or as they say, how to "take title." This has lasting importance. In most states, you have three choices:

- one person only holds title

---

[13]A "loan origination" fee is simply one extra charge the bank tacks on; commonly it runs $150-$200.

- both of you hold title as "joint tenants"
- both of you hold title as "tenants-in-common"

Here's what each means:

1. In One Person's Name[14]

This means that absent a contract to the contrary, only the person named in the deed owns the house. It isn't wise to put only one name on the deed unless in truth only one of you owns the home. Sometimes a couple who jointly owns a home is tempted to put only one name on the deed to save on taxes, avoid creditors or befuddle welfare or food stamp administrators. The tax savings is attractive if one of your incomes is very high and the other's is very low; the high-income person takes all the house tax deductions. But in general, this is a poor strategy. Even though you might fool a few creditors, there are other dangers.

Suppose the person on the deed (and the therefore presumed sole owner) sells the house and pockets the money, or dies and a passel of money-hungry relatives appear. What can the other do? Insist on a written contract which makes the true ownership clear. Absent a contract, the best the person not on the deed can do is sue to recover his or her portion of the property. But a few states have a conclusive legal presumption that the person whose name appears on the deed is

---

[14]The deed often states the name of the buyer and adds "a single man/woman." Our friend Alice put down "a singular woman" but it never made it past the escrow officer.

the owner; a lawsuit to recover your share might be difficult, or even impossible. In any case, it's absurd to risk a lawsuit. So be warned! If more than one person is buying the property, all owners should normally be named on the deed. If this is not done, see a lawyer and draft a contract clearly spelling out the interests and rights of both owners.

2. Joint Tenancy

If you take title to a piece of real property as joint tenants, it means you share property ownership equally and that each of you has the right to use the entire property. Joint tenancy also has a right of survivorship.[15] This means that if one joint tenant dies, the other (or others) automatically takes the deceased person's share, even if there's a will to the contrary.[16] And when joint tenancy property passes to the other joint tenant(s) at death, there's no necessity of any probate proceedings. Another feature of joint tenancy is that if one joint tenant sells his or her share, the sale ends the joint tenancy. The new owner and the other original owner(s) become tenants-in-common (see below). Each joint tenant has the right to sell his or her interest, regardless of whether the other joint tenants agree with, or are even aware of, the sale.

Warning! Joint tenancy can't be used if a house is owned in unequal shares. It's appropriate only when each joint tenant owns the same portion. This means that you and your lover could put a house you owned 50-50 in joint tenancy or that three people could have joint tenancy with each owning one-third of a property. If you own 60% of a house, however, and your lover owns 40%, joint tenancy won't work.

3. Tenants In Common

Tenancy in common is another way to hold title when there's more than one owner. The major difference between joint tenancy and tenancy in common is

---

[15]In some states, you must add the words "with right of survivorship." If in doubt, add them.

[16]Some lesbians and gay men who own houses as their own separate property are tempted to put the house in joint tenancy with their lovers so that the lovers will get it if the original owner dies. Think before you do this. By putting the house in joint tenancy, you make a gift of one-half of it to your lover. Not only might gift tax be assessed, but if you later split up, you have no right to have the house deeded back to you. In this situation, it makes more sense for the original owner to keep the house in his or her name and make a will or living trust leaving the house to the lover. If circumstances change, the will or trust can be changed. For a discussion of using joint tenancy as part of estate planning, see Chapter 9. A sample form for transferring property into joint tenancy is in the Appendix.

that tenancy in common has no right of survivorship. This means that when a tenant in common dies, her or his share of property is left to whomever she or he specified in a will, or if there's no will, by the process of "intestate succession" (most likely, to a child, parent or sibling). (See Chapter 9.) Also, and of particular importance in many lesbian or gay real estate ventures, tenants in common can own property in unequal shares—one person can own 80% of the property, another 15% and a third 5%. All are listed on the deed as tenants in common. You can specify the precise percentages on the deed, e.g., "the owners named are tenants in common; Sappho has a one-third interest and Joan of Arc two-thirds." Or you can simply list all owners' names on the deed and set out the shares in a separate written agreement. Especially if shares are unequal, it's important to prepare a contract. Read on.

Note: You can change title after the purchase; you need only record a new deed. For instance, if you want to start as tenants in common and later change to joint tenants, make and record a deed granting the property "from Sappho and Joan of Arc as Tenants In Common, to Sappho and Joan of Arc as Joint Tenants." But if you add a new person, the IRS will call it either a sale or a gift and tax you accordingly, which can be expensive. We discuss this soon.

G. CONTRACTS FOR PEOPLE BUYING OR OWNING HOMES TOGETHER

A house is a major economic asset. It's foolish to avoid or postpone clearly defining your mutual expectations and obligations. In this section, we discuss ways to handle joint ownership problems and give sample contracts to cover the most common.

A Last Note for People Who Hate Contracts: In the earlier chapters of this book we suggested that you prepare a living-together contract. Even if you don't take that advice, you absolutely should prepare a contract if you plan to jointly own a home. As you'll see, most of the samples we give are simple and uncomplicated. Incidentally, we have found that the people who most commonly resist contracts are those who don't really have a solid agreement in the first place. If this is your situation, sit down immediately and have a long, honest talk.

Although we recommend simple, uncomplicated contracts, some complicated home ownership arrangements will require complicated contracts. If this is your situation, you may want to have your agreement checked by a lawyer familiar with the real estate, and sympathetic to lesbian and gay couples. This doesn't mean you should take a full wallet and a basketful of problems to the lawyer. Do as much work as possible yourself and use the lawyer to help you with particular problem areas or to check the entire agreement when you're finished.

1. Agreement for Equal Ownership

Let's start with a sample agreement between two people who contribute equal amounts of money for the down payment and intend to share all costs (and eventual profits) equally.

Note that in this contract, Michael and Hadrian take title as tenants in common. As we discussed above, this means that if either dies, his heirs, or whomever he has designated in his will, will inherit his half of the property. If Michael and Hadrian took title as joint tenants, and one died, the survivor would automatically get the other's share. Taking title in tenancy in common is a cautious approach. It allows them to leave their one-half share of the property to the other by use of a will or revocable living trust, but does not require them to do so.

CONTRACT FOR EQUAL OWNERSHIP

Michael Angelo and Hadrian Rifkin make the following agreement to jointly purchase a house that both of them will live in. They agree that:

1. They will purchase a house at 423 Bliss Street, Chicago, Illinois for $180,000.

2. They will take title as tenants in common.

3. They will each contribute $18,000 to the down payment and closing costs and will each pay one-half of the monthly mortgage and insurance costs, as well as one-half of the property taxes and costs for repairs that both agree are needed.

4. Should either Michael and Hadrian decide to end their relationship and cease living with the other, and should both men want to keep the house, a friend will be asked to flip a coin within 60 days of the decision to separate.[17]

---

[17]You might have the decision made by a mediator or arbitrator rather than the caprice of a coin. If so, see Chapter 3 on mediation and arbitration, to include a clause detailing the process.

The winner of the coin toss is entitled to purchase the house from the loser, provided that the winner pays the loser the fair market value (see clause 5) of his share within 90 days. When payment is made, Michael and Hadrian will deed the house to the person retaining it in his name alone. If payment isn't made within 90 days, or if neither person wants to buy the house, it will be sold and the profits divided.

5. If Michael and Hadrian cannot agree on the fair market value of the house, this value will be determined by an appraisal conducted as follows: Michael and Hadrian will designate in writing one appraiser to do the job. If either party doesn't agree with the appraisal, he may hire a second appraiser. If the parties cannot come to an agreement with the two appraisals, then the two appraisers will choose a third appraiser. The value will be the average of the three appraisals. The fees of the three appraisers will be divided equally between Michael and Hadrian.

6. If either Michael or Hadrian dies, the survivor, if he hasn't been left the deceased person's share, has the right to purchase that share from the inheritor by paying its fair market value (to be arrived at under the terms of Paragraph 5) to the inheritors within 200 days of the date of death.

7. If one of the parties has to make a payment of mortgage, taxes or insurance on behalf of the other, who is either unable or unwilling to make the payment in timely manner, that payment will be treated as a loan to be paid back within six months, including 10% interest per annum (or the highest interest rate permitted under the state law, whichever is lower).

8. This contract is binding on our heirs and our estates.

Dated: _____   Signature: _____

                             Michael Angelo

Dated: _____   Signature: _____

                             Hadrian Rifkin

After the contract was signed, Michael and Hadrian talked about what they wanted to happen if one of them died. Michael was worried that Hadrian wouldn't be able to afford to buy Michael's share if the house went way up in value. Michael wanted to leave his mother the original $18,000 down payment, but otherwise wanted Hadrian to get the house. How could they accomplish this? They came up with the following clause, and rewrote their contract with a new #6:

6. If Michael or Hadrian dies, the survivor, if he hasn't been left the deceased person's share, has the right to purchase that share by paying the sum of $18,000 to the estate or heirs of the deceased (by giving a note for $18,000 to the estate, including 10% interest per year), in 36 equal monthly installments.

2. Owning a House in Unequal Shares

If each person contributing to the purchase of a home puts up the same amount for the down payment, pays equal shares of the mortgage and other expenses and contributes equally to any necessary labor for fixing the place up, its self-evident that each person would have an equal share of the ownership. It's common, however, for joint purchasers to contribute unequally. One person may have more money for the down payment. Another person may be able to afford larger monthly payments than the other, or has skills (e.g., carpentry) and can renovate the house while the other sits by, beer in hand, and kibbitzes.

Below, we discuss whether, and how, to own a home in unequal shares; we also provide sample contracts. Some factors to consider with unequal ownership are easily expressed in cash (making comparisons simple), while other factors are almost impossible to evaluate financially. For example, work on the house can be given a cash value by establishing an hourly wage and multiplying it by the number of hours worked. But what value do you assign to someone's ability to borrow the down payment from his parents—especially in a society structured to reward the owners of capital? We don't mean to suggest that you must arrive at a mathematically exact determination—as you'll see, we suggest that it's enough to decide on rough values that satisfy you both. Read on.

2/3 - 1/3 Ownership: Tina and Barb purchased a home. Tina had more capital, so she made two-thirds of the down payment and owns two-thirds of the house. To keep things simple, Tina will also pay two-thirds of the mortgage, taxes and insurance.

Here's their contract:

CONTRACT WITH OWNERSHIP AND PAYMENTS SPLIT 2/3 - 1/3

We, Tina Foote and Barb Bibbige, enter into this contract and agree as follows:

1. *Property:* We will purchase the house at 451 Morton Street, in

Upper Montclair, New Jersey.

2. *Contributions:* We will contribute the following money to the down payment:

| Tina | $20,000 |
| Barb | $10,000 |

3. *Ownership:* We will own the property as tenants in common with the following shares:

| Tina | 2/3 |
| Barb | 1/3 |

4. *Expenses and Mortgage:* All expenses, including mortgage, taxes, insurance and repairs on the house, will be paid as follows:

| Tina | 2/3 |
| Barb | 1/3 |

5. In the event the house is sold, the initial contributions ($20,000 to Tina and $10,000 to Barb) will be paid back first; the remainder of the proceeds will be divided two-thirds to Tina and one-third to Barb.

6. *Contingencies:*

a. We agree to hold the house for three years unless we mutually agree otherwise. After three years, either person may request the house be sold. The person who doesn't want to sell has the right of first refusal; that is, she has the right to purchase the house at the agreed-upon price, and must state in writing that she will exercise this right within two weeks of the setting of the price. She has 60 days to complete the purchase, or the right lapses.

b. If one owner moves out of the house before it's sold, she will remain responsible for her share of the mortgage, taxes, insurance and repairs. She may rent her quarters with the approval (which won't be unreasonably withheld) of the other. The person who stays in the house has the first right to rent the quarters herself or assume the cost if she so chooses.

c. If Tina and Barb decide to separate and both want to keep the house, they will try to reach a satisfactory arrangement. If by the end of two weeks they can't, they will ask a friend to flip a coin. The winner has the right to purchase the loser's share provided the winner pays the loser her fair market value within 90 days of the toss. The fair market value will be determined by the procedure in clause 6a of this agreement.

d. If either Tina or Barb dies, the other, if she hasn't been left the deceased person's share, has the right to purchase that share from the deceased's estate within six months. The value of the share will be determined as set out above.

7. *Binding:* This agreement is binding on us and our heirs, executors, administrators, successors and assigns.

Signed in _____   _____
           (City)   (State)

Dated: _____   Signature: _____
                                    Tina Foote

Dated: _____   Signature: _____
                                    Barb Bibbige

Unequal Ownership Turned into Equal Ownership: For the next example, let's fantasize that we're drawing up a contract for Gertrude S. and Alice B. Gertrude can sell a few paintings and come up with the full $50,000 down payment for a little cottage with a mansard roof. Alice can pay one-half the monthly mortgage, insurance and maintenance costs, but has no money for the down payment. They eventually want to equally own the home, but also want to fairly account for Gertrude's down payment. Gertrude could make a gift of one-half of the down payment to Alice, but she'd be liable for a gift tax and she doesn't feel quite that generous. We suggest that Gertrude call one-half of the down payment a *loan* to Alice that can either be paid back in monthly installments or deferred until the house is sold. If this is done, they should write a contract similar to Michael and Hadrian's, indicating a 50-50 ownership. They should also execute a promissory note providing a record of the loan.

PROMISSORY NOTE FOR DOWN PAYMENT MONEY

I, Alice B., acknowledge receipt of a loan of $25,000 from Gertrude S., to be used as my share of the down payment for our house located at 10 Rue de There, Oakland, California. I agree to pay this sum back, plus interest, at the rate of 10% per year, by making monthly payments of $_____, all due in seven years.[18]

If the loan and all interest due hasn't been repaid when the house is sold, the remaining balance owed will be paid to Gertrude S. before Alice B. receives any proceeds from that sale.

Dated: _____   Signature: _____
                                    Alice B.

Dated: _____   Signature: _____
                                    Gertrude S.

One Person Buys the House and Other Fixes It Up: It's sometimes common for one person to contribute a greater portion, or even all, of the down payment, and the other to contribute labor and/or materials to fix the place up. Numerous arrangements are possible. We have a strong bias for a simple contract, but if special circumstances require more complex details, have a lawyer look at the contract.

Stephan, Bob and Lyn decide to purchase a graceful but dilapidated Victorian. Stephan and Bob can put up the cash for the down payment and Lyn the expertise and time to fix it up. They can each afford to pay one-third of the monthly expenses. Like Gertrude and Alice, they want to own the place in equal shares and need only guidance on how to do it. Because Stephan and Bob are each going to contribute $17,000 to the down payment, they agree that Lyn should contribute $17,000 worth of materials and labor (at $10 an hour) to fix up the house.

---

[18]*Or:* I agree to pay the entire loan and interest at 10% per year when and if the house is sold. **Note:** A local title company can calculate for you the monthly payment necessary to pay off a loan. You need to know the original value of the loan, the interest rate, and the number of payments. Also, you can agree to pay less each month, but pay a balloon payment (large) at the end of the period.

AGREEMENT TO CONTRIBUTE CASH AND LABOR

We, Stephan, Bob and Lyn, agree as follows:

1. We will purchase the house at 225 Peaches Street, Atlanta, Georgia for $200,000 and will own the house equally as tenants in common.

2. Stephan and Bob will each contribute $17,000 to be used as the down payment.

3. Lyn will contribute $11,000 for materials over the next seven months and 600 hours of labor (valued at $10 per hour) making a total contribution of $17,000, toward fixing up the house.

4. If we all agree that more labor or materials are needed to fix up the house, the materials will be paid equally by Lyn, Bob and Stephan, and Lyn (or Bob or Stephan if they work) will be credited $10 an hour unless all three work an equal number of hours.

5. All monthly expenses will be shared equally.

6. This contract may be amended in writing at any time by unanimous consent.

Dated: _____   Signature: _____
                                        Stephan Valery

Dated: _____   Signature: _____
                                        Bob Bisell

Dated: _____   Signature: _____
                                        Lyn Rosenthal

It's easiest to determine ownership interests based on the contributions made (or promised) at the time the contact is drafted. It's possible, however, to provide for ownership shares that will fluctuate over time. Obviously, doing this can get complicated. If Stephan, Bob and Lyn want to vary their shares, with Stephan and Bob owning the place to start with and Lyn's share growing as he contributes labor and materials, they could append to their contract a sheet showing all contributions. Such a sheet might look like this when Lyn finished his work:

Nature of Contribution	Date	Value	Contributed by: Stephan	Bob	Lyn
SHEET 1					
CAPITAL CONTRIBUTIONS					
Cash	1/29	17,000	17,000		
Cash	1/29	17,000		17,000	
Paint, Roof Supplies	3/10	4,000			4,000
Wood	3/12	3,500			3,500
Floor Supplies	3/12	3,500			3,500
Labor	3/13-6/15	6,000			6,000
Cash-Hot Tub	7/20	1,500	500	500	500
Totals			17,500	17,500	17,500

Keep it Simple! We cannot over-emphasize that the best contracts are simple contracts. For example, round ownership interests off (e.g., 25% and 75%, not 26.328% and 73.672%). Why? Because trying to achieve absolute accuracy—even if such a thing were possible—is usually more trouble than it's worth. If one person puts up a little extra cash or labor, or forks out more money in an emergency, consider the extra contribution a loan to be paid back, either when the house is sold or by the other owner making a similar extra contribution, rather than redrafting the basic agreement. As long as any promissory notes are paid off before the house is sold, this approach is safe and simple.

Complicated Contribution Contracts: We do know couples who have taken a different tack. Our friends Rosemary and Glenna, for example, decided that a very detailed contract would be fairer than a rough, general division. Rosemary is a carpenter by trade, and she and Glenna agreed that her carpentry work should be valued at a higher hourly rate than the ordinary labor of either. Here's the contract they drew up. We believe it's too cumbersome for any but those with very tidy minds, but in fairness, we've seen it work very well in several instances.

DETAILED PROPERTY AGREEMENT

Glenna and Rosemary agree as follows:

1. That Glenna and Rosemary will buy the house at 15 Snake Hill Road, Cold Springs Harbor, N.Y. The initial investment (down payment and closing costs) of $24,987.07, will be contributed by Rosemary. The title to the house will be recorded as Rosemary Avila and Glenna O'Brien as tenants in common.

2. Glenna and Rosemary will each pay one-half of the monthly mortgage, tax and homeowner's insurance payments, and will each be responsible for one-half of any costs necessary for maintenance and repairs.

3. Glenna and Rosemary will contribute labor and materials to improve the house. Rosemary's labor—doing carpentry—will be valued at $14 per hour and both Glenna and Rosemary's labor making other house repairs will be valued at $7 per hour; these rates may be raised in the future if both agree. Materials will be valued at their actual cost.

4. Rosemary and Glenna will maintain a ledger marked "Exhibit I - 15 Snake Hill Road Home Owner's Record." This ledger is considered a part of this contract. Glenna and Rosemary will record the following information in the Home Owner's Record:

a) The $24,987.07 initial contribution made to purchase the house by Rosemary.

b) Monthly payments by Glenna and Rosemary for the mortgage, property taxes and homeowner's insurance.

c) Rosemary's labor as a carpenter on home improvements valued as stated in clause 3.

d) Rosemary and Glenna's labor on non-carpentry home improvements valued as stated in clause 3.

e) All money that both Rosemary and Glenna pay for supplies and materials necessary for home improvements.

f) Any other money the either Glenna or Rosemary spend for improvement of the home as long as the expenditure has been approved in advance by the other.

5. Rosemary and Glenna's ownership shares of the house are determined as follows:

a) The dollar value of all contributions made by either Glenna or Rosemary will be separately totaled, using the figures set out in the 15 Snake Hill Road Road Home Owner's Record.

b) Rosemary and Glenna may add interest to their investment totals in the amount of 10% per year simple interest. Simple interest will be calculated twice a year (January 1 and July 1), with the interest being added to each person's total investment as of that date.

c) The total equity interest in the house will be computed by subtracting all mortgages and encumbrances outstanding from the fair market value as of the date of the computation. If Rosemary and Glenna can't agree on the fair market value, each will have the house appraised by choosing a licensed realtor familiar with their neighborhood to do an appraisal. The two appraisers will choose a third realtor who will also make an appraisal. The average of the three appraisals will be the fair market value of the house.[19]

d) A fraction will be created. The numerator will be the larger share (as computed in (5a) and (5b) above) and the denominator will be the total amount of both people's shares. This fraction represents the total equity in the house of the person with the larger share. The person with the smaller share will compute her share by either subtracting the larger share from the number "1," or by also forming a fraction using the steps outlined above.

6. If either Rosemary or Glenna does not pay their share of the mortgage, taxes or insurance in a timely manner, the other person may make the payment, and that payment will be treated as a loan to be paid back as soon as possible, but not later than six months, plus interest at the rate of 10% per annum.

7. Either Rosemary or Glenna can terminate this agreement at any time. If this occurs, and both women want to remain in the house and can afford to buy the other out in 90 days, a third party will flip a coin to determine who keeps the house. If only one person wants the house, she will pay the other her share within 90 days. If the person who wants to keep the house is unable to pay the other within 90 days, the house will be sold and the proceeds divided according to the shares established under Paragraph 5(d).

Dated: _____   Signature: _____
                                      Glenna O'Brien

Dated: _____   Signature: _____
                                      Rosemary Avila

---

[19]Or, a simpler and less costly approach would be for the contract to provide that Rosemary and Glenna average the first two appraisals.

3. When Not All Owners Live in the House

If only some owners live in the house (as often happens when a group invests), those living in the house usually pay a fair rental value to the "partnership," i.e., the group of owners. If this rent doesn't cover the monthly expenses, then each owner (including those living in the house) will need to pay their share of the difference. If the rent exceeds the monthly expenses, deposit the profits into a "partnership" bank account and divide it amongst the owners, in proportion to ownership shares, once a year. The fair rental value should be adjusted every year or two.

There are other considerations when some owners live off the premises. Those living in the home want low "rent" and will resist sale of the home. This is their home, not just an investment. The outside investors might want high "rent," low maintenance and sale for peak profit. And the expectations can differ considerably concerning the quality of maintenance and improvement, or what happens when the occupants want to put in a hot tub costing $1,500, of no immediate benefit (but perhaps an expense) to the investors? There's potential conflict, which should be addressed in advance, not surprisingly, in a contract. Some items to include in the contract are:

- A set period of time after the purchase in which the house will be sold or the non-occupant investors may withdraw their money and profit.
- The fair rental value to be paid by the occupants. Rental value often (but by no means always) equals the total of all ordinary monthly payments for mortgages, insurance and taxes, plus something extra for minor repairs. The rental value ought to be adjusted every year or two.

- An understanding that the occupants may improve the premises, but that purely decorative improvements are at their own expense. Necessary improvements and major repairs are usually charged to the entire "partnership."
- The right of the occupant-owners to buy out the non-occupant-owners at a specific time for the net fair market value. Net fair market value means that expenses such as termite clearances, a broker's fee and loan prepayment penalties are subtracted from the appraised value.

Let's assume that Sappho Clarke and Teresa Marie are lovers who want to buy a little island of peace. Their friend Vita has some money, is looking for an investment and wants to help. Here's their contract:

Note: These contracts can easily be modified if there are more than three owners. It's our experience that some lesbians and gay men live with lovers and then the relationship evolves into loving friends. As friends still living together, one or both may bring a new person into the relationship and, as a group, they all join forces and buy a home.

CONTRACT WHEN ONE OWNER DOES NOT LIVE ON THE PREMISES

We, Sappho Clarke, Teresa Marie, and Vita Sackville agree as follows:

1. We agree to purchase the home known as 21 Island Retreat.
2. We will contribute the following money for the down payment:

   Vita $10,000
   Sappho $5,000
   Teresa $5,000

3. We will own the property in the following proportions: Vita—50%, Sappho—25% and Teresa—25%. If we sell the house, each person will be repaid her initial contribution; then the remaining profit or loss will be divided: Vita—50%, Sappho—25% and Teresa—25%.
4. Sappho and Teresa will live on the property and pay rent of $400 per month for the first two years. At the end of two years, we will decide what is a fair rent, taking into consideration that Sappho and Teresa do all the work necessary to maintain and manage the property.
5. Mortgage payments, insurance and taxes total $398 per month. These expenses will be paid from Sappho and Teresa's rent. Sappho and Teresa will be responsible for all maintenance and repair.
6. We will sell the house within five years unless we unanimously

agree in writing to keep it longer. If at any time after two years and before five years Sappho and Teresa desire to purchase Vita's share, they may do so at the fair market value of Vita's interest.

7. Mediation—Arbitration clause (see Chapter 3(H), Arbitration and Mediation).

8. Moving on clause (see Section G(4) following).

9. If one of us isn't able to make a timely payment, then either one or both of the other women may make the payment, and the payment will be considered a loan at 14% interest (or the highest allowed by law, whichever is lower) to be paid back within six months.

10. If any one of us dies and doesn't leave her share to the other owners, the survivors have the right to purchase that share from her estate. The value of that share will be the initial down payment plus an increase of 3% per year (simple interest). The surviving owners may buy this share with no down payment and pay the estate over a 10-year period, including interest of 10% per year on the share.

11. This agreement is binding on our heirs, executors, administrators, successors and assigns.

Dated:_____   Signature: _____
                                    Sappho Clarke

Dated:_____   Signature: _____
                                    Teresa Marie

Dated:_____   Signature: _____
                                    Vita Sackville

Another example of group ownership is provided by Sarah, Guy and Millet. They bought a duplex together with the understanding that Sarah and her children would live in one-half and Guy would live in the other half. Millet joined the venture to invest some money and aid her friends. Here's their contract:

ANOTHER CONTRACT (WHEN NOT EVERYONE LIVES ON THE PREMISES)

We, Sarah Wren, Guy Wright and Millet Victor, on _____, 19__, agree to enter into a joint venture as follows:

1. *Purpose:* The purpose of the joint venture is to purchase the property known as 1 Lake Front, Jefferson, Iowa.

2. *Duration:* The joint venture will commence this day and will continue until dissolved by mutual agreement or sale of the property.

3. *Contributions:* The parties will make the following contributions, which will be known as their Capital Contribution:

Guy Wright	$20,000
Sarah Wren	$12,000
Millet Victor	$8,000

4. *Responsibility for Loans:* In addition to the Capital Contribution, the parties agree to be responsible for the loans and mortgages as follows:

a. Sarah will be responsible for 50% of all payments due to The Jean Mortgage Company.

b. Guy will be responsible for 50% of all mortgage payments due to The Jean Mortgage Company.

c. Millet will have no additional responsibility beyond her initial capital contribution.

5. *Mortgages:* If at any time Sarah or Guy cannot make her or his half of a mortgage payment in a timely manner, one or both of the other parties, at their option, may make the payment in order to keep the property from being foreclosed. The person(s) making the payment will be repaid within six months, with 10% annual interest.

6. *Rights and Duties of the Parties:* Guy has the right to live in the upper unit of the building or to rent it out at whatever rate he may choose. If he rents it out, he remains responsible for 50% of the Jean Mortgage Company payment, and, in either case, he's responsible for all repairs and maintenance of the upper unit.

Sarah has the right to live in the lower unit of the building or to rent it out in whole or part at whatever rate she may choose. If she rents it out, she remains responsible for 50% of the Jean Mortgage Company payment, and, in either case, she's responsible for all repairs and maintenance of the lower unit.

Millet isn't responsible for any payments beyond her initial Capital Contribution.

7. *Repairs:* Either Guy or Sarah may need to make extensive repairs to the building. The cost of major repairs (like the roof or boiler) will be divided evenly between them. If either wants to improve her or his unit,

either may do so under the following rule:

• Any repairs or additions costing more than one thousand dollars ($1,000) will be considered a capital investment, credited to the party's Capital Account and paid back upon sale of the building.

• Repairs or additions above $1,000 must be approved by Sarah, Guy and Millet in writing if they want to be paid back.

8. *Forced payments:* If Guy or Sarah can't make a payment in timely manner, then the other may make that payment for them, and the payment will be considered a loan at the highest interest rate allowed by law, to be paid back in six months.

9. *Shares:* Sarah will own 30% of the property, Guy will own 50% and Millet will own 20%.

10. *Profit and Loss:* Upon the sale of the building, the respective capital investments, reflected by the Capital Accounts, will first be returned to the parties. The remaining profit or loss will be distributed as follows: Sarah 30%; Guy 50%; Millet 20%.

11. *Regular books* will be kept that are open to inspection by all parties upon reasonable notice.

12. *Time:* Sarah, Guy and Millet agree to hold the property for five years; no sale or encumbrance will be made without unanimous consent. At the end of five years, any one of the parties may request a sale of her or his share by giving four months written notice.

13. *Election to Keep Building or Sell:* If the venture is dissolved due to the death, withdrawal or other act of any party before the expiration of the five years, the remaining parties may continue to own the building. If the remaining owners so elect, they will have the right to purchase the interest of the other person in the building by paying to such person, or the legal representatives of such person, the value of such interest as follows:

Appointment of Appraisers. The parties desiring to continue ownership will appoint one appraiser; the withdrawing person or the legal representative of a deceased or incapacitated person will appoint a second appraiser. The appraisers will determine the value of the assets and liabilities of the venture, and the parties desiring to continue ownership will pay to the other, or the representative, his or her capital investment plus the share (as set out in clause 9 above) of the gain or loss of the venture. The withdrawing person or the legal representative will execute the documents necessary to convey such person's interest in the venture to other parties.

Additional Appraiser in Event of Disagreement. In the event the appraisers cannot agree on the value of the venture within 15 days after their appointment, they will designate an additional appraiser whose appraisal will be binding on all parties. If any selected appraiser becomes unable or unwilling to serve, the person(s) originally selecting him or her shall appoint a substitute. In the event the two appraisers first appointed cannot agree on a third appraiser, such appraiser will be appointed by the director of the _____ (e.g., local gay rights organization).

Rights and Obligations of Continuing Parties. The parties continuing the venture will assume all of the existing obligations and will indemnify the withdrawing party against all liability.

14. *Dissolution:* In the event that all parties agree to dissolve the venture, the building will be sold, the debts paid and the surplus divided among the parties in accordance with their interests as set out in clause 9.

15. *Amendments:* This agreement may be amended at any time in writing by unanimous agreement.

Executed at _____ on _____

       (City, State)   (Date)

_____

Sarah Wren

_____

Guy Right

_____

Millet Victor

Note on Limited Partnership: In the last two contracts, the owners agreed that the persons not living in the house shouldn't be responsible for maintenance and repairs. Often, the non-occupant wants to limit her or his liability. A simple method for this is clause 4c or clause 5 in Sarah, Guy and Millet's contract, where Millet isn't obligated to make any payments beyond her initial capital contribution. Although this is binding between the three partners, you should also know that if a new roof is added, and Sarah and Guy fail to pay the roofer, the roofer could sue Millet. To insure that Millet wouldn't have to pay the roofer in this situation, or face any other liability on the basis of another partner's acts, they could form a corporation (which is costly, cumbersome and not really necessary) or a limited partnership.

In a limited partnership, each investor is called a "partner" and some of the partners have limited liability. These are the "limited partners." The partners fully liable are called "general partners." A disadvantage is that a limited partnership is a legal entity of its own, and, as such, requires a tax number and a tax accounting each year. Another disadvantage is that limited partners cannot claim some of the tax deductions general partners can claim. This may be reason enough not to form a limited partnership. But a limited partnership is an excellent idea if one investor (who cannot have a management role) wants to fully protect herself or himself. The limited partner is liable only for the money she has invested; she's not liable for anything beyond that. To learn more about limited partnerships, see *The Partnership Book* (Nolo Press), Warner and Clifford.

If One Person Moves into a House Already Owned by the Other: Sometimes, it seems that even the mildest people have problems when their turf is invaded. For example, our friend Nate fell in love with Alan and wanted to move in with him. Alan agreed, asking Nate to share equally the monthly house payments, property taxes, fire insurance and utilities. Nate agreed, "but only if I somehow get to own part of the house." Alan, in the rush of first love, murmured he'd be willing to give Nate half of everything, but then thought again. The house is worth $220,000; the existing mortgage is $120,000, so Alan's equity is $100,000. After careful thought, Alan told Nate that if he paid one-half of all the monthly payments, it would be fair to give him some of the equity in the house; then Alan asked two questions. First, "I already have a $100,000 equity in the house; how can you ever hope to accumulate anything more than a negligible share?" His second question logically followed the first. "I agree it's fair for you to have some equity in the house, but how can we work out the details?" We offered four solutions:

- The simplest (if not the wisest) was for Nate to forget buying part of the house and instead pay Alan monthly rent. We pointed out to Alan that with this alternative, Nate's rent should be considerably less than one-half the mortgage, tax and insurance because Nate would be getting no equity. A fair rent could be determined by ascertaining the rent for a portion of similar homes in the neighborhood.

- Another easy solution would be for Nate to pay Alan $50,000. This is one-half of Alan's equity in the house and Alan could then deed the house to himself and Nate as either "joint tenants" or "tenants in common." We didn't get too far with this discussion before Nate stood up and emptied his pockets. He had $68, some change and a battered Swiss army knife, which he said was a significant part of his net worth.

- Next we offered a less simple suggestion. The two men could sign a contract where Nate agreed to pay one-half (or all, or any other fraction) of the monthly mortgage, tax and insurance in exchange for a share of equity in the house equal to the percentage his total payments bear to the total amount of money invested in the house by both men.

Sounds complicated? Well, it's really not that difficult to understand.[20]

Example: After one year of payments of $7,000 each, Alan would own ($107,000/$114,000) x 100 or 94% and Nate, ($7,000/$114,000) x 100 or 6%.

- We liked our next idea best, because it was so simple and clear. We suggested that Alan sell Nate one-half of the house at present fair market value, and take a promissory note for the payment. The note would be paid in full if the house was sold or refinanced. This method is very generous to Nate because he'd be get the advantage of ownership (tax advantages and market-caused value increases) with no money down. But the simplicity appealed to both, and that's what they did. Here's the agreement they prepared.

SELLING A SHARE OF YOUR HOUSE TO YOUR LOVER

We, Alan Zoloff and Nate Nichols agree as follows:

1. Alan now owns the house at 1919 Church Street, Seattle, Washington, subject to a mortgage for $120,000.

2. The present value of the home is $220,000.

3. Alan hereby sells one-half of the home to Nate for $110,000 and retains a one-half interest in the house, also valued at $55,000.

4. The $110,000 will be paid by Nate as follows:

$60,000: Nate agrees to assume[21] one-half of the $120,000 mortgage and to pay one-half of the monthly mortgage payments.

$50,000: Nate will sign a note to Alan for $50,000 plus 10% (simple) interest per year to be paid in full when the house is sold.

(They could certainly select a different payment schedule, and/or secure the note by the property.)

5. All other costs for the home, including taxes, insurance, utilities, repairs and maintenance will be divided evenly.

6. When the house is sold, after all other costs are paid, Alan will first

---

[20]It's important to realize that the payments made do not increase actual equity ownership by the amount listed below because most of the money goes to pay the mortgage interest and taxes, not principal. Still, as long as the total payments of both people are treated similarly, this approach produces rough equity. If Alan and Nate had chosen this alternative, they would have had to write a contract with a ledger similar to the one used by Glenna and Rosemary to show their contributions.

[21]The lender will probably not want to let Nate officially assume one-half of the note without considerable expense, so this is a contract solely between the two men.

receive the payment on Nate's note plus the interest due, and the remaining profit (or loss) will be divided evenly between Nate and Alan.

(Other clauses, such as including separation provisions, arbitration clauses, etc. may be included.)

Dated:_____   Signature: _____
                                         Alan Zoloff

Dated:_____   Signature: _____
                                         Nate Nichols

A Note on Taxes: There are tax consequences of selling a share of a home. If you receive no money for the sale, there's no immediate taxable gain (hence, nothing to tax) from the sale. If you receive money from the sale, you'll need to determine what percentage was a return on your capital investment or capital improvement (not taxed), and what percentage was interest on the note or profit on the sale (taxed). And just to keep you muddled, the IRS keeps changing the rules on "installment sales." Because these rules are confusing, spend an hour with an accountant if you put together a house deal like Alan and Nate's. Remember that if Alan wanted to give Nate one-half interest in the house, Alan would be liable for a gift tax on this gift.

4. Moving On

Relationships can end—especially when a group lives together. Planning for this contingency in advance is always wise. If you don't, and a person wants to move and sell her share, the entire household could be forced to sell and move out. Problems can also develop for the person wanting to move. If she's required by the agreement to continue to pay some expenses after moving out, because she can't find a buyer, she may become a prisoner in the house and quite bitter. Here's a clause to cover the contingency of one person moving on. Include it in the original contract, as an amendment to the original contract, or as its own "moving on" contract.

SAMPLE MOVING ON CLAUSE

If one owner moves out of the house, she or he remains responsible for her or his share of the mortgage, taxes and insurance. She or he may rent her or his quarters with the approval (which won't be unreasonably withheld) of the rest of the household. The remaining owners have the first right to rent the quarters themselves or assume the cost if they so choose at a fair market value. The remainder of the house owners must rent the quarters themselves or assume the cost if they reject at least three people the owner moving out proposes as renters.

At the end of two years following the owner's moving out, that owner will have the right to sell her or his share to the remaining owners or to a new person completely, subject to the the approval (which won't be unreasonably withheld) of the remaining owners.

Contracts for Dividing Your Property: We hope you don't have to read this because you've already signed a real property ownership contract carefully defining each person's rights and responsibilities should you separate. But what if you're in the process of separating and made no agreement in advance? Take heart! While it's harder to make an agreement after a relationship has ended than when all is sweetness and light, it can be done. Here are your alternatives:

- Keep the property and run it as a joint venture (if one of you continues to live in it, that person should pay fair rental value of the home to the joint owners).
- Have one person buy the other out.
- Sell the property and divide the proceeds.

AGREEMENT TO SELL

This is an agreement between Art Phillips and Lee Aaronson to sell their house at 1618 Bestview Lane, Fort Lauderdale, Fla.

1. Art and Lee bought the house with each putting up one-half the money. As each has made one-half of the payments, they currently own the house 50-50.

2. They agree to sell the home and divide the profits (or losses) equally.

3. Art is moving out as of July 31, 19___. Lee will stay in the home, keep it presentable for showing to prospective buyers and pay Art a monthly rent of $350. All monthly expenses for repairs, mortgage, taxes and insurance will be paid equally until the house is sold. Lee will pay utilities and simple maintenance. He will keep track of all reasonable expenses incurred to prepare the house for sale, including his labor, valued at $12 an hour. He will be reimbursed from the proceeds of the sale.

Dated: _____   Signature: _____
                                                    Art Phillips

Dated: _____   Signature: _____
                                                    Lee Aaronson

---

Now let's take a different example. Erna and Ann owned a house and decided to go separate ways. Erna paid 60% of the down payment, Ann 40%, and they agreed they owned the home according to those percentages. The difficulty was that Erna had a seven-year-old son and wanted to keep the home. But she didn't have the cash to buy out Ann. Their solution was to agree on an appraiser—who valued the home at $186,500. The couple then calculated the value of each person's share if the house was sold (the net fair market value) as follows:

Determining Net Equity

Agreed upon fair market value:	$186,500

Balance of mortgages:

1st mortgage:	104,500
2nd mortgage:	30,000

Expenses of sale:

Prepayment penalty on 1st mortgage:	5,360
Prepayment penalty on 2nd mortgage:	none
Realtor's commission of 6%	11,190

Other expenses necessary to get full price:

Termite work necessary	2,000
New paint for kitchen	400

Total Mortgages and Expenses	153,450
Net Equity	33,050

Erna's interest—60%	= $19,830
Ann's interest— 40%	= $13,220

There may or may not be prepayment penalties on the mortgages. Also, Ann may argue that if Erna keeps these mortgages, these penalties will not need to be paid. so she, Ann, should not be charged for them.

Now, they had to deal with the fact that Erna didn't have $13,220 to pay Ann. Their options:.

- Erna could try to get a loan to raise the cash to buy out Ann. This could be done by: (1) refinancing the home and giving her a larger mortgage, say $150,000 at 10%. She could then pay off the existing mortgages of $104,500 and $30,000,[22] leaving $15,500. But she'd probably be stuck with a higher interest rate and higher monthly payments. (2) obtaining a third mortgage from a loan company for $13,220 at 18%. (This is also expensive.)

- Erna could write Ann a promissory note for her share, payable monthly, to be paid over a long enough period of time so that Erna could afford the payments. This would work only if Ann had no pressing need for cash.

- If Ann didn't need immediate cash, she could move out, let Erna stay and pay rent or Ann's share, and have Erna either pay Ann her total share—or sell the house—in two years. This would allow Ann to remain an owner, receiving tax and investment advantages, while Erna got two years to either come up with the money or move. If the

---

[22]She'd have to pay re-financing fees too, though if she used the same bank, she'd eliminate pre-payment penalties. Most bank contracts charge you extra for paying off your loan early, but generously waive this requirement if you get a new loan with them at a higher interest rate.

house went up in value in the meantime, it would be easier for Ann to refinance. Here's their agreement:

AGREEMENT FOR ONE OWNER TO RENT THE HOUSE FOR A PERIOD AND THEN SELL

1. This agreement is made between Erna Plank and Ann Cruz.

2. We own 637 Happy Hollow Road, Falmouth, Massachusetts, with Erna owning 60% and Ann owning 40%.

3. The monthly payments are:

Mortgage	$1,006
Taxes:	$50
Insurance:	$30
	$1,086 per month

4. Erna will rent the house for $1100 per month for two years (which we have determined is a fair market rent, giving Erna consideration for managing the property). Erna will be responsible for all maintenance and repairs. If a major repair (over $300) is required, we both must authorize the repair and will share costs in proportion to how much we own (Erna, 60%; Ann, 40%).

5. At the end of two years, we will sell the house and divide the profits (or losses); Erna will get 60% and Ann 40%. Erna has the right to purchase the house at any time during the two years for the fair market value by paying Ann her total net equity. (Add the clause on determining value, found in the "Agreement for Equal Ownership," in Section G1 above.)

Dated:_____   Signature: _____
                                              Erna Plank

Dated:_____   Signature: _____
                                              Ann Cruz

-6-

MARRIAGE, CHILDREN AND DIVORCE

Many lesbians and gay men have been married and become parents. These marriages often end dramatically—sometimes with bitterness, sometimes with real understanding. We have no statistics on the number of lesbians and gay men who have married and become parents, but the number is certainly large. The great variety of experiences, such as those outlined below, gives some indication of how hard it is to generalize about lesbians and gay men and marriage.

A. SOME EXPERIENCES

- *Paul* has enjoyed an open gay lifestyle and is about to enter a marriage with Lucy. Both want children. Lucy knows Paul well and understands that he is gay, and at the same time believes they will make good partners and excellent parents.

- *Don Clark,* a therapist in San Francisco, has chronicled his own story as a gay married man and father. His books[1] describe his "coming out" to his wife and children and his attempt to live within his marriage as a gay man. When that didn't work, he and his wife divorced. Fortunately, their divorce was civilized, and they remained friends. When he moved in with his lover, who also had children, both maintained close relationships with their kids.

---

[1]Don Clark, *Loving Someone Gay* (1977), and *Living Gay* (1979). Celestial Arts Press.

- *Jean* is married, has a child and is just discovering she is a lesbian. She is filled with excitement for a new life, but she is also filled with guilt and contemplates suppressing her sexuality for the sake of her husband (whom she dearly loves) and her child. Right now, she's confused and uncertain as to what she should do.

- *Sarah* met a woman, fell in love and left her husband a note that she had taken the two kids to live in a lesbian collective. She's full of anger at the past, has "great expectations" for future freedom and adventure and cannot relate to her ex-husband, who's having difficulty accepting Sarah's decision, at the same time that he's anxious to maintain a continuing relationship with his children.

- *Martin and Jane* went through an amicable divorce with each moving on to enjoy a gay life. But before parting ways, they went to Hawaii, with their three children for a short celebration. They plan to cooperate closely to see that the children are raised in a warm, loving and stable environment.

The development of a lesbian or gay identity and the emotional consequence that "coming out" can have for spouses and children have been rich subjects for contemporary novelists. But, as is often the case, writers were hardly two exclamation points and a question mark ahead of lawyers, and recently many lesbians and gay men have had their dreams unravel in courtrooms. Even people who have not been dragged into the legal arena realistically fear the possibility. We're regularly asked questions like:

- Can my ex-husband get custody of the children if he learns I am a lesbian?

- My ex-wife says I can't have my lover with me when I take our boy for a weekend. Does she have that power?

- Is it okay to live with my new lover while I am getting a divorce?

- My husband knows I am a lesbian. What should I tell my lawyer— and the judge?

- Will my being gay make a difference when it comes to dividing property or deciding on child custody and support?

- Can I just take the kids and move from this crazy place?

The purpose of this chapter is to discuss what can legally happen when marriages break up and one spouse is lesbian or gay. The legal rules governing divorce, child support, alimony, custody and property division are basically the same for gays and lesbians as for straights, but it is essential to examine them from a lesbian and gay perspective. Our goal is to help you to understand the legal risks and consequences of your actions so you can effectively enforce your rights.

B. DIVORCE—A GOOD DIVORCE CAN BE AS PRECIOUS AS A GOOD MARRIAGE

Egos are commonly bruised whenever a couple splits up, but when the split occurs because one partner has found a new sexual identity, bruises can quickly turn into fractures. We don't have any magic formula to dispense with the pain and anger, but we do know three ingredients that are bound to help:

1. Be as sensitive as possible to the feelings and needs of your (ex) mate.

2. Avoid a court battle if at all possible.

3. Even if you're sure that avoiding a court battle is hopeless, try again, and keep trying.

And even if you're not in a mood to be sensitive, points two and three are still valid—a fight is almost certain to be emotionally draining, costly and, at bottom, unpredictable, even if you're lucky enough to appear before a non-prejudiced judge, which it doesn't take a genius to know is no sure thing.

Practical problems (e.g., who gets the house, custody of the kids, pays the bills, etc.) and paranoia are almost always part of ending a marriage; they are not, however, sufficient reason to hire an attorney and charge off to court. Most people simply need to get upset as part of separating. Even if they're lucky enough to have nothing major to argue about, they'll often argue about who owns the waterbed or the antique lamp. When one partner is lesbian or gay, especially if that person ended the marriage, there's obviously ready focus for the other spouse's pain.

Think of it this way—even if there are real disputes about money and property, fighting about them in court only decreases what's left to divide; a sign in one courtroom reads "litigants should be aware that this court cannot resolve insoluble financial problems." Seeing a therapist, involving yourself with a gay, lesbian or bisexual support group, engaging in mediation or arbitration, or even moving ten miles away, can be more effective ways of handling serious disputes than battling them out in court.

Compromise does not require capitulation. We know lesbians and gay men who left their marriages and gave up everything, even all rights to their children. Reasons varied. Some did it for the sheer joy of moving on, some out of shame over "coming out," others to be rid of the past and a few out of a fear of public disclosure of their sexual orientation. In essence they all said, "I'll give up everything. I just want out!" Obviously, this kind of rash action is unwise; many people later spend months or years trying to obtain custody, support or property that they impulsively abandoned. Getting out of a heterosexual relationship normally doesn't require that much drama. There's no sensible reason to abandon all your rights when you move on.

1. Getting a Divorce

Will the fact that you are lesbian or gay be significant in obtaining a divorce? The answer is, "It depends." In every state, some type of no-fault divorce is available. In a "no-fault" divorce, the court won't be interested in either partner's sexual identity, peccadilloes, moral faults or virtues as far as the divorce itself is concerned.

In adopting no-fault divorce, states have recognized that a court is not suited to determine what happened in a marriage, and it is both wasteful and degrading to encourage couples to drag each other through a morass of petty wrongs, unfulfilled expectations or betrayals. This isn't to say that moral wrongs haven't been committed—only that the courts have sensibly left them to be worked out by higher laws. All that is legally important is that the marriage no longer works and at least one partner wants out. No matter how much the other insists on staying married, he or she can't force it. In no-fault divorces, the common grounds for ending a marriage are separation for a certain length of time, "irretrievable breakdown," "incompatibility" or "irreconcilable differences."[2]

Although every state has some type of no-fault divorce, 33 states and the District of Columbia[3] kept their traditional fault-based divorces as well. This means that your spouse, if in one of those states and so inclined, could request a fault divorce and show that you've mistreated him or her. Thus, if your state still has fault divorce, and your spouse is angry, hurt, jealous and bitter because of your new-found lifestyle, you may find your living arrangement and lifestyle dragged into court.

The question, of course, is "What does this mean practically?" Can you be awarded less than your share of the marital property or be awarded less (or ordered to pay more) alimony because you're gay or lesbian and have ended your marriage? Maybe. Some of the states, such as Florida and Hawaii, have done away with fault divorces, but have retained fault as a factor in dividing property and awarding alimony. And just to confuse things further, some states

---

[2]In California, the ground is "irreconcilable differences have arisen that have caused an irremediable breakdown in my marriage." This is a fine example of legislative poetry, and aside from saying "we just can't stand each other," it's hard to think of a way to describe the reason for the end of the marriage more succinctly.

[3]The 17 states with only no-fault are: Arizona, California, Colorado, Florida, Hawaii, Indiana, Iowa, Kentucky, Michigan, Minnesota, Montana, Nebraska, Nevada, Oregon, Washington, Wisconsin and Wyoming.

which retained fault divorces, such as Alaska and New Jersey, don't allow fault to influence property division or alimony. Yes, we agree that it's all illogical, but when you deal with the law for any length of time, you'll realize that illogic is routine. Finally, in all states, no matter what type of divorce is obtained, "fault" (homosexuality or any other) may be raised in a child custody or visitation dispute.

Here are the state-by-state breakdowns:

GROUNDS FOR DIVORCE[4]

The grounds for divorce are the legal reasons a spouse (or the couple) must give to request a divorce. This chart sets them out state by state:

State	Fault Grounds	No-Fault Grounds	Separation	Length of Separation
Alabama	•	•		
Alaska	•	•		
Arizona		•		
Arkansas	•		•	3 years
California		•		
Colorado		•		
Connecticut[5]	•	•	•	18 months
Delaware	•	•	•	6 months
Florida		•		
Georgia	•	•		
Hawaii		•	•	2 years
Idaho	•	•	•	5 year
Illinois[6]	•	•	•	2 years
Indiana		•		
Iowa		•		
Kansas	•	•		
Kentucky		•		
Louisiana	•		•	1 year
Maine	•	•		
Maryland	•		•	1 year
Massachusetts	•	•		
Michigan		•		

---

[4]The information and charts on the following few pages are taken from the *Family Law Dictionary*, Leonard & Elias, Nolo Press.

[5]Separation-based divorce must also allege incompatibility.

[6]Must allege irretrievable breakdown and separation for no-fault; if both parties consent, 2 years reduced to 6 months.

GROUNDS FOR DIVORCE (cont'd)				
State	Fault Grounds	No-Fault Grounds	Separation	Length of Separation
Minnesota		•		
Mississippi	•			
Missouri[7]	•	•		
Montana		•	•	180 days
Nebraska		•		
Nevada		•	•	1 year
New Hampshire	•	•		
New Jersey	•		•	18 months
New Mexico	•	•		
New York	•		•	1 year
North Carolina	•		•	1 year
North Dakota	•	•		
Ohio	•		•	1 year
Oklahoma	•	•		
Oregon		•		
Pennsylvania	•	•	•	3 years
Rhode Island	•	•	•	3 years
South Carolina	•		•	1 year
South Dakota	•	•		
Tennessee[8]	•	•	•	3 years
Texas	•	•	•	3 years
Utah	•		•	3 years
Vermont	•		•	6 months
Virginia[9]	•		•	1 year
Washington		•		
West Virginia	•	•	•	1 year
Wisconsin		•	•	1 year
Wyoming		•		
Washington, DC	•		•	6 months

[7]If contested, plaintiff must show adultery, abandonment, incompatibility or separation.
[8]Separation-based divorce allowed only if there are no children.
[9]May be reduced to 6 months if there are no children.

FAULT CONSIDERATIONS IN DISTRIBUTING MARITAL PROPERTY

Marital Fault Irrelevant to Property Division	Marital Fault May Reduce Share of Property
Alaska	Alabama
Arizona	Arkansas
California	Connecticut
Colorado	Florida
Delaware	Georgia
Idaho	Hawaii
Illinois	Maryland
Indiana	Michigan
Iowa	Mississippi
Kansas	Missouri
Kentucky	New Hampshire
Louisiana	North Carolina
Maine	North Dakota
Massachusetts	Rhode Island
Minnesota	Texas
Montana	Utah
Nebraska	Vermont
Nevada	Virginia
New Jersey	Wyoming
New Mexico	
New York	
Ohio	
Oklahoma	
Oregon	
Pennsylvania	
South Carolina	
South Dakota	
Tennessee	
Washington	
West Virginia	
Wisconsin	
Washington, DC	

FACTORS IN SETTING ALIMONY		
Fault May Bar or Limit Alimony		
Alabama	Louisiana	Tennessee
Arkansas	Massachusetts	Texas
California	Missouri	Utah
Connecticut	North Carolina	Maryland
Florida	Oklahoma	Virginia
Georgia	Pennsylvania	West Virginia
Hawaii	Rhode Island	Washington, D.C.
Idaho	South Carolina	Wisconsin
Illinois	South Dakota	

2. Dividing Things

If your marriage has lasted long enough for the silver wedding presents to tarnish, you and your spouse have probably accumulated both property and debts. Property includes houses, furniture, cars, motorcycles, savings accounts, patents, invention royalties, stocks, bonds, income tax refunds, money owed to you by other persons, interests in retirement funds or pensions, some disability benefits, vacation pay, a business, etc. How a court will divide the property accumulated during your marriage depends on where you live, as different states follow different property division schemes.[10] States have either community property (Arizona, California, Idaho, Louisiana, Nevada, New Mexico, Texas, Washington and Wisconsin) or equitable distribution (everywhere else but Mississippi).[11] Under both these systems, virtually all property acquired during marriage is basically divided equally. (Gifts and inheritances, however, remain the separate property of the spouse receiving them.)

In states (except Mississippi) where fault has no bearing on property division, the court evenly allocates the property and the debts acquired during marriage. But remember—a few states allow fault to be considered by the court when allocating property.

Example: Hawaii has eliminated fault divorce; only "irreconcilable differences" may be alleged to end the marriage. Hawaii, however, considers marital fault when dividing the property. So, your personal life may be dragged into court anyway. On the other hand, Alaska still has fault divorces, but in either a fault or a no-fault divorce, fault cannot be raised while dividing the material property.

3. Alimony

Alimony is in bad repute these days. This is largely because it no longer fits our times, now that both men and women routinely work. Indeed, when younger couples break up, and both work outside the home, alimony is rarely granted or requested. Does this mean that the concept of alimony is dead? No. Fading away slowly perhaps, but far from dead. For many couples where one spouse earned the money while the other raised the children, alimony is still appropriate—at least until the children enter school full-time or the non-wage earner develops skills necessary to enter (or re-enter) the work force.

Just as some states allow fault to influence property division, a few consider fault when awarding alimony. Again, Hawaii (a no-fault divorce state) allows fault evidence into court when setting alimony, but Alaska, a "fault" state, doesn't.

In addition, if you do receive alimony, it will, most likely, terminate if you remarry. But what if you (or your ex) "cohabit"—that is, live with a lover? Can you lose (or stop paying) alimony? This is a relatively new area of law, and only

---

[10]In most states, publications explaining the ins and outs of marital property are not easily available for nonlawyers. California is an exception; see *California Marriage and Divorce Laws* (Nolo Press), Warner, Ihara and Elias. Check your law library for materials in your state.
[11]Mississippi uses a "division by title" approach—that is, whoever's name is on an item, or whoever earned the money used to buy it, gets it.

few states have rules; so far, all statutes and most court decisions involve heterosexual cohabitation. In New York, cohabitation is ground for cutting off alimony only if the woman receiving the alimony holds herself out as the wife of the man she lives with. Other states with alimony/cohabitation laws have adopted tighter rules. In California, for example, Civil Code 4801 states:

> *Except as otherwise agreed to by the parties in writing, there shall be a reputable presumption... of decreased need for support if the supported party is cohabiting with a **person of the opposite sex**. Upon such a finding of changed circumstances, the court may modify the payment of support... [Emphasis is ours.]*

It's not common, but one California court applied the policy of this statute to a case where a woman receiving alimony moved in with her lesbian (wage-earning) lover. California isn't the only state to do this. In another case, a woman was awarded alimony "until death or remarriage" as part of her divorce. When her ex-husband learned that she was a lesbian, he asked the court to set a date when the alimony would end. The court did so, finding a fixed time appropriate because there was no chance the wife would remarry.[12] In a Minnesota case, an ex-wife's alimony was terminated when her ex-husband proved she had "entered into an apparently stable relationship with a woman." This trend may continue. Alimony is based on the ex-spouse's need, and if in reality that need decreases, alimony probably should be ended or reduced. Logically, it should make no difference whether an ex-spouse has remarried or is living with a gay lover—it's the financial reality that counts.[13]

4. Conclusion

It's possible to get a sensible, civilized divorce even in a state where fault divorces are still available. Many people make decisions about children, support and property in a spirit of common sense and compromise rather than "who is more right." (As the saying goes, "Being right is the consolation prize of life.")

If your state considers fault in dividing property, and you've accumulated a lot of property and are having difficulty dividing it, reconcile yourself to a long court struggle and start saving money for lawyer's fees. And realize that if you're the higher—or only—wage earner during the marriage, you may be ordered to pay your spouse's lawyer's fees too.) But if you've agreed on a plan for dividing

---

[12]5 Family L. Rptr. 2127 (1979).

[13]You may want to check your state's law; see Chapter 12, Lawyers and Doing Your Own Research.

your property, considering each person's needs and earning abilities, congratulations.

COOPERATIVE SEPARATION AGREEMENT

Herb and Carol Fitzroy agree as follows:

1. That they have decided to separate and no longer plan to live together.

2. That their children, John age 7, and Phillip age 4, will live with Carol, and that Herb will visit and babysit as much as his job allows—at least two nights and one weekend day per week.

3. That Herb will pay child support to Carol. Initially, it will be $400 per month; it will increase yearly by the same percentage that Herb's net salary increases.

4. That neither Herb nor Carol plan to marry again immediately, and that it's clearly understood and accepted that both will have friendships that may involve sexual relationships with people of the same or opposite sex.

5. That Herb and Carol will cooperate in getting an amicable divorce, and that neither will attempt to influence the court's decision by raising the point that the other is having a sexual relationship, or living, with a person of the same or opposite sex.

Dated: _____   Signature: _____
                                              Carol Fitzroy
Dated: _____   Signature: _____
                                              Herb Fitzroy

Note: This sort of agreement is not enforceable in court, especially as it relates to custody of children and child support. As we explain below, when deciding matters relating to kids, a court must look at all factors and decide what's in the "best interests of the child." Still, an amicable agreement can be a valuable reminder that you both want to avoid a court battle. Also, if you find yourself in court with your spouse complaining of your gay or lesbian lifestyle, a judge might give the agreement considerable weight. She's likely to ask, "If you didn't object to her (or his) sexual orientation the day you signed the agreement, why are you objecting to it now?"

C. Child Custody

Child custody is usually the most difficult legal problem a formerly married lesbian or gay parent faces. In a court fight over custody, judges are supposed to consider all factors and arrive at a decision in the "best interests of the child." This means that virtually anything relating to your lifestyle, sexual identity and behavior can be legally dragged into court. Obviously, you must insist that your sexual identity is irrelevant to your being a good parent. If you and your spouse agree on custody, the court will almost certainly accept your arrangement with no questions asked. Court battles develop because parents can't agree, and one or both bring the dispute to the judge.[14] We don't need to tell you that a lesbian or gay parent faces a difficult struggle trying to gain custody in most American courtrooms, especially if the parent is living with a lover. Indeed, in the past many gay parents chose to remain in nonsupportive, non-loving marriages, or to live secretive, guarded gay lifestyles after separation, for fear of losing their children.

But lo! We see a glimmer of light at the edge of the black sky. In the last few years, some courts have held that a parent's homosexuality cannot be grounds for automatic denial of custody. But while we hope this is a growing trend, we think it is fair to say that the majority of judges are prejudiced against, or at least suspicious of, gay or lesbian parents. Be careful. Only if compromise with your (former) spouse is impossible should you fight in court. But if you must fight, prepare well, and then, as one writer put it, "Hold on tight! For you are about to

---

[14]It is technically possible for a state agency to seek to remove a child from the custody of a lesbian or gay parent because of the parent's homosexuality. This was a substantial fear a few years ago, but we know of no recent cases. We still recommend discretion in conservative areas of the country.

enter a maze of decisions central to your life and your children's, to embark on a roller coaster of emotions, and to be politicized in every area of your life."[15]

A parent with custody has the legal right to have the child live with her or him, and to make the important decisions—such as where to make the home, what school to attend, what doctor to use and what medical treatment to seek. Visitation (discussed later in this chapter) is the non-custodial parent's right to see and be with the child; the right to visit is far more limited than the right to custody. Obviously, the first decision a gay or lesbian parent must make is whether to seek custody at all, and if so, whether to share it.

If you think there's a serious possibility you and your spouse will fight in court over custody, the cautious legal advice is not to live with your lover, and to be very discrete, at least until the court has made a decision. Many judges have an easier time giving a lesbian or gay parent custody if she or he lives alone. This advice applies to both fault and no-fault divorces because, as we've stated, the living arrangements of both parents are always admissible in determining the "best interests of the child."

Before 1900, children were considered property, and as such, custody was almost always given to fathers. For most of the twentieth century, mothers have been awarded custody, especially of children under age 5, unless they were found to be "unfit." Today, the automatic preference for mothers has been rejected by almost every state, and many men are winning custody. Sadly, however, this is especially true if the mother is a lesbian. Although under the "best interests" standard, each parent has an equal right to custody, the reality is that the judge has almost complete discretion when two fighting parents come to court.

In some states, joint custody is possible. We recommend it when the parents get along amicably and are equally dedicated to raising the children because it equalizes the balance of power between the parents and gives each an equal say in raising the children. In our experience, fathers are more likely to support and maintain close relationships with their children when they're involved in decision-making. A common criticism of joint custody, however, is that because neither parent has the final say, arguments can go on forever. This is a valid point, and we suggest parents with joint custody use family counseling to help them through rough spots. We haven't seen a lot of marriages "saved" by counseling, but we've seen many families save much anguish by using it.

---

[15]Mary L. Stephens, "Lesbian Mothers in Transition," found in *Our Right to Love*, p. 207, 1978, Prentice-Hall.

Contested custody is full of uncertainties, not just related to sexual orientation. We've been asked such questions as:

- My wife is a real fascist. Will she be able to get the children just by proving I'm gay?
- I was convicted for possession of hashish in the sixties. Does this mean I can't get custody of the kids?
- My former husband is way behind on his child support. Can he try to get out of paying and take the children from me by claiming he just learned that I live with my lover?
- I go to school and earn only $8,000 a year; my husband is a veterinarian and earns $75,000 yearly. Does this mean he'll get the children?
- Tell the truth—is there any chance for a gay father to get custody of young children?

The answer to all of these questions, including even the last one, is, "It depends." In spite of what you "learned" at the movies, or what your bartender or brother-in-law has told you, the laws of most states do not say that homosexuality or living with your lover automatically results in the loss of custody. The judge will make a decision after hearing all sorts of negative and positive evidence and, in doing so, he will necessarily apply his own standards and prejudices. Some judges are teetotalers or are adamantly opposed to marijuana; others don't give heavy weight to old criminal convictions (unrelated to child welfare); some do; some will let a parent's poverty or politics influence them; many are biased against lesbians and gay men. Of course, there are also judges who are themselves lesbian or gay. So, don't over-generalize or jump to conclusions. Each judge is different and each case unique.

As a generalization, courts are less concerned with sexual conduct than they used to be. Not surprisingly, this change first occurred with heterosexual unmarried couples.[16] Gradually, as more and more opposite sex couples began cohabiting, judges decided that living together without a permission slip from the county clerk didn't necessarily mean that people were "unfit parents." Here are two early court holdings:

> *We have long passed the point where sexual misconduct automatically disqualifies a mother from obtaining custody of her minor children.*[17]

---

[16]In this connection, we'd like to recognize the pioneering work in the area of rights of heterosexual couples in *The Living Together Kit* (Nolo Press), by Toni Ihara and Ralph Warner.

[17]*Greenfield v. Greenfield*, 260 N.W.2d 493 (Nebraska 1977).

> *The fact of the mother's adulterous relationship is of importance in a*
> *child custody case only as it may affect the best interests of the child.*[18]

It is still possible to find cases in which courts have held that heterosexual cohabitation is reason to deny custody, but these decisions are fast becoming historical anachronisms. This more tolerant trend is slowly spreading to cases involving lesbian or gay parents. An excellent reference guide is *The Lesbian Mother Litigation Manual,* available from the Lesbian Rights Project.[19] It is also imperative that you get a sympathetic at least, knowledgeable if possible, lawyer for any contested case. Don't be shy about bringing your attorney the materials we mention if she doesn't have them. Of course, there is still a long way to go, but there is now some hope for lesbian and gay parents in contested custody cases.

1. How Does a Court Decide a Contested Custody Case?

In most states, judges do not decide contested custody cases simply by inviting the parents to present their arguments. Much happens long before the parents have their nervous day in court. A custody battle is part of a divorce proceeding, a paternity proceeding or a post-divorce or post-paternity modification request. The lawyers (or parents, if they represent themselves) tell the court there's a disagreement over custody. The court refers the case to a county agency (such as child welfare, social services, etc.) with authority to look into the dispute. A case worker (usually a trained social worker) investigates all relevant facts and makes a written report and recommendation to the court. The case worker interviews the parents and children, and often teachers, day care workers, neighbors, friends and family. Arrest, health and employment records of the parents and children are gathered. The case worker may suggest psychological testing or request that a parent release his or her therapist's report.

Case workers have different interests, skills and approaches in preparing reports and recommendations. Some are so overworked or lazy that they do very little; others do quite a bit. There is really no such thing as an objective investigation, as each worker is bound to let his or her own values color the recommendation. It's probably fair to say that the average case worker is more liberal and tolerant of different lifestyles than is the average judge, but don't count on it. Normally, the case worker, no matter how tolerant of gays and

---

[18]*Bonjour v. Bonjour,* 566 P.2d 667 (Alaska 1977).

[19]Their address is 1370 Mission Street, 4th Floor, San Francisco, CA 94103. As of Spring 1989, they are changing their name to the National Center for Lesbian Rights. Another good source is the *Family Law Reporter.*

lesbians, will reveal your sexual orientation (if known) or your living situation (if apparent) in the report. And even if the case worker does not think your sexual orientation or living situation is important, the judge may.

After the case worker writes the report and makes the recommendation, the judge and both attorneys receive copies. Your lawyer should discuss it with you in detail. Although nothing compels judges to follow the recommendations, most do. If the recommendation is in your favor, you are in excellent shape to get custody; conversely, you're in trouble if the recommendation is against you. It doesn't mean custody is impossible, but it does mean you'll have to do a significant amount of preparation for the hearing. At the hearing, either parent may ask the case worker to come to court to be questioned about the report and recommendation.

In California and some other states, courts require the disputing parents to attend at least one mediation session with a court-sponsored professional mediator to try and settle the custody dispute. This mandatory mediation occurs before the parents ever go to court.

During the hearing, the judge may want to talk with the children. Each judge handles this differently. Many talk to children they believe are old enough to have a sensible opinion; others never consult with kids. Most judges give little weight to the views of children under seven, and give considerable respect to the desires of teenagers. For children between seven and eleven, it usually depends on their maturity. In any event, most judges try to keep brothers and sisters under the same roof unless there's a strong reason not to.

Caution! There is yet another strong reason for a lesbian or gay parent to avoid a mudslinging battle. No law requires judges to award custody to either parent; if both are really good at slinging mud, the court may find neither fit to raise the kids and may turn them over to a relative or even the state.

Another Caution! In most states, courts have the power to order a custody investigation even if the parents are not disputing. Although most court calendars are overcrowded and this is unlikely, don't automatically assume that all is fine if you've reached a compromise. If a judge knows, or finds out, that a parent is gay, the case worker may come a-knocking.

Finally, remember that custody disputes are never truly settled until the child reaches majority. As long as the child is a minor, the court retains power over child custody. Custody decisions can be reopened and changed, if a parent shows "change of circumstances" and that the status quo is not in the child's "best interest."

2. The Gay Parent's Fight for Custody

We know this is repetitive, but if we could, we'd put it in neon. Custody battles are a last resort. They are bitter, emotionally and financially draining and pose special problems for lesbians and gays. If it's humanly possible, work out your custody arrangement with your (ex) spouse. Do it even if you feel you're going more than halfway. Only if your spouse adamantly refuses to be fair should you go to court. We are not suggesting that you give up without a struggle or that you compromise in areas you consider essential, but remember—the odds are still heavily against lesbian and gay parents in custody disputes.

If you do fight, be prepared for a dirty battle. Many non-gay parents mount nasty courtroom attacks with the hope that a conservative judge will deny custody or even visitation to a gay parent. More than one heterosexual parent has stooped incredibly low—even going so far as launching a media campaign designed to brand their former spouse a flaming queer or bull dyke.

The first step in any custody battle is to decide exactly what you want, and then to decide what you're willing to settle for. Your strategy is to pursue your wants, and be willing to compromise to obtain what you'll settle for. If you get to court, however, you'll have to be prepared to persuade a judge why your "wants" are in your children's best interests.

Don't worry about legal technicalities or rules of evidence. That's your lawyer's job. In most custody cases, judges cut through legal gobbledygook to learn all the facts and decide what's in the child's best interest. Most judges flatter themselves that they try to be objective; while convincing a judge that your sexual orientation is irrelevant will be an uphill battle, it's possible. You need a good grasp of the basic facts. Don't lose track of what is in your child's best interest and just try to punish your ex. The judge may be prejudiced, but is probably not dumb. If she feels that one parent (gay or straight) is putting vengeance over concern for the children, the judge will award custody to the other parent. So from the start, be calm, rational and caring.

Warning! When you first separate, stay with your children (keep custody) if at all possible. If you leave to "get your head together," you're risking creating a situation where it's easy for a judge to give custody to the parent who's taking care of the kids. Courts don't like to disrupt the status quo, and often put a high value on keeping kids with whomever they've been living. If you have to get away for a period of time, try to first reach an understanding with your spouse that, when you return, the two of you will share custody—and put it in writing!

Let's assume you're facing a custody fight. How do you proceed? Start by getting yourself a good support system. Find people or groups concerned with gay or lesbian custody issues. A local lesbian mothers' or gay fathers' group is ideal. You will need a great deal of support if you are going to engage in a court struggle, and no one can give it to you better than folks who've been there.[20]

Your next step is to get a sympathetic and knowledgeable lawyer—and you do need one. As you have no doubt gathered, we favor people doing their own legal work where feasible, and are convinced that our laws and procedures must be changed to make it easier for people to represent themselves. But a custody battle is not the place to do it. You face an uphill struggle even with a lawyer, and you need someone who knows the local judges, probation officials and custody laws. It's sad but true, but some judges evaluate litigants by the quality of their attorneys.

How do you choose an attorney? If you find a support group, ask around for names of attorneys other gay parents have used. If that doesn't work, we've provided a list of lesbian and gay legal organizations in Chapter 12. Call one for referrals. Get the names of more than one lawyer; call and speak to them before making an appointment. You've got to feel comfortable with the one you hire.[21]

Just because you hire a lawyer, don't give up control of your case. You must be involved in the day-to-day preparation and decision making. Gather the facts and do other legwork; you'll be involved and save some lawyer fees. Don't pay your lawyer $100 to $200 an hour to do background preparation you can do. Here are some things you can do to help prepare your case. Of course, you should discuss these with your lawyer before doing any of them:

- Find stable, respectable people (religious officials are always good) who know your situation, will tell the case worker why you should have custody and will later testify in court, if necessary.
- Have stable, respectable people send letters to the case worker stating that you're a good parent. (The case worker can't talk to everyone.)
- Prepare a list for your attorney of friends, relatives, children's teachers or day care workers, neighbors, clergy and anyone else willing to speak on your behalf. Outline what each is prepared to say and who is likely to impress the judge.

Here is a sample letter to send the case worker. It's included to give you an idea of what is needed, not to copy. The letters you get should be personal, focused on your situation and succinct. Thomas Jefferson once began a long letter

---

[20]The National Gay and Lesbian Task Force in Washington, D.C. can help you find a local support group.

[21]If you can't afford an attorney, don't give up. Legal services might help. Or, a lawyer might take the case "pro bono"—that is, for free. Also, several lesbian organizations have helped raise funds to pay lawyers representing lesbian mothers and gay fathers in custody battles.

by writing "If I had the time, I'd have written you a short letter." Case workers and judges have quite a bit of paperwork, and rarely give much attention to anything more than a page or two.

May 10, 19___

To Whom It May Concern:

I have been a neighbor of Sandra Welch for six years. I know her family intimately, including her children, Joy and Teresa.

Sandra is a warm, sensitive and dependable person and parent. She is wonderfully patient and loving with her children. Her husband, Frank, never seemed very interested in his children and did not spend much time with them.

Sandra has discussed with me the fact that she and Georgia Conrad are lovers. I have visited their home; it is my observation that they are a very stable and caring couple who provide a warm, loving, clean and nurturing home and environment for the children. The children seem comfortable with both women and in a way act as if they have two mothers. Knowing the family background as I do, I am convinced that they are happier with Sandra than they would be living with Frank.

I am a mother and I happen to be heterosexual. Like many others, I had a bit of difficulty accepting that my friend, Sandra, is a lesbian. It took some getting used to, but I know that it in no way negatively affects her being a good parent. My two children, one boy and one girl, are about the same age as Sandra's. All the kids are in and out of both of our houses all the time and they are very fond of Sandra and Georgia. I have no hesitation about my children being with Sandra and Georgia, and I often leave my children with Sandra when I go out.

After thinking carefully about all the issues involved, I can see no way in which Sandra's sexual identity has adversely affected her children. And I don't see any problem in the future. It's just not related to her being the children's mother.

I would be willing to testify to my observations and beliefs in court if this would be helpful.

Sincerely,

Joyce Johnson

3. Making Your Case a "Political" Statement

Some organizations have urged that any lesbian or gay man involved in a custody fight "politicize" it—take a militant gay rights stand, focus media attention on their struggle and use it to advance lesbian and gay culture, causes and acceptability. Obviously, this is a decision only you can make. Our personal feeling is that tactically, you're more likely to succeed by down-playing the political concerns of gay custody unless you have no other choice. Winning your right to custody (or visitation) seems enough of a political statement to us. Maybe we're being overly lawyerly, but in most courts, most of the time, you'll do better if your sexual orientation is not known to the judge, or if it is known, not made into a political issue. There are many arenas for fighting for lesbian and gay rights; a child custody case is usually legally difficult and emotionally traumatic enough without running the added risks that politicization brings. If you know that your ex-spouse will raise your sexual orientation, strategically it may be wise for you to bring it up first to eliminate any shock value and to present yourself as open and honest. Obviously these are tactical and legal decisions you need to discuss with a lawyer you trust.

4. Looking for a Judge Who Understands Your Lifestyle

Parents caught in custody battles often think of moving to a part of the country where judges are likely to have more liberal views. San Francisco can judge to decide the case in your new locale. Although legally you can take a child to a new state unless a court order prohibits you, a law called the Uniform Child Custody Jurisdiction Act limits a judge's power to make a custody decision. If you move to San Francisco from Oklahoma and eventually request custody, the San Francisco judge doesn't have the authority (called "jurisdiction") to hear your request, and will send you back to Oklahoma. One purpose of the law is to stop parents from moving about in a search for a court that will grant them custody. The mere presence of a child in a state does not mean that the state has the power to make a custody ruling. Rather, the law provides that a court can make a custody ruling if (in this order):

- The state was the child's "home state," generally being the state where the child lived at least six months before the custody case was filed in court.

- It's in the best interests of the child that the court make a decision because the child and at least one parent have significant connection with the state, *and* there is available in the state "substantial evidence concerning the child's present or future care, protection, training, and personal relationships."

- The child is physically present in the state and has been abandoned or needs emergency protection from mistreatment or abuse.

- No other state has authority over the case.

Be warned that the act disfavors giving custody to a parent who relocates just to create a "home state" or "significant connections." If you've moved, you'd better be able to convince the judge it was for a better job and therefore a better life for your kids, not that it was to look for a more "enlightened" court.

If custody proceedings are started in more than one state, the court of the state with lower ranking jurisdiction under the act must stop all proceedings or dismiss the case. In other words, unless you can show a dire emergency, all you'd get for your trip from Enid to San Francisco would be a determination that Oklahoma had jurisdiction. You might even get fined. The act provides that a court can order the parent to pay the other's attorney's fees and travel expenses.

If there's an existing court order establishing custody, your chances of moving and persuading a court in another state to modify that order are extremely slim. By taking a child in violation of a court order, you are guilty of kidnapping. The Uniform Child Custody Jurisdiction Act provides that a court, in declining to hear a custody case, can notify the prosecuting attorney of the original state that the child has been illegally removed. And the Parental Kidnapping Prevention Act can be used to prosecute you for kidnapping.

The Uniform Act should work for both parents. Although it greatly limits a gay or lesbian parent's power to move to a more favorable state, it also limits the non-gay parent's power to take a child to a conservative jurisdiction, hoping to get a custody change by proving the other parent is gay.

Despite our words of caution, there may be some extreme situations when discrimination in your home area is so severe that a move to a new state is a lesbian or gay parent's only hope of gaining custody. Although it doesn't work often, shopping for a better court has been known to work occasionally. If you are contemplating this course of action, please see a lawyer who knows the field well. As we said above, your chances of success are poor and you are risking a kidnapping charge if there is already a court order. And think of the effect that running, hiding and living with fear will have on your children.

5. Resources Available to Lesbian and Gay Parents Seeking Custody

If you're involved in a contested custody case, your sympathetic and experienced lawyer may need assistance. Chapter 12 includes names and addressees of gay and lesbian legal rights groups; contact one near your home. These groups will probably have resources beyond what we list below. Nonetheless, some resources which should prove quite helpful to your lawyer are:

- Achtenberg, *Sexual Orientation and the Law* (1985)
- Hitchens, *Lesbian Mother Litigation Manual*, Lesbian Rights Project (1982); the Lesbian Rights Project's address is 1370 Mission Street, 4th Floor, San Francisco, CA 94103
- Susoeff, *Assessing Children's Best Interests When a Parent is Gay or Lesbian*, 32 UCLA Law Review 852 (1985)
- National Lawyers Guild, Anti-Sexism Committee, *A Lesbian and Gay Parents Legal Guide to Child Custody*, San Francisco (1985)
- Goldzband, *Custody Cases and Expert Witnesses: A Manual for Attorneys* (1980)

6. Use of Expert Psychiatric Witnesses

As you may have noticed, the last resource we list relates to "expert witnesses." Who are expert witnesses? They're psychiatrists, case workers, psychologists and other professionals who testify about an area where most people don't have "expert" knowledge. Experts are often used in custody cases, and can be extremely helpful for a gay parent. An expert can evaluate your home environment, and testify about your fitness as a parent, your child's health, welfare, relationship to you and relationship to the home environment. An expert can also educate the judge about lesbian and gay parents in general. The judge is probably dying to ask questions, and a sympathetic expert can provide positive answers.

Whatever you personally feel about psychologists and therapists, courts are frequently impressed by credentialed "experts." It takes the wisdom of Solomon to decide many custody cases, and although few judges publicly admit it, most welcome all the help they can get. This is one reason judges rely on case workers' reports and recommendations. An expert also allows a judge to pass the buck to another "professional" when having to make a difficult decision.

So, if you can afford it, seriously consider having an expert or two testify on your behalf. Be sure they're clearly on your side and that you and your lawyer know exactly what they will say ahead of time. Ideally, an expert should testify that:

- You are a well-adjusted, stable and fit parent.
- The children are, or will be, well-adjusted, healthy and happy with you.
- It is in the best interest of the children to live with you.
- In general, gay and lesbian parents provide loving, stable homes and that all studies show that children raised by gay or lesbian parents grow up to be happy, healthy and well-adjusted.

An expert should also be able to address issues concerning the children's relationships to their peers and anyone significant to you. In other words, the expert should explain away all the fears the judge may have about homosexuality.

There has been extensive positive research and writing done regarding gay and lesbian parents and their children. You'll want to review some of this information with your expert. Start with the *Gay Parent Support Packet*, distributed by the National Gay and Lesbian Task Force, 1517 "U" Street, N.W., Washington D.C. 20009. This packet includes information about a study on children of gay and lesbian parents done by Dr. Evelyn Hooker, which concluded that:

- The children were well-adjusted regarding their lifestyle and sexual identity.
- There was no evidence of proselytizing by the gay parents.
- There was no adverse effect on the children growing up knowing that the parent was gay.

In addition, there are questions the judge might have that your expert should be able to answer:

- Are children of gay or lesbian parents going to be "normal?"
- Are the kids apt to be molested or seduced by the gay parent or the parent's friends?
- Aren't all gays and lesbians promiscuous and unstable?
- What is the effect of AIDS on the home life of the child?
- Are gay people as "adjusted" and happy as heterosexuals?
- Do the children of gay parents have problems typical of, or different from, children of the average divorced parents?

Your expert might be countered by an opposing one. Lawyers know that you can find an expert who will support almost any position, provided you have the money. Cross-examining and discrediting an opposing expert is a job for your lawyer, which is another reason why you'll need someone knowledgeable about lesbian and gay issues.

D. Visiting Your Child

Judges have hindered and obstructed gay parents' rights to visit their children with the same coldness and caprice that they have exhibited when denying custody. And hypocrisy? How about the following statement supposedly protecting the constitutional rights of a gay father:

> *Fundamental rights of parents may not be denied, limited, or restricted on the basis of sexual orientation, per se. The right of a parent, including a homosexual parent, to the companionship and care of his or her child, insofar as it is for the best interest of the child, is a fundamental right protected by the First, Ninth, and Fourteenth Amendments to the United States Constitution. That right may not be restricted without a showing that the parent's activities may tend to impair the emotional and physical health of the child.*[22]

Beautiful words, aren't they? Yes, until you realize they were part of a decision in which a father was allowed to see his children as follows:

> *...on alternate Sundays and some holidays and three weeks' visitation during the summer, at some place other than his home, during which he is ordered not to sleep with anyone other than a lawful spouse nor to involve the children in any homosexual-related activities or publicity nor to see his male companion in the presence of his children.*

---

[22]*In Re J., S. and C.,* 129 N.J. Super. Ct. 486, 324 A.2d 90 (1974).

In general, the problems confronting a lesbian or gay parent in a custody proceeding are ones to be addressed in a visitation case. But there are significant differences too—considerable legal precedent states that to deny a parent the right to visit, the showing of potential harm to the child must be extremely high, much higher than when custody is denied. Even judges have recognized that if you are going to deny (or greatly restrict) a parent's right to see his or her child, you must show that the parent is a true ogre. The legal lingo for this finding is that the visitation would be "actually detrimental" to the best interests of the child.

A lesbian or gay parent can't legally be deprived of visitation with his or her child just because a court feels it's in the child's best interest to live with the other parent. It takes extreme behavior (child abuse, violence, repeated drunkenness, etc.) for a court to deny any parent visitation. Once your (ex) spouse learns this, she or he should be much less inclined to fight over visitation; if she or he insists and takes the case to court, you should win.

Our advice to parents worried about visitation is the same that we gave in the custody section above—compromise if you can. If you and your spouse agree that you should be granted visitation, the court will probably give you "reasonable visitation rights" and leave you and your spouse to work out the details.[23] If, however, you're relating so poorly that you cannot agree on when, where and how the visitation will take place, a judge will specifically define visitation rights. For example, a court might make the following order:

> *Herb Fitzroy is awarded the right to visit with John and Phillip Fitzroy every weekend from 10:00 a.m. Saturday to 8:00 p.m. Sunday, plus six weeks during the school vacations, the weeks to be agreed upon by the parties.*

or

> *Carol Fitzroy is awarded the right to visit with her children on the first and third weekends of each month from 5:00 p.m. on Friday to 8:00 p.m. on Sunday, and for the children's entire summer vacation, on the condition that she pick up the children from, and deliver them to, the home of Herb Fitzroy.*

---

[23]This assumes that you and the other parent were married. If you were never married, there will be no divorce and no court proceeding unless one of you initiates a paternity action. An unmarried father has both an obligation to support his child and the same visitation and custody rights as if he and the mother had been married, assuming he maintained a close relationship with his child and acknowledged paternity. The rules differ if he has "abandoned" his child. For more information, see *The Living Together Kit* (Nolo Press), Ihara and Warner.

Sometimes a judge will impose specific rules on visitation. A non-custodial parent may be required to give the custodial parent 48 hours notice before coming to visit. Or, a court may prohibit the visiting parent from removing the child from the country or the state, or, in rare situations, from the child's own home or the home of a third party. It's common for courts to require that parents with histories of drinking not use alcohol while visiting the children. But can the court restrain Herb from visiting with his children in the presence of George Wilcox (the man with whom he lives)? Can the court prohibit the children from spending the night with Herb if George Wilcox is present? Some courts have said yes; others no. Can a court prohibit a gay father with AIDS from visiting with his children? Because the children are not at risk of catching AIDS from their father, there's no medical ground for a prohibition. In most cases, visitation has been permitted. But some judges will prohibit visitation, supposedly to "protect the children." In any of these situations, you will want an expert or two to testify on your behalf. If the court rules against you, especially in the case of a gay father with AIDS, consider appealing—but it's rarely wise to violate the court order.

Once a visitation order is entered, it's enforceable just like any other court order. Parents with custody have been known to refuse to comply with visitation orders, to spite their ex-spouse. Whatever the motive, it's not in the best interests of the children, and it's illegal. A parent violating a court order can be held in contempt of court, fined and even jailed.

E. SUPPORTING YOUR CHILD

In every state, parents are required to support their children if they are financially able to do so. It makes no difference whether the parent has custody or has been denied visitation, or whether the parents were married when the child was born. All parents have equal obligations to support their kids.

Example: Toni is a bank president and Mort, a bank guard. After a whirlwind courtship behind the vault, they marry. Before long they have twins, Gold and Silver. Everything is smooth until Toni goes to a bankers' convention and meets Keija, who is also in bank management. Toni returns home and informs Mort that she and Keija are having a relationship and plan to live together. Mort, who has some new romantic notions of his own, is not terribly upset and agrees to Toni having custody, but he feels that because she makes more than he does, he shouldn't have to pay child support. Is this a reasonable position? Perhaps, but it will not do Mort any good in court. Support is based on both the ability of parents to pay and the needs of the children. Mort may be ordered to pay less than if Toni didn't work outside the home, but he will be ordered to pay something.

Example: Now assume that Mort has custody. Mort's salary is $15,000 per year and Toni's is $50,000. A court would clearly order Toni to pay considerable support. She has the ability to do so, and Mort will find it impossible to keep the twins clothed without Toni's help.

Example: Assume now that custody is joint and the kids spend roughly half the year with Toni and half with Mort. Mort probably won't have to pay when the kids are with Toni, but Toni will be required to pay some support when the kids are with Mort.

Example: Now let's get Keija into the picture. Assume that Toni has custody, but that she and Keija act as if they were both the kids' mothers. Keija commonly spends large chunks of her salary on the kids. When combined with what Toni spends, the twins are lavishly taken care of. Does Keija's voluntary spending reduce Mort's obligation? Under the letter of the law, probably not. Keija's contributions are voluntary—she is not a parent, while legally Mort still is. If Mort asked a court to reduce his support obligation, however, a judge might be informally influenced by Keija's spending and reduce Mort's obligation slightly. Mort should argue that because Keija contributes to the household expenses, Toni now has more of her disposable income to spend on Gold and Silver, and he can pay less.

Example: Now assume that Mort starts living with Alex and Alex's two kids. Between raising the kids and doing carpentry work, Alex can barely pay for groceries and Mort finds himself chipping in to help support the family. Before long, he's short of money to send Toni for Silver and Gold. He asks the court to reduce his child support obligation, explaining that he is helping support Alex's kids, who really need it. Will the judge reduce Mort's support obligation? No. Mort has no legal relationship with Alex's kids and no legal duty to support them.

Note: This last example is obviously troubling, and we've seen it cause great hardship. Often people such as Mort, who are trying to be decent and caring, are hauled into court for nonpayment of support, when in fact they're working hard to support a new family. We feel it's time that our child support laws be re-examined to take into consideration the way people actually live. At present, often only the support collectors—lawyers, judges, case workers and district attorneys' investigators—end up with adequate support—not the kids who are in need.

Important—Failure to Support Is a Crime: In all states, it is a crime to fail to support your kids, whether you were ever married. It also doesn't matter if you've separated, but not yet divorced.

A parent sometimes tries to avoid paying child support by moving to a different part of the country. Hiding out is hard to do, however, because of a law called the Uniform Reciprocal Enforcement of Support Act. This law connects state and federal governments in their support enforcement efforts. In addition, federal laws make social security, internal revenue service and other federal files available to child support enforcement officials.[24] If someone with the ability to work refuses to do so (and therefore claims inability to pay child support), he'll probably be ordered to pay support and be fined or jailed if he fails to do so. Many judges define "ability to support a child" to mean "able-bodied," and demand that parents who aren't employed show up in court periodically with lists of potential employers they've contacted.

If you're a parent with custody and are not receiving support, speak to your district attorney for assistance.

F. CHILD SUPPORT WHEN VISITATION IS DENIED

Suppose your ex-spouse arbitrarily refuses to comply with court-ordered visitation. Can you retaliate by refusing to pay child support? In most states, no. Most courts have ruled that support and visitation are not intertwined, and that you must pay support no matter what happens with visitation. Not all courts are this tough, however. Some have granted requests to reduce child support on the ground that a visitation order wasn't being honored. And in Oregon, a court held that a father did not have to pay any child support for each week that he was denied visitation. A few other states, while not allowing parents to withhold support, do allow parents to seek reimbursement from the custodial parents for all costs incurred in trying to exercise visitation. So, if you're being denied visitation, you may be able to go to court and get either your support reduced or your costs incurred in attempting to visit reimbursed. You must go to court, however, before actually reducing the payments; if you reduce them without

---

[24]Even if you move from Maine to Oregon, it is not usually difficult for a district attorney to locate and prosecute you. In most states, child support collection officers have the authority to take unpaid support directly from your paycheck.

court authorization, you may be held in contempt of court under the original support order.

G. AFTER THE DIVORCE

Finally, your marriage is over; custody, support, visitation and property division are settled. You and your lover are settling down to enjoy your new life. It's nice to be able to forget all about courts, lawyers and hassles about who cares for and supports the kids. Sound too good to be true? You're right. It probably is. Questions of custody and child support are never finally settled. Either parent can request the judge to modify custody or child support if the circumstances have significantly changed since the making of the previous order.

Example: Remember Mort and Toni? Assume that Toni (the banker) got custody and Mort (the security guard) was ordered to pay $400 a month in child support. All went well for a year, until Toni quit her job to go back to school to learn the piccolo. Can she ask the court to raise the amount of Mort's support? Of course she can ask. Will the court do so? Perhaps, depending on what the judge thinks of Toni's decision. Obviously, the kids' need for support from Mort has increased, but as a result of a voluntary decision on Toni's part; she could still earn a good salary if she chose. Had Toni been fired and unable to get another high-paying job, the court would almost surely order Mort to pay more.

Example: At the time of the divorce, Mort made $15,000 a year. He later quit his job and went into sales, eventually earning $100,000 a year. Can Toni ask the court to raise the child support? Yes. Does the court have the power to do so? Yes. Will it? Almost certainly.

Example: At the time of the divorce, Toni was living with Keija, but the judge never knew this. Later, they moved to a lesbian commune with the kids. Mort asks the court to change custody, claiming that living on the commune is not in the children's best interests. Will he win? There is a good chance he will if he can show that the commune is detrimental to the children and he can offer them a good home—and if the judge is biased against lesbian mothers.

Many people ask, "What can I do to keep my former spouse from taking me back to court?" The answer, unfortunately, is "Very little." You both have the right to ask the court to change child custody, support and visitation at any time. The best way to avoid or minimize future court hassles is to establish good communications with your ex. Go more than halfway in the small areas; you'll be in a good position to work out larger ones, such as a major change of lifestyle. If you are unkind and uncooperative, your ex will be too. Be flexible. As incomes go up and down, be ready to adjust, even if it means you pay more or receive less. If you agree on a change, have the court approve it; it's easy and requires no more than a pro forma hearing. If you don't have the court approve it, at least write it down and sign it. This will give you some protection.

SAMPLE SUPPORT CHANGE AGREEMENT

Herb Fitzroy of 27 Apion Way, Spokane, Washington, and Carol Fitzroy of 11 State Street, Yakima, Washington, make the following agreement concerning a change in the amount of child support for their children, John and Phillip:

1. Herb has suffered an attack of hepatitis making it impossible for him to work for nine months; his income has been reduced by 60 percent because of his inability to work.

2. Herb and Carol want to avoid a court fight and have agreed to change the amount of support to fit the new circumstance.

3. They agree that commencing July 1, 19__ and continuing until April 1, 19__, the amount of Herb's child support obligation shall be reduced from $600 per month to $240 per month.

4. They further agree that this agreement may be presented to a court with jurisdiction over John and Phillip's child support at any time.

Dated: _____   Signature: _____
                                              Herb Fitzroy
Dated: _____   Signature: _____
                                              Carol Fitzroy

ANOTHER SAMPLE SUPPORT CHANGE AGREEMENT

Veronica Lee of 17 Leafy Lane, Palos Verdes, California, and Robert Lee, of 311 Hennepin Drive, Minneapolis, Minnesota, make the following agreement:

1. Because Veronica has received a promotion to chief buyer at Racafrax Department Store and now earns $3,000 per month, it is fair and equitable that she increase the child support she pays Robert for Ricky and Sharon.

2. Therefore they agree to raise child support from $400 per month to $750 per month to continue at this new rate indefinitely or until they make a subsequent modification.

3. This agreement may be presented by either party to a court having jurisdiction over this case at any time.

Dated: _____   Signature: _____
                                          Robert Lee
Dated: _____   Signature: _____
                                          Veronica Lee

Note: Let us repeat. It is not difficult to have an agreed-upon child support (or visitation or custody) change entered as part of a court record. *How to Modify and Collect Child Support in California*, Nolo Press, shows Californians how to change child support themselves. It's especially wise to file your papers with the court if your ex has given you trouble or has a history of "forgetting" or ignoring agreements.

-7-

So You Want to Become a Parent?

The desire to be a parent and raise a child is perhaps as prevalent among lesbians and gay men as it is among non gays, and the reasons are as complex. Some believe that having a child ensures their immortality; others wish to meet their parents' insistence on grandchildren; still others feel the basic human urge to parent and nurture. Indeed, for many lesbian women and gay men, the only undesired consequence of their sexual orientation is the inability to have a child with the person they love.

Lesbians and gay men who wish to raise a child face social and legal problems. Therefore, we've devoted this chapter to discussing how you, as a lesbian or gay couple, might bring a child into your home and your life. Besides the obvious opportunities to become a "Big Brother" or the loving "aunt" to the little girl down the street, or to teach cub scouts (which may be ample involvement for many), there are ways to legally cement your relationship with a child. Women, obviously, can bear children, and men may be able to arrange to have a child with a "surrogate mother." And men and women can become foster parents, adoptive parents or guardians.

These possibilities are discussed in the beginning sections of this chapter. The last section contains contracts between the adults who'll raise the child, and can be useful if one partner already has a child.

A. A FEW PRELIMINARY STEPS

1. Legal Parent

If you're a gay or lesbian couple and you want to raise a child, you face a major practical problem: in almost all cases, only one of you'll have the legal rights of a parent. Why? Because only one of you can be the biological parent, or, if you adopt or foster a child, usually only married couples or single people can adopt or become foster parents. No matter how strong the bonding between the child and the other parent, or "co-parent," the role isn't legally recognized.

What does it mean if only one of you has legal parental rights? If you split up, only the legal parent will have the right to custody and the obligation of support. In a few states, however, agreements by couples to jointly raise a child have been enforced. Non-legal parents have been given visitation rights and have paid child support when courts concluded that the agreements were in the "best interests of the child." In this chapter, we provide several contracts on co-parenting, which include provisions in the event you separate.

2. Practical Realities

Also, let us remind you of something you probably already know. Don't underestimate the power of a child. The entry of a small being into your lives will change you drastically. The mother of one of the authors, who raised seven children, wrote:

> *Most people take on the job, whether it's their own child or an adopted one, with unreasonable expectations as to the amount of pleasure versus the amount of frustration and resentment. Maybe children should come labeled "Warning, the Surgeon General advises that child raising may be dangerous to your health, way of life, and peace of mind."*

Still, children offer fulfillment and fun, and most parents we know (including one author's mom—he thinks) are pretty pleased with their lot, all things considered.

A lesbian or gay couple must put in time and effort discussing the practical and legal concerns in raising a child. Who will provide support? Who will make the day-to-day decisions? How open do you want to be with neighbors, officials or the child? Will one of you remain at home, or will homemaking duties be shared? If both of you will work, how will you deal with the problems all working parents face—illness, emergency calls from schools, etc.? These are only some of the issues. We aren't authorities on child raising. We know, and have spoken to, many gays and lesbians who are raising children, and are cheered by what we've seen and been told. Love and understanding are clearly what matter most in parenting. The best creative expression of this we know is the film "Choosing Children," about lesbian mothers who chose to become parents *after* coming out.[1]

3. Changes! Changes!

Laws relating to lesbian and gay couples and children are changing with fascinating rapidity. After centuries in which it was impossible for a person to be openly gay and raise a child, a few segments of American society have begun to understand that a person's (or couple's) sexual orientation has no bearing on the ability to love and raise a child. In California, an adoption by an avowedly gay man was approved by the superior court. Some foster parent agencies in major cities will consciously try to place "gay-identified" teenagers with gay foster parents. And in the San Francisco area, a lesbian couple was allowed to jointly adopt a child.

There are many excellent materials on the emotional and financial realities of raising a child.[2] In this chapter, we provide the most up-to-date information we've gathered. But again, let us emphasize, this area of law is changing so quickly that there may be new legal developments by the time you read these words. Don't rely on our information as being definitive, but treat it as a place to start your own exploration of the process of bringing a child into your home.

4. Lawyers—Lawyers—Good Grief, Lawyers!

Children and their custody, education, support and general well-being are subjects to which government has traditionally staked a claim. This means that in bringing a child into your lives, you may deal with state agencies and courts. Inevitably, the question arises as to how much formal legal assistance you'll need. In some cases—particularly in adoptions—you'll probably want a lawyer. Adoptions require court proceedings, and, right or wrong, judges are comforted by the presence of lawyers, especially if the proceeding is even slightly

---

[1]Available from Cambridge Documentaries, P.O. Box 385, Cambridge, MA 02139.
[2]See especially, Cheri Pies, *Considering Parenthood: A Workbook for Lesbians*, Spinsters Ink, 1985 (contains an excellent annotated bibliography) and Jeanne Jullion, *Long Way Home: the Odyssey of a Lesbian Mother and Her Children*, Cleis Press, 1985.

controversial. A lesbian or gay person adopting a child faces enough legal obstacles and societal prejudices without adding the burden of judicial hostility to appearing in court without a lawyer. We hope, however, that legal forms will be developed so that prospective adoptive parents can handle their own legal work.

Adoptions aside, there may be times when lawyers will be useful or necessary, but in most situations, they aren't. For example, you can learn about—and use—foster parenting or artificial insemination without judicial proceedings or lawyers. (See Chapter 12, "Lawyers and Doing Your Own Research.") If you do hire a lawyer, keep control over decision-making and save money by educating yourself about your proceeding and the precise reason you're hiring a lawyer.

B. HAVING YOUR OWN CHILD

The birds and the bees are doing it,
Lesbians, even Lebanese are doing it,
Guys in heels and silk chamois are doing it.[3]

---

[3]Not Cole Porter.

They are having babies. With great planning and consideration, lesbians and gay men are bringing much wanted and well loved children into the world. Some lesbians and gay men have married just to have children. We won't discuss this here; there's ample literature—both fiction and non-fiction—about the consequences of such arrangements. (We also refer you to Chapter 6, "Marriage, Divorce and Children," because gay married parents face all the same obstacles that other married parents face.) Aside from marriage, there are other ways to have your own child. Lesbians can get pregnant. Gay men don't have the same biological opportunity, but can try to find women willing to bear their children.

If you decide to have a child, questions arise about parenting, custody, visitation and support:

- I want to have a child but my lover and I want to raise it without help or interference from the father. Is that possible?
- If I agree just to be a biological father, can I later be held liable for support?
- If the biological father now agrees to let me bring up the child myself, how can I be assured he'll never seek custody?

There are no blanket answers to these questions. A man and a woman can write an agreement concerning their rights and obligations to each other and the child, but neither the child nor the state is bound by the agreement. A child has the legal right to receive support from both biological parents (unless she's been adopted) until she becomes a legal adult. Agreements regarding custody or visitation are recognized by courts, but courts have independent power to conclude that an agreement isn't in "the best interests of the child," and set it aside.

A lesbian who doesn't want to share parenting with her child's father has several choices. The most obvious is to not let him know he's parenting. While this approach can sometimes work well, it often presents problems. For one, it often takes more than one or two leaps in the hay to get pregnant and thus a continuing relationship with a man may be necessary. If the woman plans to raise her child with her (female) lover, an ongoing relationship with a man may raise havoc. It also raises the possibility that the man will learn that he's the father; this gives him the legal power to request custody or visitation. And there's the question of whether it's wise (healthy, moral, etc.) to hide a father's identity from a child when the mother knows it.

1. Biological Parents' Agreements

In some situations, the biological parents agree to conceive a child outside of marriage, understanding that both will be legal parents, though otherwise not be emotionally involved with each other (aside from being friends). For example, Julie wanted her own child. She decided to parent with one of her male friends so that the child would have the emotional and financial support of a father. She ruled out her straight male friends, fearing that they'd be automatically preferred if any custody dispute developed. On the other hand, Julie was very concerned that the father be HIV negative. She talked to her friend, Victor, who'd also been thinking he'd like to be a parent. After some hesitation, Victor agreed to be tested for the AIDS virus every other month for six months. If the results were negative, he would parent with Julie and allow her custody, as long as they both acted as parents. Julie and Victor knew they were each obligating themselves for support until the child reached legal adulthood.

They discussed their decision and arranged for counseling, to both get support for their arrangement, and test the sincerity of their commitment. Julie and Victor realized that anything they agreed to would probably not be legally binding if either ever challenged it in court, but they knew it was important to write down their agreement, both for clarity and to refresh their memories in the future.

Here's the agreement Julie and Victor made regarding their child (a girl, named Leslie.)[4]

---

[4]Also see the "Agreement to Jointly Raise Our Child" in Section F(1) of this chapter.

CONTRACT BETWEEN UNMARRIED PARENTS REGARDING
CHILD SUPPORT AND CUSTODY

This agreement is made between Julie Roberts and Victor Lawrence to express our understanding as to our rights and responsibilities to our child. We fully realize that our power to make this contract is limited by state law. With this knowledge, and in a spirit of cooperation and mutual respect, we wish to state the following to be our agreement:

1. Victor shall sign a written statement acknowledging that he's the father within ten days after birth; his name will be on the birth certificate.

2. Our child shall be given the last name Roberts.

3. Julie shall have physical custody and Victor shall have reasonable rights of visitation. Julie shall be sensitive to Victor's needs and shall cooperate in all practical ways to make visitation as easy as possible.

4. Both of us shall do our best to see that our child has a close and loving relationship with each parent.

5. Victor shall provide support in the amount of $200 a month for the first year after our child is born. Thereafter, the amount Victor will pay will be determined annually by mutual agreement, by taking into account:

> a) The needs of our child;
> b) Increases in the cost of living;
> c) Changes in Victor's salary and income;
> d) Changes in Julie's salary and income.

6. We shall make a good faith effort to jointly make all major decisions affecting our child's health and welfare.

7. If either Julie or Victor dies, our child shall be cared for and raised by the other.

8. If any dispute or problem arises between us regarding our child, we agree to seek counselling and professional help to try to resolve those problems.

Executed at_____

                (County, State)

Dated: _____   Signature: _____
                                Julie Roberts

Dated: _____   Signature: _____
                                Victor Lawrence

Parenthood Statement: Anytime the biological father will be involved with raising the child and he isn't married to the mother, he should sign a written statement acknowledging parenthood as soon as possible after the child's birth. In addition, the mother should sign a statement acknowledging that the father is, in fact, the biological father. Regardless of whether the statement is signed, the father is legally responsible for support, but signing a statement is the simplest way to avoid the brambles of the law concerning legitimacy, father's rights, etc. Signing it as soon as possible after the baby is born (i.e., before any disputes can arise) is the best protection for the mother, the baby and especially a father who wants rights of visitation as well as duties of parenthood.

Following is a parenthood statement. The form should be prepared in triplicate, dated, signed and notarized. The mother and father should each keep a copy, and the third copy should be kept safe for the child. While legal distinctions between "legitimate" and "illegitimate" children for inheritance, social security, insurance, etc. purposes are fast disappearing, they still can arise. Having the father sign this statement makes a child legitimate in almost all states, as if the parents had been married.

ACKNOWLEDGMENT OF PARENTHOOD

Julie Roberts and Victor Lawrence hereby acknowledge that they are the biological parents of Leslie Roberts, born April 18, 1989, in Eugene, Oregon.

Julie Roberts and Victor Lawrence further state that they've welcomed Leslie Roberts into their lives and that it is their intention and belief that they've taken all steps necessary to fully legitimate their child for all purposes, including the right to inherit from and through Victor Lawrence.

Julie Roberts and Victor Lawrence further expressly acknowledge their legal duty to properly raise and adequately support Leslie Roberts.

Dated: _____   Signature: _____
                                    Julie Roberts, Mother

Dated: _____   Signature: _____
                                    Victor Lawrence, Father

Notarization

---

2. Having Your Own Child by Artificial Insemination

Artificial insemination isn't artificial from the point of view of reproduction, and for this reason and others, many people now refer to artificial insemination as alternative fertilization. Sperm is injected into the uterus and, if it fertilizes an egg, a child develops. The woman doesn't have intercourse. For lesbians, and possibly for a gay man who finds a woman amenable to bearing his child, artificial insemination is a highly desirable way to parent.

Artificial insemination has become an accepted practice in the United States. Married couples use it when the husband is sterile. The couple locates a sperm donor (often chosen because he has characteristics similar to the husband's) so the wife may become pregnant. More recently, there have been cases (some well publicized) where the wife is unable to bear children and the couple seeks out a surrogate mother to be impregnated by semen from the husband.

For lesbians, there are many advantages to conceiving by artificial insemination. It can be done without medical personnel or any great expertise.[5] Also, artificial insemination avoids entanglement with the state; no agency comes snooping into your life. Finally, if the woman uses a sperm bank,[6] the identity of the donor can be (and usually is) kept secret, thus eliminating future problems of custody and visitation. Of course, if the donor is anonymous, there can be disadvantages, or at least areas of potential difficulty. The mother must be the sole provider, financially, and emotionally, for her child. Also, there may be potential problems in not knowing the child's hereditary history (more about this below).

a. The Legal Background of Artificial Insemination[7]

Artificial insemination was first used by women at the end of the eighteenth century and it has disturbed self-appointed "moral" guardians ever since. Many churches have declared artificial insemination sinful and "repugnantly wicked." The Catholic Church's views are represented by the following statement of Gannon F. Ryan, Chaplin, St. Thomas More Chapel, Syracuse University, discussing whether the church would ever condone artificial insemination:

---

[5]So we've been told. We make no claims that we are authorities on artificial insemination beyond our reading and our interviews.

[6]There are now women-controlled insemination clinics, such as the Oakland (California) Feminist Health Center.

[7]For a thorough discussion of the legal issues involved in artificial insemination, see *Legal Issues in Donor Insemination*, available from the Lesbian Rights Project, 1370 Mission St., 4th Floor, San Francisco, CA 94103.

> *We reply no and under no circumstances, because the evil of both masturbation and adultery are involved, thus making the procedure most repugnantly wicked. The agreement of all parties doesn't alter the immorality of the procedure. We cannot vote to violate the Laws of God. Even a desirable End, such as children in the home, cannot justify an evil means to achieve it. This is elementary.*[8]

While churches have struggled with moral issues, courts have struggled with legal ones in determining who's the father, and morality has certainly played a role. The history of court responses to artificial insemination is found in Achtenberg, *Sexual Orientation and the Law* (1985).[9] Some highlights (or lowlights):

- An Illinois court in 1954 was irate about artificial insemination by a donor not the woman's husband; "with or without consent of the husband [it] is contrary to public policy and good morals, and constitutes adultery on the part of the mother. A child so conceived isn't a child born in wedlock and therefore illegitimate."[10]

- Some judges have ingeniously tried to make the consenting husband the father. *In Straad v. Straad,*[11] a New York court found the consenting husband had quasi-adopted the child and therefore had the same rights an adoptive father would.

- Finally, in *Adoption of Anonymous*[12] (wonderful, these court names), the court found that the husband, who had consented to the insemination by a donor, was the lawful father and stated: "... that a child born of consensual artificial insemination by a donor during a valid marriage is a legitimate child entitled to the rights and privileges of a naturally conceived child of the same marriage." This rule has become the norm.

All these cases ask the fundamental question: Is the husband the legal father of an artificial insemination baby born to his wife? To most courts, the answer is yes. But what happens when there's no husband? What are the rights of a male donor who's the biological father of a child? In an early unmarried-woman-artificial-insemination case,[13] a donor petitioned a court to be recognized as the child's father, and be authorized to visit and support the child. The man and woman had agreed that his semen would be used to artificially impregnate her because she wanted to have his child, but didn't want to have sexual intercourse.

---

[8]7 Syracuse L. Rev. 96, 101 (1955).

[9]See also Schultz & Shapiro, *Single-Sex Families: The Impact of Birth Innovations Upon Traditional Family Notions,* 24 Journal of Family Law 271 (1986).

[10]*Doornbos v. Doornbos,* 40 U.S. Law Week 2308; No. 54-S-14981 Super. Ct. Cook County, Illinois (1954).

[11]78 N.Y.S.2d 390 (Super. Ct. 1948).

[12]345 N.Y.S.2d 430 (Super. Ct. 1973).

[13]Reported in 3 Family L. Rptr. 2690 (1978).

Although the parties had at one time contemplated marriage, the relationship ended following an argument during which the donor learned that he wouldn't be permitted to establish a parent-child relationship. The court ruled for the donor, stating:

> *The courts have consistently shown a policy favoring the requirement that a child be provided with a father as well as a mother. In a situation where there's an anonymous donor, the courts have required that the husband who consents to the use of sperm not his own be responsible for fathering the child.*

Here the woman wasn't married, and the donor wasn't anonymous. The judge concluded that if an unmarried woman conceives a child through artificial insemination from the semen of a known man, "that man cannot be considered to be less a father" simply because he isn't married to the mother. Finally, the court said that it was most concerned with the best interests of the child and "in granting custody or visitation, wouldn't make any distinction between a child conceived naturally or artificially."

b. Choosing a Donor

The semen used for artificial insemination can be from a donor known to the mother or from someone whose identity is and remains secret (and who never knows the mother's). Choosing a donor is critical both to the genetic makeup of your child and to your legal relationship with the donor. We aren't concerned here with genetics; you'll have to study this question yourself. Our job is to explain the legal implications of choosing a donor. Their are several ways to proceed:

- Ask a medical doctor to obtain sperm from a sperm bank for you. These banks are usually associated with medical schools and donors are quite often medical students. You can specify coloring, race, religion and often even height. The donors are supposedly tested for diseases—both personal (such as syphilis and AIDS) and hereditary (such as sickle-cell anemia). The donor remains anonymous and will never have rights or obligations of a parent. Some state laws, such as California Civil Code Section 7005, specify that if semen is delivered to a licensed physician for use in artificial insemination, the donor isn't considered the legal father.

- Do the insemination yourself without medical supervision and take precautions so that the donor remains anonymous. Taking precautions is crucial. For example, in a California case,[14] a court held that where a licensed physician hadn't been used, a sperm donor chosen by the mother, with no attempt at anonymity, was the legal father of the child, entitled to full parental rights and responsibilities.

We have a friend who chose to take control of her own conception not only because she views clinical procedures as cold, impersonal and male-dominated, but also because she wants to make the insemination a shared experience with her lover. There are gay men willing to be donors who respect the mother's desire to raise the child without interference. An excellent booklet entitled *Artificial Insemination: An Alternative Conception*[15] goes into great detail on finding donors, screening them, getting medical information, planning the time of the insemination, and arranging for the delivery of the semen. The details are handled through a third person (liaison), thus protecting the anonymity of the donor (only the liaison knows.) Often people take the added precaution of having more than one donor.

- The mother can find a donor herself.

TIME OUT FOR A STORY

Our friends Regina and Susan wanted to have a child. They talked a long time about bringing a baby into their relationship, and were satisfied that the difficulties would be more than balanced by the joy and fulfillment. Regina wanted to bear the child, which was fine with Susan. Neither woman wanted to bring a fourth person (the father) into the relationship. Regina especially didn't want to have intercourse with a man, fearing emotional problems if she had to experience intercourse repeatedly to get pregnant.

---

[14]*Jhordan C. v. Mary K.*, 179 Cal.App.3d 386 (1986).
[15]Write to the San Francisco Women's Center, 3543 18th St., San Francisco, CA 94110.

At one point, Susan suggested that her friend Tom, who was attractive, intelligent, healthy and had nice teeth (she liked the idea of her child having nice teeth), would be wonderful. But Regina pointed out that, no matter how sure they were that Tom didn't want to be involved in raising the child, there would always be the possibility that he would change his mind and seek custody or visitation. And there was no way to guarantee to Tom that neither Regina nor the state would ever ask him for child support. The best they could offer Tom would be a written agreement, saying he wouldn't be financially responsible, but all concerned knew that such contracts aren't enforceable.

Finally, after several consultations with a lesbian rights counselor, Regina and Susan decided that Regina would have a child by artificial insemination, with the father never being involved. As part of their investigation, Susan found the booklet *Artificial Insemination* we mentioned above. It suggested saving the doctor and sperm bank fees and assuring anonymity by having a friend act as a liaison. This made sense, but Regina decided that because she was in California, which means the donor isn't the father if a doctor is used, and because she knew an understanding doctor and was near a sperm bank, she opted for medical assistance. The doctor arranged for Regina to obtain sperm from a local sperm bank.

Regina and Susan were reassured by the doctor that the donor had no history of inheritable mental or physical illness, or communicable disease. They gave hair, skin and eye color, as well as racial and ethnic background preferences. After five months of inseminations, Regina became pregnant. She was fortunate to find two other women who had been inseminated about the same time and they started a weekly "support group." They discussed questions common to all mothers and some unique to artificial insemination mothers, such as what "father's name" to put on the birth certificate. All were concerned about what they would tell their children in later years.

Susan and Regina went to classes on natural childbirth. Finally the great day arrived. Regina gave birth to a beautiful, healthy girl in a San Francisco hospital. They were surprised that their child was a girl, however, since they knew that 75 to 80 percent of children conceived by artificial insemination are boys. The family is doing very well.

c. Other Questions Concerning Artificial Insemination

The Hospital and Birth Certificate: It's important to decide what last name you'll put on the birth certificate. Also consider the blank for the father's name. What should you write down? Here are your alternatives:

- Put down the name of the father (if known); don't do this, however, if you don't want the donor to have any rights or responsibilities.
- State the father is "unknown." (Consider whether this might later lead to embarrassment for the child.)
- State "Name withheld."
- State the father was "by artificial insemination." (Again, consider any later embarrassment for the child.)
- Invent a fictitious name. (In most hospitals, nobody's going to bother about whatever name you list for the father—but providing incorrect information is technically a misdemeanor.)
- Don't put your lover's name (even if it's sex-neutral, like Chris or Lee). This is illegal and could raise many eyebrows.

Note: In most states, you can mark the hospital form "Do Not Report" so that the information isn't given to the newspaper "Births" columnist.

What if the Child Wants to Find the Donor Later? Several women have asked us if there's a way to have the best of all worlds—anonymity now, with the possibility that little Veronica will be able to find the donor later, perhaps when she's a teenager or older. This is a good question, especially given the fact that many adopted children are demanding to know who their biological parents are. Unfortunately, we've no good answer. If you want to be sure of having no interference from the donor and want to assure him that he will never be liable for support, anonymity must be maintained. It's possible for your liaison to keep secret records, but this isn't really satisfactory; the records could be subpoenaed by the state or someone acting on behalf of the child in a paternity-support suit. If any arrangement is made whereby donor, mother and child might be able to find each other in the future, we advise complete disclosure of all the risks and a signed consent.

d. Artificial Insemination Agreements

The following agreements can be used or adapted when a woman doesn't know the identity of a donor, and the woman and donor want to ensure that the donor isn't the legal father of the child. The first agreement is probably legally enforceable even if the donor subsequently learns the mother's identity and demands the rights of a father. (We say probably because there are very few court decisions, and it's possible some judges might refuse to honor such an agreement.) If anonymity is maintained, however, it should be impossible for the donor to discover the mother's identity.

ARTIFICIAL INSEMINATION DONOR'S AGREEMENT

I, [name of donor], have been given the opportunity to donate my semen for the purpose of artificial insemination of a woman whose identity is unknown to me, and wish to protect my interests and those of all concerned. In furtherance of this desire, I freely state that:

1. I understand the purpose of such artificial insemination is to produce a child or children.

2. I don't expect to have divulged to me the identity of the woman, or of the child or children who may be produced as a result of such insemination, nor do I expect to learn whether such insemination(s) result in the birth of a child or children.

3. I agree not to seek the identity of the child or children, or of the mother, and I waive all parental rights which I might have regarding the child.

4. I donate my semen with the understanding and agreement that the person who's responsible for its collection will undertake to keep my identity confidential and unknown to anyone except those directly involved in the collection.

5. I agree to submit to a standard physical examination carried out by qualified medical personnel, as well as to tests for the detection of any inheritable disease or other defects, after each test and procedure are explained to me; I further agree to supply true and full answers to the doctor (or intermediary) in connection with all relevant questions bearing upon my health and family background. It's my understanding that such information will be treated in confidence, and not linked to my identity in any documents outside the confidential files of the doctor (or intermediary) responsible for the semen collection.

6. I understand that any and all financial compensation I receive will be payment for the expenditure of my time in medical examination and semen collection, as well as reimbursement for loss of income and travel expenses because of my donation. This amount is estimated to be $_____.[16]

Place: _____

Date: _____   Donor Signature: _____

Date: _____   Doctor (or Intermediary) Signature:_____

---

[16]If it is impossible to estimate accurately, substitute an hourly amount. If the donor wants no compensation, eliminate this clause.

RECIPIENT'S AGREEMENT

I, [your name], hereby engage the services of [name of doctor or intermediary] to collect semen and perform one or more artificial insemination procedures on me from an unknown donor. I make this agreement in order to fully protect the interests of myself, any child born as the result of such artificial insemination, the donor, the doctor(s) and any laboratory used in supplying the semen.

In this connection I agree that:

1. I understand that the purpose of the insemination is to attempt to produce a pregnancy in me; that any pregnancy involves the risk of a miscarriage or other complication, difficulties in delivery and birth defects; and that the risk of such problems is also present in pregnancies resulting from artificial insemination.

2. The doctor (or intermediary) engaged by me to collect the semen and perform the procedure will obtain the necessary semen from a donor who won't be advised of my identity, nor of the success or failure of the insemination, and who'll agree in writing not to seek out my identity or the identity of any child who may be born from the insemination. Furthermore, I acknowledge that the identity of the donor isn't to be divulged to me and I agree not to seek out his identity.

3. I hereby authorize the doctor, in [her/his] sole and absolute discretion, to use fresh or frozen semen from one or more unidentified donors, to select the donor(s), and to select the laboratory that has collected, processed and stored frozen semen.

4. It's understood that the religion of neither the donor nor myself will be considered in selecting the donor.[17]

5. I fully understand that the doctor performing the insemination procedure isn't responsible for the physical or mental characteristics of any child so produced and do hereby absolve and release the doctor, [her/his] collaborating colleagues, the institution in which [she/he] practices, the donor(s), and the laboratory involved in sperm collection from any liability whatsoever arising out of, or resulting from, the collection and processing of semen or from any other aspect of the artificial insemination procedure.

6. I agree that the nature of this agreement is such that it must remain confidential and, therefore, agree that the sole copy of it may be given to the doctor for [her/his] confidential files.[18]

Place: _____

Dated: _____ Mother Signature: _____

Dated: _____ Doctor (or intermediary's) Signature:_____

---

[17]Obviously, if religion is to be taken into account, change this provision.

[18]If you want to keep a copy of the agreement as well, state that. If you do decide to keep one, store it in a safe deposit box or other secure place where you child won't just happen upon it before you are ready to deal with the question.

3. Surrogate Motherhood

The *Baby M.* case[19] brought the possibility and problems of surrogate motherhood to public attention. In *Baby M.*, a married couple (Elizabeth and William Stern) chose not to try to have a child because Elizabeth had multiple sclerosis, and pregnancy, in some MS patients, poses a serious health risk. They contracted with Marybeth Whitehead for her to be impregnated with William Stern's semen, to carry the baby to term, and then to give up the child to be adopted by Elizabeth for the Sterns to raise. All went well until baby M (Melissa) was born, and Marybeth didn't want to part with her. The Sterns sued Marybeth to enforce the contract.

The legal question was whether the contract was enforceable. The trial judge said yes, terminated Marybeth's parental rights, allowed Elizabeth to adopt Melissa and ended the case. The New Jersey Supreme Court reversed, invalidating the contract

> *because it conflicts with the law and public policy of this state. While we recognize the depth of the yearning of infertile couples to have their own children, we find the payment of money to a "surrogate" mother illegal, perhaps criminal, and potentially degrading to women. Although in this case we grant custody to the natural father, the evidence having clearly proved such custody to be in the best interests of the infant, we void both the termination of the surrogate mother's paternal rights and the adoption of the child by the wife/stepparent.*

---

[19]537 A.2d 1227 (N.J. Supreme Court 1988).

Baby M. is binding only in New Jersey. In response, however, legislatures and courts of other states are now struggling with the problems of surrogacy. (Surrogacy contracts are now illegal in Michigan.) Political groups wrestle with their concerns. What we know, however, is that couples and single men are making surrogacy arrangements, usually using a lawyer to help prepare the contract. In most arrangements, the mother carries the child and gives it up at birth for the father to raise without the fear that mother will return to seek custody. The mother is compensated for her medical care and expenses, although in most states it's illegal to make any payment construed as "payment for a child."

In the cases we've heard about, the mother goes through a psychiatric evaluation before being accepted by the father, and she must already have children of her own. The fathers fear that the mothers will want to keep the children; mothers fear that the fathers will not want to take the children.

We believe that surrogacy arrangements should become legally accepted, with sensible regulation in case there is conflict. We have a friend who recently brought home from the hospital his wonderful baby girl born by a surrogate mother. She agreed that the child would be raised entirely by the father, and didn't contest the adoption proceedings where her parental rights were legally terminated.

C. ADOPTING A CHILD

The most permanent, binding way of becoming a nonbiological parent is by adoption. If you adopt a child, you become the legal parent of that child. As part of the process, the biological parents' rights and responsibilities are terminated. An adopted child has the right to inherit from your estate and not from the biological parents, and the child, or the state, can sue you for child support if you fail to provide it; after the adoption, the biological parents have no such obligation.[20]

Adoption is an ancient practice, used in Roman, Babylonian, Assyrian, Greek and Egyptian societies, primarily to provide an heir for the adoptive parent (read: father). Adoptions were equally important in feudal times, when land could be passed to only a male heir. Land couldn't be conveyed to anyone else by will, and

---

[20]It's a crime to willfully fail to support your biological or adopted child, if your parental rights haven't been terminated.

usually couldn't be conveyed at all except with the consent of the heir, and often the local king or duke. If a landholding baron or knight had no male heir, adopting a son was the one method to keep the property in his family.

Today, adoptions always involve a court. Prior to the adoption, the court terminates the biological parents' rights (this may be done weeks, months or years before the adoption); then the adoption occurs, and the court issues an order declaring the child adopted and stating that you're the legal parent. Before you go to court, an official agency (usually social services or juvenile probation) will investigate you and your home. The investigating agency recommends whether you'll be allowed to adopt, unless it's a private adoption, but even then, most states' require that the adoption be investigated by a state agency before being judicially approved. If the biological parents' rights were terminated prior to the adoption, the court adoption, whether agency or private, won't be contested. And unless the judge won't permit an adoption by a lesbian or a gay man, the court proceedings will be routine, with the judge following the agency's recommendation.

While only two states absolutely prohibit lesbians and gays from adopting,[21] this doesn't mean other states are supportive. In all adoptions, the investigating agency and court must be persuaded that the adoption is in the "best interests of the child;" this may be more difficult if your sexual orientation is revealed. In the past, the fact that the would-be adoptive parent was lesbian or gay was used to declare her or him unfit to raise a child. (Read Chapter 6, "The Gay Parent's Fight for Custody.") Slowly, however, the prohibition against gays adopting is changing. In a well-publicized California adoption, an openly gay man living with his lover was permitted to adopt a child. In addition, some states' statutes don't explicitly require that a couple be married in order to jointly adopt. California's law states that "any person desiring to adopt a child" may petition a court to do so. Under this statute, the Lesbian Rights Project in San Francisco was able to arrange for a joint adoption by a lesbian couple; both women became legal adoptive mothers.

If you want to adopt, you should hire an attorney to handle the legal issues. Adoptions aren't very complicated, but a judge will be reassured by the presence of a lawyer, and probably disturbed by the absence. To utter the obvious, a lesbian or gay man who's adopting a child wants the judge to be as acquiescent as possible. Also, a lawyer with good local connections, who has handled gay and lesbian legal issues before, will know the ropes and can disqualify a judge likely to be hostile to your adopting.

---

[21]Florida and New Hampshire.

The biological parents must consent to the adoption unless their rights have been terminated or there's another reason their consent isn't necessary, such as they've abandoned the child, become insane or transferred legal control over the child to an adoption agency. If the child is under the care of an agency, the agency's consent is required.

Although there are no statistics about gay parent adoptions, single people are adopting in increasing numbers. Surely some, perhaps many, of these people are gay. But the increase in single-parent adoptions doesn't solve the major problem with adoption today: The number of children available to be adopted has decreased. Birth control has reduced the number of "illegitimate" children, traditionally the major source of adopted children. And the stigma against having a child outside of marriage has decreased, increasing the number of unmarried parents who keep their children. Agencies are trying to find homes for "hard-to-place" children—usually minorities, disabled or older kids. Don't be discouraged, but be realistic. Adoption is a difficult process. Your chances of adopting a non-handicapped infant are slim. But lesbians and gays have done it, and if you long for a child and cannot, or choose not to, give birth, explore adoption.

Start with your local lesbian or gay organization. Its members will know what's been done and what's possible in your area. If you proceed, find a friend in the adoption agency—someone sympathetic to your cause. Even in the best situations, be prepared to wait about two years between the initial application and the placement of a child in your home.

1. Methods of Adoption

There are basically four ways to adopt:
- through a public or private agency;
- through the mother (or an intermediary);
- through an international agency, i.e., a "foreign adoption";
- as a stepparent.

Agency Adoption: An agency adoption is the usual method. The agency (either a state agency such as the county welfare department or a private adoption agency) locates children available for adoption. (Foster children are often adopted by foster parents this way; in fact, foster parenting is one of the most common avenues for adopting in many states. See the next section on foster parenting.) Would-be adoptive parents are interviewed by the agency, which has obtained consents to adopt from the biological parents. The agency recommends to the court who the adoptive parent(s) will be. Traditionally, most agencies favor married couples over single parents. No agency we know of "favors" lesbians or gays, though some treat them like any other single people. More likely, however, the agency will rule out gays from adopting. In other words, if you're open and frank about your sexual orientation, few agencies will recommend you as an adoptive parent. There are, however, advantages to using an agency:

- An agency adoption provides maximum assurance that a child's biological parents won't change their minds.
- The procedures are established, and the agency is known to the court, which means the judicial procedure should go smoothly.

Private Adoptions: In a private adoption, no official agency is involved (except to investigate the home and report to the court). You find the child yourself, or with the aid of a private "open adoption" firm. Private adoptions are legal in many states and are common for adopting infants. The adopting parent(s) normally pay the biological mother's medical expenses and sometimes her living expenses, in addition to paying all the legal fees; however, paying any other "fee" is illegal almost everywhere.

In fact, in a case where a couple obtained a child by paying a lawyer a substantial sum, the judge discovered the truth, angrily ordered the infant removed from the home in which he'd lived for a year and placed him in a state institution. Fortunately, an appeals court recognized that this was literally throwing the baby out with the bathwater, reversed the trial judge's decision and allowed the baby to stay in the home.

In many states, it's illegal to advertise for an adoption, and the legality of using an intermediary to locate or place an adopted child varies. For example, in Virginia and Washington, an intermediary may place a child; in Arizona, the intermediary may assist the biological mother in the placement. In California, however, it's a misdemeanor for anyone except a parent or a licensed agency to place a child.

Consent of the Biological Parent(s): Once you locate a baby, you'll need the consent of the biological mother, and the biological father, if his identity is known and he hasn't abandoned the child or otherwise forfeited his rights. The biological parent(s) sign a consent-to-adopt form, and an adoption proceeding is filed in court. There may, however, still be problems. The law may require, or the judge may order, an investigation and report. And although your attorney and friends can help you decide whether the child's biological mother should be told of your sexual orientation, there's usually no reason to tell the agency (i.e., the court), and it could cause you trouble if you do.

Important! If you don't go through a formal court proceeding, you haven't adopted the child. This is true even if the biological mother has signed a consent-to-adopt form. Without the court proceedings, all you have is an informal guardianship, and the biological mother, or parents, can attempt to reclaim the child. If you formally adopt, the biological parents can withdraw consent any time before the adoption decree is issued by the judge (about three months to a year after you receive the child), but once the decree is issued, the biological parents have lost all rights over the child.

A Note on "Black Market" Adoptions: Almost everyone has heard the term "black market adoptions." The idea of people skulking down dark alleys to buy a baby from a mother or an intermediary isn't pleasant. Moreover, black market adoptions are illegal. One way this "adoption" works is to have the biological mother register at a hospital in the name of the adoptive mother so that the birth certificate contains the "adopting" parent's name. But, however handled, it leaves the adoptive parent open to blackmail and the risk of losing the child should the biological mother change her mind and try to reclaim the child.

Foreign Adoptions: It's possible to adopt a child from another country. US immigration laws provide a special visa for a child who's to be adopted by an American citizen. There are two methods of adopting an "alien" child. (That's what our government calls any foreigner.)

- The child may be adopted in his or her own country. The child must be personally seen by the adoptive parent(s) before the adoption is completed.
- The child may be admitted to the United States for adoption if the adopting parent(s) have met the pre-adoption requirements of their state of residence.

In either case, it's possible for a single person to qualify as an adopting parent. Many countries, however, strongly prefer that infants be adopted by married couples. Also, the United States isn't alone in its societal bias against lesbian or gay adoptions. So if you are involved in a foreign adoption, you may need to keep your sexual identity private.

Adoptions by going abroad are rare. You must locate the would-be adoptive child yourself, and then travel to the child's country and go through its adoption procedures.[22] Many countries don't quickly issue final adoption decrees; Chile, for instance, issues an interim decree, and requires a two-year wait for a final decree. You must obtain a special visa for the child from the Immigration and Naturalization Service (I.N.S.) to bring the child to the United States before the adoption is final.

---

[22]There are also requirements imposed by U.S. immigration law and state adoption laws. For instance, federal law requires that a single adopting parent be at least 25 years old, and that a full investigation of the adopting parent be done before the I.N.S. issues an immigration visa for the child.

Foreign adoptions through an agency in your state are slightly more feasible than traveling to a foreign country. There are adoption agencies in some states that can, and do, locate foreign orphans to be adopted by U.S. citizens. The prospective adoptive parent is investigated by the adoption agency. If it determines that an adoption is suitable, it certifies to the I.N.S. that the state's pre-adoption standards have been met, and I.N.S. issues a visa so the child can be brought to the United States. In general, agencies aren't being asked to find homes for children from Europe, North America or Japan.

There are substantial costs in intercountry adoptions, including:

- the child's transportation to the United States
- the fees of the adoption agency in the child's country
- the fees of the U.S. adoption agency
- attorneys fees and I.N.S. charges

Foreign adoptions, however, have been successful for gay and lesbian people. Be prepared to be very patient and persevering.

Stepparent Adoptions: In all states, a stepparent may adopt his spouse's child if the child's other biological parent is absent, consents to the adoption, or has abandoned the child. Stepparent adoptions are not available for lesbians and gay men involved in raising their lover's child, no matter how much the person wants to adopt.[23]

2. Legal Aspects of Adoption

The following information is general. State laws vary considerably; treat what you read here as a starting place for your research.

Age Limits: Some states have age restrictions for the adoptive parent. In California, the adoptive parent must be at least ten years older than the adopted child. Other states, such as Delaware, require the parent to be over 21, and some states, such as Rhode Island, simply state "any person older than the child may adopt."

Residence: You, and normally the child as well, must reside in the state where the adoption proceedings are filed. The legal concept of "residence" is vague—it combines an intent to live in a certain place with actually being there. In practice, authorities rely on a driver's license, living address, voter registration, etc. to decide residence. Many states require that adoptive parents bringing a

---

[23]See Zuckerman, *Second Parent Adoption for Lesbian Parented Families; Legal Recognition of the Other Mother,* 19 U.C. Davis Law Review 729 (1986).

child into the state for adoption notify the state or a county adoption agency. These laws don't apply if the biological parent brings the child into the state. If a child you want to adopt resides in another state, you may have to establish residence in that state before adopting.

Who May Be Adopted: Some states permit the adoption of adults; most limit adoptions to "minors." Interreligious adoptions used to be, and sometimes still are, refused by adoption agencies and therefore courts as not considered in the "best interests of the child."

Betty, an American Indian friend of ours, noted that with the adoption or foster placement of an Indian child, federal law requires preference be given to (1) a member of the child's family; (2) other members of the child's tribe or (3) other Indian families.

Change of Name: All states permit the adoptive parent(s) to change the child's surname (last name) at the time of adoption.

Records and Birth Certificates: Nearly all states seal adoption records, allowing them to be inspected only if the court orders. Adoptive parents can obtain a new birth certificate with the child's new name which gives no information about the biological parents.

Consent of the Adopted Child: Once the child reaches a certain age, his or her consent is required for an adoption. This age varies by state: It's usually from age 10 (Michigan) to age 14 (Texas). In a few other states, such as West Virginia and Vermont, the adopted person may have an adoption vacated by filing a dissent within one year after it's final.

D. BECOMING A FOSTER PARENT

If you have an urge to be a parent, you may find foster parenting a viable way to accomplish your goal. Several foster-home placement agencies have placed children with lesbians and gay men, and some have recognized the appropriateness of placing gay teenagers in stable gay households. In some progressive cities, such as New York, San Francisco and Trenton, agencies have actively recruited gay foster parents for such placements. On the other hand, Massachusetts and New Hampshire have made it very difficult for a lesbian or gay person to be a foster parent. Non-traditional households (i.e., single or gay) are given low priority and in Massachusetts, the applicant must state his or her sexual orientation. North Dakota allows only married couples to become foster parents.

A foster parent is only a temporary guardian of a child. The state has simply granted you a license to be a foster parent, that is, to run a foster home. You have no other legal relationship with the child. This means, for example, that the child won't inherit from you unless you provide for him or her in your will. (See Chapter 9, Estate Planning.) The placement might be emergency placement for two days, or might last years. Similarly, the details of the placement varies among agencies. Before you even consider being a foster parent, talk to someone at an agency.

The state pays foster parents a monthly amount for support of each foster child. The amount varies among states, but in many urban areas the range is $200 to $275 per month. Clearly this isn't generous, and we can't imagine that anyone becomes a foster parent for the pay. Still, if you become a foster parent, the monthly allotment can help.

What children are put into foster homes? Traditionally, they are children who, for one reason or another, have been dumped into the cold lap of Mother State. Most of these kids have had emotional difficulties. A foster child's parents may have died; or either the child is considered delinquent (incorrigible) or the parent was delinquent (abused or neglected the child, or in jail). Physically disadvantaged children are also common foster children.

And then there's the category that you may be most interested in—teenagers who are gay. These kids often find themselves in foster care because, as a consequence of their sexuality, they are unable to stay at home. Sometimes they're kicked out; often they run away, and occasionally, their parents just seem to have evaporated.

1.   APPLYING FOR A FOSTER CHILD

Single people (except in North Dakota) as well as married couples (and in many states "roommates") can get foster parents' licenses. In some areas, openly gay households have been licensed. So, if a gay or lesbian couple wants to become foster parents, should one of them apply to the licensing agency as a single person, or should they apply as a couple? We can't tell you how to apply, but we can give you information to help you decide.

If you want to keep your relationship private (secret, if you prefer), have one person apply as a single individual. A single adult, sharing space with another adult, can become a licensed foster parent in most states. But foster care placement is at the agency's or court's discretion, so busy little social workers (sometimes wonderfully helpful social workers) will march into your home to look about. They have an odd view that the right to privacy is exercised only by people who have something to hide. Of course, they don't put it that way, and instead turn people down because of "lack of openness." At any rate, plan in advance how "open" to be. And when you decide, be consistent; if there's one thing you can count on when dealing with social workers, it's that they'll be back.

In some instances, it may be foolish to tell all to a foster agency that you're gay or lesbian. Generally, however, maintaining secrecy and applying for a child is risky. The agency may find out the truth; more likely, the child will, and it's not appropriate to ask the child to lie. The question of "to be, or not to be—out" is raised often in this book. However you answer that question for your own life, we believe that kids should be dealt with honestly (it's our hippie backgrounds). And once a foster kid knows the truth, it's going to be hard to keep it secret. If you can locate a sympathetic social worker, you may be able to resolve your coming-out dilemma informally and personally.

2. Placing Gay Kids In Gay Homes

As we've said, in some areas of the country, agencies will approve stable, caring, gay households for placement of gay-identified (the agencies' term) teenagers. These agencies realize that few heterosexual foster parents can adequately deal with gay teenagers. They simply don't know the problems the kids have. And placing gay kids in the large group homes could be problematic—many of these homes are terribly cruel environments for gay teenagers. So, reluctantly, some states have realized that gay foster parents can provide a positive alternative.

It's often easier for a gay person or couple to become licensed foster parents than it is to actually have children placed in their home. And because foster placement is always considered temporary, the child can be removed at his or her request, your request, or the request of the agency or government probation officers. So there are uncertainties to being a foster parent, especially for a lesbian or gay foster parent.

The changes in gay foster parenting have been largely brought about by the dedicated work of many lesbian and gay people. Sue Saperstein,[24] for example, worked with the director of the San Francisco Department of Social Services to get a gay caseworker in the department to handle the foster placement of gay kids. In response, the San Francisco Foster Licensing Division of the Department of Social Services has licensed known lesbian and gay foster homes.

Linda Graham worked with Project Lamdba in Boston, helping place gay teenagers in gay households. Amazingly, Project Lambda was funded by an agency of the United States Department of Justice and was very successful for a few years.[25] Linda explained the reasons for her project's success.

The relationship between the mature person and the youth has been a part of the homosexual experience since Socrates and should be both explored and encouraged. The older person provides maturity and stability, wisdom and usually some material well-being to the relationship, while the youth brings whatever youth's all about— excitement, wonder, adventure. It's analogous to the role of the teacher and the student, plus a lot more. This interaction has been sought by many adults and youth through the centuries and can be a very rich and rewarding experience for both.

When asked what she thought made a successful foster placement, Linda responded:

Foster placements must emphasize stability. It must be understood by everyone that sexuality is involved in this relationship as it is in every relationship—but it should be just as clear that it is very inappropriate for any foster parent and foster kid to have sex together. Any teenager who has found himself or herself in a foster home is most likely to have difficulty adjusting to their life. If they have been sexually active, then the last thing they need is another adult to have sex with. The teenager needs a responsible, stable role model as well as a home. Sex has a way of confusing issues. My advice is that, before a gay teenager comes into a gay household, the sexual issues be thoroughly discussed. All

---

[24]She coordinated the Youth and Sexuality Services at the Center for Special Problems in San Francisco.

[25]Now, of course, Massachusetts makes it nearly impossible for gays or lesbians to be foster parents.

concerned should know that it's perfectly normal to have sexual fantasies. These should be discussed so that it can be determined what to do about them. In other words, neither the teenager not the adults should have any hidden agendas or hidden demands on the relationship.

Most sexually active kids know how to relate to adults primarily through sex. They are accustomed and prepared to use sexuality both to relate to adults and get what they want from them (whether it's warmth, real and kind attention, or money). They need to learn another way to relate, and the adult must be responsible for the direction of the relationship so that they can do so. The child must be made to accept responsibility too. If there's too great a sexual attraction between the child and the adult, then it's best not to enter into a foster situation.

She continued,

A teenager is demanding and disruptive as well as a delight. If the foster parents are a couple—and they could be simply roommates or lovers—they must have a commitment to each other and the placement. There will be a strain as well as a benefit in their new relationship with the child, who'll demand time, and, in conflict, will often side with one adult against the other. I recommend everyone sit down and discuss expectations. A written agreement would be helpful as a guideline. I would even advise writing down each's fears and fantasies. I highly recommend that both the adults and the child create a strong support group for themselves. It's very useful if the social worker is made a part of this.

Success shouldn't be measured by the length of the time that the teenager lives with the foster parent(s), but by the feeling of security which the kid is allowed to feel, and the amount of growth toward self-sufficiency and independence. If the teenager and the adults can learn to live together and to live their own lives in an environment of security and caring, then a great deal has been accomplished. Use the counselors, social workers and friends to help guide this process.

Alternative Family Services Agency in San Francisco[26] licenses the homes of lesbians and gay men, single people, unmarried heterosexual couples and groups. This private foster-care agency places gay teenagers with gay homes and provides follow-up support. Prior to placement, Alternative Family Services provides three weeks of orientation and five weeks of "skills" training (i.e., how to get along with a new teenager in your home) for prospective foster parents. After the eight weeks, an agency social worker matches foster parents with foster children, considering race, sexual orientation and religion. There's an initial meeting between the parents and the teenager, and then a trial visit. If all goes

---

[26]Located at 5352 Mission Street, San Francisco, CA.

well, the foster parents and kid sit down and work out a detailed agreement—including things like drug use, pets, hours, non-negotiable demands, etc.

Sue Saperstein finds that, on the average, the teenager stays in a foster home between six months and a year. We were surprised and disappointed to hear this, as it shattered our images and dreams of a foster parent-child relationship becoming lifelong with "lots of homemade cookies and adorable grandchildren." Sue noted that the shortness wasn't an indication of failure. The reality is that any teenager's life, and especially a foster teenager's life, is chaotic and changing; "success" of a placement isn't measured by duration, but by the love between the parent and the child, and the teenager's growth toward self-sufficiency. Sue herself took a foster teenager for one year and it worked very well, aided by realistic expectations.

3. Practical Steps to Becoming a Foster Parent

There's a Foster Home division in almost every county welfare department. Call it and ask for a list of agencies, both state-operated and private, that license fosters homes. Finding an agency willing to place gay-identified teenagers with lesbian and gay couples may take a little work. Ask a local lesbian or gay organization which agencies are sympathetic to placing a gay-identified teenagers in gay homes. Agencies or particular social workers willing to make such placements often keep a low profile, believing themselves to be more effective that way.

Because most states have several agencies who place foster children and because you can be licensed by only one agency at a time, investigate carefully. Once you select an agency, the licensing process itself is usually quite simple. You fill out an application, are interviewed by an employee of the agency, who is, or should be, concerned only with whether you'd make a good foster parent and are visited at home. In addition:

- You should have a separate room for the child.
- You must have a medical exam.
- Usually you must get fingerprinted; ex-felons and ex-sex offenders aren't eligible.
- If you're asking for a young child, you must have time to care for the child, or have arranged for child care.

But the most important criteria are intangible—stability and responsibility.

You may have a choice of becoming licensed as a foster home for a particular child or getting a general foster home license and having the agency place a child. When on the general list, you have the option of refusing a child if you and the child don't hit it off.

Becoming licensed for a specific child works a bit differently. For example, Michael and Ron had befriended Scott, a boy in his early teens who was gay. Scott was living at an institution and on weekend days caught a bus to Michael and Ron's; they drove him back in the evenings. After two years of this, at Thanksgiving lunch, Scott said to Ron, "Wouldn't it be great to live here all the time?" Ron sighed. "It'd be wonderful—but it's impossible. We all know that." Later, Michael and Ron wondered if it really were impossible. They decided they really liked the idea—they'd simply accepted the belief that it was impossible because they hadn't been ready to make the commitment. They contacted Scott's social worker, who (to their surprise) agreed that placing Scott in Michael and Ron's home would be good for him. The social worker sent Michael and Ron the application forms, and a license was granted. Scott lived happily in Michael and Ron's home.

Note on the Legal Paperwork: Usually the agency will assist you with paperwork, so you shouldn't need an attorney. If, however, you think you're being discriminated against and want to fight it, you'll need legal help. Bringing a sexual orientation discrimination lawsuit can be very expensive and, when dealing with kids, an uphill struggle. Unless you're wealthy, approach a public-interest law firm (see the list in Chapter 12, "Lawyers and Doing Your Own Research"). If a lawyer advises you against suing, take her advice.

E. GUARDIANSHIPS[27]

A guardianship means an adult other than a legal parent is responsible for taking care of a minor. Usually the adult is given physical custody of a minor, and sometimes the adult is given authority to manage the minor's assets. Sometimes a parent arranges a guardianship informally; other times a parent, relative, other adult, teenager on his own behalf[28] or state agency (usually over the parent's objection) asks a court to establish the guardianship. Our discussion is with uncontested guardianships, where the parents consent to the arrangement. Contested guardianships are birds with different (and usually

---

[27]For more information in California, see *The Guardianship Book*, Brown & Goldoftas, Nolo Press.

[28]Check your state's law to find out how old a child must be to petition on his own.

nasty) chirps. Almost by definition, contested guardianships are messy and bitter; someone—the parent, or the proposed guardian—is charged with being unfit. It's unusual for a lesbian or gay couple to gain a child through a contested guardianship, but it's happened.

Informal guardianships are temporary and can be changed at the decision (or whim) of whoever placed the child. They're commonly used when, because of illness, jailing or extended travel, a parent asks a relative or friend to temporarily take over parenting. With informal guardianships, there are no legal proceedings. The parent simply delivers the child to the guardian with a document of authorization.

Formal guardianships do involve court proceedings. A petition is filed and the court decides whether the guardianship is "in the best interests of the child." As long as everyone agrees, the judge usually grants the guardianship (why not?) and issues an order establishing its terms.

1. Informal (Voluntary) Guardianship

An informal guardianship without a court proceeding is almost always preferable to a court proceeding, likely to involve hassles, expenses and also presenting the risk (in some areas, the likelihood) that the judge will be outraged at the idea of a child living with gay adults. If you hide your sexual orientation from the judge and it comes out during the proceedings, the judge will probably be angry with you.[29]

If a child is eligible for welfare, the welfare benefits usually follow the child to the guardian's home, but be sure to check your state's laws. Normally, if the guardian is a close relative or meets the welfare department formalities (which are less rigid than with formal guardianships), the benefits should follow. If you're confused or anticipate trouble, find a friendly social worker and casually explain your problem. We've found that for every welfare rule saying you can't do something, there's another saying you can.

In most states a guardian (whether it's formal or informal) isn't legally or financially responsible for a child's actions. For example, if a child causes damage by vandalism, a parent (in most states) is liable, but a guardian isn't. There's usually an exception if the guardian agrees, on the child's driver's license application, to be financially responsible for any damage the child causes while driving.

---

[29]Sometimes, a formal guardianship may be necessary in dealing with schools, hospitals or insurance companies.

How One Informal Guardianship Worked

Dear Ben:

Remember how we talked last summer about my parents' divorce? Well, I find there's another reason I want to come to Boston to go to school. I am gay. I just told mother and she said, "No 15-year-old can be queer!"

Can you write her and ask if I can come stay with you for the school year? I can't even get any studying done around here! She respects you. Please!

Love,

Mark

Mark's mother, Paula, wrote to Ben almost the same time. Her letter was a little different:

Dear Ben,

I need to talk to you. Mark has just been impossible lately, and nothing I can do or say seems to help. Of course I have known that he's gay for a long time, but he has come out to me very belligerently and accuses me of never understanding him. Frankly, right now, I don't. He has been talking about writing you. I sure hope he does.

Love,

Paula

This was a situation in which an informal, voluntary guardianship made sense. To fill you in, Ben, a gay man, and Paula were old friends. Mark had confided in Ben the summer before coming out to his mother. Paula wasn't shocked to learn that Mark was gay, but was finding him hard to handle. She had no intention of relinquishing custody or abandoning her duties as his mother. She just knew they needed time apart. Paula reflected on the various possibilities and concluded that allowing Mark to live with Ben, a mature gay man in Boston, made sense. Fortunately, it made sense to Mark and Ben, too. And Mark's father readily agreed—he'd taken little interest in raising Mark for years and was for any solution that didn't involve work or money on his part. A formal court proceeding was unnecessary and undesirable. Paula's concern was with Mark's well-being. And going to court could produce a nasty reaction from a judge. So Mark lived happily with Ben during the school year, and returned to his mother during the summer.

2. Informal Guardianship Documents

While written documents aren't essential to establish an informal guardianship, they're desirable. To continue our story, suppose Mark suffered a deep cut on his arm while in Ben's custody. The wound would have been sewn up by a doctor, under laws authorizing doctors to do what's necessary in an emergency. But what if the doctor also recommended plastic surgery, surgery that had to be done (if at all) within 24 hours? As this is "elective," not "emergency" surgery, the doctor would require Mark's parents' permission before operating. If Ben had no document authorizing him to make medical decisions for Mark, there would be an obvious problem if Paula couldn't be located. Or, to switch to a more pleasant example, suppose Mark wanted to go on a school picnic and needed written permission to attend. Ben would need written authorization in order to give permission.

In addition to parental responsibility, there's the question of support. Who pays Mark's living expenses? Paula and Ben must discuss it, and write down their agreement. Other issues come up as well—school attendance, curfews, drug use, etc. Again, Ben and Paula must talk about them, and may want to write down their understanding. Because Mark is a teenager, we recommend that he be in on the discussion and sign any agreement. After all, if Mark doesn't like what Paula and Ben decide, he can vote with his feet.

Important: The forms we include aren't court orders. Have them notarized; you may also want an attorney to look at them. We believe they're valid, and should suffice when a school official, doctor or someone similar needs proof that the guardian can act for the child. If someone refuses to honor a form, you've got a problem. Insist that you have the legal authority to act for the child. After all, that's what the agreement says. If that doesn't work, call the child's parents fast— and you may have to hire a lawyer.

Note on Dealing With Schools: Schools, like other public agencies, often like their own forms. Don't argue. If they insist you use their form, use it.

TEMPORARY GUARDIANSHIP AGREEMENT[30]

We, Paula Ruiz, and John Ruiz are the parents of Mark Ruiz, born to us on August 18, 1973. Paula resides at 1811 Main Street, Cleveland, Ohio, and John resides at 493 Oak Street, Cincinnati, Ohio. We hereby grant to Ben Jacobs, living at 44 Tea Road, Boston, Massachusetts, the temporary guardianship of Mark Ruiz. We grant to Ben Jacobs the power to act in our place as parents of Mark Ruiz, to authorize any medical examination, tests, operations, or treatment that in Ben Jacobs' sole opinion are needed or useful to Mark Ruiz.

We also hereby grant to Ben Jacobs the power to act in our place as parents of Mark Ruiz in connection with any school, including, but not limited to, enrollment, permission for activities, and medical authorization.

During the period while Ben Jacobs acts as guardian of Mark Ruiz, the costs of his/her upkeep and living expenses shall be paid as follows. [Insert what has been agreed on.]

Dated: _____   Signature: _____
                                               Paula Ruiz

Dated: _____   Signature: _____
                                               John Ruiz

Dated: _____   Signature: _____
                                               Ben Jacobs

Notarization

[30]Make at least four originals: one for the school, one for the hospital, etc.

AUTHORIZATION TO CONSENT TO MEDICAL, SURGICAL, OR DENTAL EXAMINATION OR TREATMENT OF A MINOR

I, Paula Ruiz, being the parent with legal custody of Mark Ruiz, born August 18, 1973, hereby authorize Ben Jacobs, into whose care the minor has been entrusted, to consent to any x-ray, examination, anesthetic, medical or surgical diagnosis or treatment and hospital care to be rendered to Mark Ruiz under the general or special supervision and upon the advice of a physician or surgeon licensed to practice medicine in any state of the United States, or to consent to an x-ray, examination, anesthetic, dental or surgical diagnosis or treatment and hospital care to be rendered to Mark Ruiz by a dentist licensed to practice dentistry in any state of the United States.

This authorization is valid from April 29, 19__ to April 29, 19__.

Dated: _____   Signature: _____
                                      Paula Ruiz

Dated: _____   Signature: _____
                                      Ben Jacobs

Notarization

---

3. FORMAL COURT-APPOINTED GUARDIANSHIP

In some cases, a court-ordered, voluntary guardianship is preferable to an informal one. In this situation, the parents, the guardian and the child (if old enough), agree on the guardianship. A court-ordered guardianship makes sense if the parent is mentally ill, incarcerated, or if a third party (usually a relative) may try to intervene and get custody. It also may be necessary to obtain benefits, deal with school authorities or manage the child's money. (An adult must be legally authorized to care for the child's financial assets.)

We don't cover contested guardianships, where relatives or other persons may object to the guardianship. In this situation, you'll need an attorney's help. If you anticipate problems with the guardianship process, you should see an attorney before you start the court process.

The court proceeding and the social service investigation into the guardian's life vary from state to state.[31] Before proceeding, discuss your situation with a knowledgeable lawyer sympathetic to, and aware of, lesbian and gay concerns. Unless you're convinced, you won't face a biased, hostile judge, don't file a formal guardianship. And while heterosexual couples can safely handle their own guardianships, you'll probably want to hire a lawyer. The patina of respectability that an "Esq." carries will help you gain your result, however much of an illusion that patina really is.

F. Co-Parenting Arrangements

A lesbian or gay couple who raises a child together must outline, in writing, their understanding and arrangement; if the child is old enough, they should write out something among the three.

1. Raising a Child Jointly

As we've said, usually only one member of a lesbian or gay couple can be the legal parent of the child. Legal rules aside, you both want to raise the child. You entered into the adventure together, and you both want to make financial and emotional decisions. What you need is a written agreement stating your understanding. As with living-together agreements, the purpose is to identify ambiguities, uncertainties and disagreements, and to resolve them before trouble arises.

Example: Remember Regina and Susan, who had a little girl by artificial insemination? Although Regina gave birth, she and Susan want to jointly raise their daughter. To whatever extent possible, Susan wants to be as legally responsible for the child as Regina is. Psychologically, both women see themselves as mothers. They came to us before the birth and asked us many questions. If Regina died, what would be Susan's rights to custody? If they both contributed to the child's support, what would Susan's rights be regarding visitation if she and Regina split up? Could the child inherit from Susan? After several discussions (with a little kibitzing from us), they drew up the following agreement:

---

[31]Investigations, if any, are usually conducted by the county social services or juvenile probation authorities. Because a guardianship is not "final" (as is an adoption), the investigation isn't intense. A friend, or a friend of a friend, in the county agency can tell you what to expect.

AGREEMENT TO JOINTLY RAISE OUR CHILD

We, Regina Miller and Susan Carlson, make this agreement to set out our rights and obligations regarding our child who'll be born to us by Regina. We realize that our power to contract, as far as a child is concerned, is limited by state law. We also understand that the law will recognize Regina as the only mother of the child. With this knowledge, and in a spirit of cooperation and mutual respect, we state the following as our agreement:

1. It's our intention to jointly and equally parent, including providing support and guidance. We will do our best to jointly share the responsibilities involved in feeding, clothing, loving, raising and disciplining our child.

2. Regina will sign a temporary guardianship or a power of attorney giving Susan the power to make medical decisions she thinks are necessary for the child in Regina's absence.

3. We both agree to be responsible for our child's support until she or he reaches the age of majority (or finishes college). We each agree to contribute to our child's support in proportion to our net incomes. This agreement to provide support is binding, whether or not we live together. If we dispute the amount of support our child needs, or the percentage that either of us is to pay, we agree to submit our dispute to binding arbitration, as laid out in Paragraph 9.

4. Our child will be given the last name "Carlson."

5. Regina agrees to designate Susan as guardian of Regina's estate, and of the child, in her will. We understand that naming Susan legal guardian of the child in Regina's isn't legally binding, but believe it should be persuasive in court.

6. Because of the possible trauma our separation might cause our child, we agree to participate in a jointly agreed-upon program of counseling if either considers separating.

7. If we separate, we will both do our best to see that our child grows up in a good and healthy environment. Specifically, we agree that:

a. We will do our best to see that our child maintains a close and loving relationship with each of us.

b. We will share in our child's upbringing, and will share in our child's support, depending on our needs, our child's needs and on our respective abilities to pay.

c. We will make a good-faith effort to jointly make all major decisions affecting our child's health and welfare.

d. We will base all decisions upon the best interests of our child.

e. Should our child spend a greater portion of the year living with one of us, the person who has actual physical custody will take all steps necessary to maximize the other's visitation, and help make visitation as easy as possible.

f. If we disagree about what's in the best interests of our child, we will undergo jointly agreed-upon counseling with the hope that we'll work out our differences and avoid taking our problems to court.

g. If either of us die, our child will be cared for and raised by the other, whether or not we are living together. We will each state this in our wills.

8. We intend that this agreement be binding not only between ourselves, but between each of us and our child.

9. Should any dispute arise between us regarding this agreement, we agree to submit the dispute to binding arbitration, sharing the cost equally. In the event of such dispute, the arbitrator will be _____.[32]

10. We agree that if any court finds any portion of this contract illegal or otherwise unenforceable, the rest of the contract is still valid and in full force.

Executed at: _____
           (Place)

Dated: _____   Signature: _____
                                 Regina Miller

Dated: _____   Signature: _____
                                 Susan Carlson

A Note on Enforceability: We believe that the financial provisions, the visitation clause and the arbitration clause are enforceable by either party, and by the child, as a "third-party beneficiary" of the agreement, in many states.[33] But, as the contract itself states, the custody and parenting provisions may not be.

---

[32]You can name anyone you want to be the arbitrator. Because the agreement will be in effect for 18 years, name non-specific arbitrators, such as the director of a gay/lesbian center you trust, or the minister at a gay/lesbian church. See Chapter 3, "Arbitration and Mediation," for more details.

[33]In a California case, a (former) lover of a lesbian who had a child by artificial insemination was awarded visitation rights based on the couple's child-rearing agreement. There's always the possibility that some troglodyte judge would refuse to enforce the agreement, claiming that sin or sodomy was involved, but we think that under traditional contract rules, it should be enforced. After all, it's a contract to support a child, something the state has traditionally been interested in. It would take a small-minded judge to deny

Whenever a lesbian or gay couple plans to parent together, a written agreement is essential. A sincere understanding and an honest intention to honor an agreement are at least as valuable as the benediction of a black-robed bureaucrat. It's rare for these contracts to wind up in court, but discussing the contract will help you understand each other's concerns, and anticipate any possible problems before they loom large; having a contract will help refresh memories when disagreements arise. And if you ever need help settling a dispute, arbitration is a sensible forum.

You have great freedom in drafting your agreement and should include whatever seems fair and necessary. Our contract is only one example. But if you change ours substantially, have a sympathetic lawyer look at it (see Chapter 12).

2. Adoption By the Co-Parent

Traditionally, Susan, as the "other" parent or co-parent, has no custody or visitation rights if the couple breaks up and can only be recommended as the guardian if Regina dies. At least two states, however, Alaska and Oregon, have permitted the co-parent to adopt the child, and two California judges have granted joint adoptions to lesbian couples. For more information, contact the Lesbian Rights Project, 1370 Mission St., 4th Floor, San Francisco, CA 94103.

3. Arrangements Between a Teenager and the Adults Who'll Care for the Teen

For most of this chapter, we've discussed legal aspects of parenting. Now, let's look at the practical concerns when teens come into a home (by guardianship, foster parenting, etc.). Our sample agreement concerns Eric, a sixteen-year-old who has come to live with John and David. The purpose of this contract isn't to create a document they can use to sue each other if the garbage isn't dumped, but to formulate their understandings and expectations.

---

support to a child because of the judge's hostility to the couple's sexual orientation. Also, with this agreement, any dispute would first go to arbitration, and judges are reluctant to overturn arbitrators' decisions, no matter what the issue.

CONTRACT BETWEEN A TEENAGER AND THE ADULTS HE'S ABOUT TO LIVE WITH

1. *First things*

General: Eric's coming into John and David's home; we are making this agreement to help make our family life together as harmonious and enjoyable as possible. We realize that circumstances change and we agree to review this agreement every six months.

Disputes: All disputes will be carried out in English. This means no punching. It also means that we will do our best to communicate openly and not assume that the others "ought to know what concerns us."

Eric's Parents: Eric's parents will be encouraged to visit if they wish to do so and will be made as welcome as possible.

2. *Finances*

John and David will receive $225 from the welfare department as stipend for Eric's support. The money will be used as follows:

$60 for rent;

$100 for food;

$25 for clothing;

$40 for Eric for spending money.

John and David will contribute more to Eric's support than they are compensated by welfare. Further, Eric's $40 per month spending money isn't conditioned upon his doing chores. John will be the banker.

3. *Hours*

Eric agrees to be home by 7:00 p.m. on school nights and by 1:00 a.m. on weekends. He agrees to generally let John and David know what he's doing. He also agrees to call home by 6:30 p.m. on school nights and by 9:00 p.m. on weekends to request any later hours.

John and/or David agree to be home by 6:30 p.m. on weeknights and by 1:00 a.m. on weekends, and agree to leave a note on the refrigerator and/or call if there's any change.

4. *Meals*

Dinner is considered a special time, and will be served around 7:30 p.m. Everyone's expected to be present if at all possible.

5. *Drugs*

Eric will obey all laws regulating drug use.[34]

---

[34]This may not be realistic. Many teenagers use (or experiment with) drugs. The French traditionally allow wine at meals for everyone. Drug use should be discussed honestly and,

6. *School*

Eric will be enrolled in public school and agrees to attend regularly.

7. *Chores*

Eric will keep his room neat—but it's his room and as long as he confines his mess to this area, there will be peace. Eric won't spread his belongings around the rest of the house. If he does, they will be placed in his room.

John and David will shop, do the general cleaning, cook, keep the household accounts, do the wash and do the maintenance around the house.

Eric's responsible for his own room; he will clean up after dinner and wash dishes twice a week. He will also take out the garbage—without being asked—and pitch in on small chores and large cleaning jobs. Yard work will be divided.

8. *Time Together*

John agrees to be home at least two nights a week and David agrees to be home two nights a week. Tuesday night and Saturday afternoons are times together and no plans can be made unless they include everyone—except if we all agree otherwise.

9. *Stereo Equipment*

The stereo equipment is David's. He admits he's fanatic about it, but it was expensive. So everyone agrees only David will use it. He will attempt to either play music everyone enjoys or use earphones. He's willing to put albums, tapes and CD's on for others. The radio and TV can be used by all, and the volume is to be kept at a moderate level.

10. *Smoking*

Smoking is permitted only in the back room.

11. *Space*

Eric has his room and is free to lock it if he chooses. John and David have their room, and they may lock it if they choose. Everyone's privacy is respected.

12. *Guests*

John and David aren't used to sharing their home with a lot of people so Eric is permitted only one guest at a time and only when someone else is home unless other arrangements have been made; Eric is

---

hopefully, a realistic agreement can be reached. It is not wise to sign an agreement that expressly approves violating drug laws.

responsible for his guest's behavior.

No guests after 9 p.m. without agreement.

13. *Social Welfare*

We agree to meet with Jeff Lakely, the social worker, every other week and candidly discuss our joys and problems.

14. *Length of this Agreement*

Eric, David and John understand that their living together must be enjoyable for everyone, and that they must all give a lot for it to work. If one person can't make it work, they will terminate the agreement and it will expire.

Dated: _____   Signature: _____

Eric

Dated: _____   Signature: _____

David

Dated: _____   Signature: _____

John

-8-

Medical Emergencies[1]

A. Introduction

All gays and lesbians, whether in a couple or not, should consider what will happen if they become seriously ill or suffer a medical emergency. Who will have authority to act for them if they are incapacitated and cannot make their own health care decisions? Who will be allowed to visit them in intensive care?

Unfortunately, if no advance legal work has been done, serious problems can arise. In a fairly well-known case from Minnesota, Karen Thompson has been forbidden, for years, to have any contact with, or authority to act for, her incapacitated lover, Sharon Kowalski. Sharon was seriously injured in a car accident. Her mother and father ran to court to remove her from Karen's care after learning that the women were lovers. Since being placed in her parent's care, Sharon first regressed and, since then, has shown no improvement.

In another case, the lover of a man with AIDS, and other people the patient chose as "family," have been excluded from visiting him in the hospital by his biological family. There have also been cases where biological family members have fundamental religious —and medical—ideas that the ill person has rejected. Because hospitals and doctors conventionally look to the immediate family for

---

[1]Because of space limitations, this chapter necessarily gives only a broad overview. A more thorough discussion of planning for medical emergencies can be found in Clifford, *The Power of Attorney Book* (Nolo Press).

authority to act (absent a document giving the lover that power), the lover is sometimes forced to look on in horror while the doctor is instructed in ways which the lover knows are contrary to his or her mate's wishes.

Some Definitions

Attorney in Fact: the person given the authority to act on behalf of the principal in a power of attorney.

Conventional Power of Attorney: a power of attorney used when a competent principal is unavailable and wants someone else to make decisions for her. This power of attorney automatically terminates if the principal becomes incapacitated or dies.

Durable Power of Attorney: a power of attorney which remains valid even if the principal is or becomes incapacitated and doesn't terminate until the principal's death.

Guardianship/Custodianship/Conservatorship: a court proceeding where someone is appointed to manage the finances for and make medical decisions about an incapacitated person.

Power of Attorney: a legal document in which one person authorizes another person to act in the former's behalf.

Principal: the person who executes (writes and signs) a power of attorney.

Springing Durable Power of Attorney: a durable power of attorney which doesn't become effective until the principal becomes incapacitated; e.g., it's used only if the principal has a medical emergency.

In addition, if someone becomes incapacitated, financial matters must also be attended to. The authority to make financial decisions has traditionally belonged to a spouse, not a lover or friend. Only a few years ago, court proceedings were almost always necessary to authorize anyone else to handle financial matters.

Fortunately, gays and lesbians now have the power to decide in advance, who will have legal authority to make medical and financial decisions if they become incapacitated. By creating a "durable power of attorney," you select who will act for you. We recommend that you create two separate durable powers of attorney: the first one is for health care, to ensure that your lover, or whoever else you choose, can make medical decisions for you, and visit you in intensive care; the second one is for finances, so that the person you choose can pay your bills and handle your money. Because the incapacitated person decides in advance, her loved ones, doctors, and even attorneys, are working together to care for her, not fighting over who makes decisions.

This chapter explains what durable powers of attorney are, and provides sample forms so you can create your own. The chapter is designed for those caught in an emergency, as well as for those foresighted enough to prepare in the event an emergency develops (which we hope are all our readers).

Durable powers of attorney are of vital importance for people with AIDS. As we are all sadly aware, the AIDS epidemic has been responsible for the death of thousands of gay men and has drastically effected their lifestyle. It has made people aware of their mortality and their need to be responsible to themselves and their community. "Medical Emergencies" have, tragically, become realities for many gay people, their family and friends. We provide a list of AIDS organizations in the Appendix.

All medical emergencies are frightening and stressful. Recently a friend of ours was diagnosed with AIDS. One of us was a close member of his extended family, as well as his attorney. These roles were to some extent conflicting, and the process painful, but I think I was able to share with Jan his dignity in life and death, and to be of some assistance regarding his affairs.

Within approximately a week and one-half after diagnosis, Jan had recovered sufficiently to leave the hospital. We were all so elated that he was out of the hospital and doing so much better that we didn't want to consider death. We became jubilant as he improved. His mother baked a dozen pies and after a week his parents flew back home. Within a month, however, Jan had to go back into the hospital. Because his fever was so high, he was incompetent to make any personal, let alone business, decisions. His parents flew out again.

This time it was clear that we had to be prepared for future times when Jan would be unable to make medical or business decisions. We also had to prepare for his death. We were fortunate because Jan's parents talked and listened to Jan's lover, business partner and friends. The question we had to resolve was, if Jan didn't recover sufficiently to make his own decisions, who should have the power to decide business and financial matters, medical care, hospital visitation and burial plans? When Jan became coherent we urged him to consider these questions and to prepare the necessary documents.

Jan died in the summer. No legal papers can lessen that tragedy. The documents we provide here, though, can help to prevent needless additional pain and confusion, as well as the denial of ill gay and lesbian people's wishes.

Following is a checklist of the topics and forms we provide for anyone planning for the possibility of incapacity (which we believe all lesbians and gays should plan for) or dealing with a medical emergency:

Section B. Authority over Property

- Form: Durable Power of Attorney for Finances

Section C. Authority over Medical Decisions

- Form: Durable Power of Attorney for Health Care
- Form: The California Statutory Durable Power of Attorney for Health Care

Section D. Self-Deliverance and the Right to a Natural Death

- Form: Directive to Physician

Section E. Estate Planning Note

Section F. Burial and Body Disposition

- Form: Written instructions

B. AUTHORITY OVER PROPERTY

A person with a medical crisis is frequently incapable of managing his or her own financial affairs. A person with AIDS, for example, may become incompetent for a period of time, recover sufficiently to handle practical matters and then become incompetent again. During periods of incompetency, bills must be paid, bank deposits made, checks drawn, insurance requested and social security applied for. Many other concerns may need to be addressed, from running a business to buying Christmas presents. During the incompetency, someone else must have legal authority to handle these affairs, or all sorts of trouble, trauma, confusion and financial injury are possible.

One method of authorizing a person to handle another's financial affairs is through a court proceeding, called a "guardianship," "custodianship" or "conservatorship," depending on the state. Whatever they're called, in these proceedings a court appoints someone to have legal authority to handle the incompetent person's financial affairs. These court proceedings are costly, and take considerable time. They can also be ugly if, for example, the lover and the parent of an ill gay person both ask to be appointed. We recommend court proceedings only as a last resort. They won't be necessary if the ill person signs a "durable power of attorney."

A *power of attorney* is a legal document in which one person, called the "principal," authorizes another person, called the "attorney in fact," to act for the principal. A conventional power of attorney is used when the principal isn't available to handle her affairs; for instance, she goes out of town and wants someone to make decisions while she's away. It automatically terminates upon her incapacity (or death), and therefore isn't useful in a medical emergency. A relatively new type of power of attorney, called a "durable" power of attorney ("DPA"), remains valid even if the principal becomes incapacitated, and doesn't terminate until her death. In fact, one type of durable power of attorney, called a "springing durable power of attorney" in legalese, becomes effective *only* if you become incapacitated. In other words, you can prepare a durable power of attorney to be used only if you have a medical emergency.[2]

A durable power of attorney is very flexible. You can include any reasonable limitation on the attorney in fact's authority, as well as setting forth any specific direction. For example, you could restrict your attorney in fact from having the power to sell your home, or require him to use money from specified bank accounts to pay certain bills.

Clearly, the most important decision when creating a durable power of attorney for financial affairs is the choice of the attorney in fact. It's wise to choose an alternate as well, in case your original choice can't serve. These choices are obviously very personal. Those selected should be people you fully trust and who have good business sense. If there isn't such a person, a durable power of attorney isn't for you.

There are different technical requirements applicable to durable powers of attorney in different states. For example, in California, and many other states, a durable power of attorney for finances must be notarized. In any case, any durable power of attorney should be notarized. Even if it's not required, it's always a very good idea. Notarization promotes acceptability with banks, hospitals and other institutions. Also, a notarized DPA may be recorded with the county recorder's office, which can further promote acceptability. If the attorney in fact will be handling real estate matters, the durable power of attorney must be recorded in the county where the property is located.

Because of state law variations, we recommend that a lawyer review your durable power of attorney for finances (see Chapter 12). It's an important document which potentially transfers great power; you'll want to be sure it's valid.

Now let's get to work. The following form is an example of a completed durable power of attorney for financial affairs, which takes effect only if you

---

[2]Again, durable powers of attorney are explained in depth in *The Power of Attorney Book* (Nolo Press).

become incapacitated. We've derived this form from California statutes which require that the "warnings" be included. Other states don't require warnings, but they're always a good idea.

This durable power of attorney is signed by two witnesses. Witnessing isn't a legal requirement, but, it too, helps promote acceptability.

DURABLE POWER OF ATTORNEY FOR FINANCES

Recording requested by and
when recorded mail to:
Lucas Wilkes
147 Iris Street
Lansing, Michigan

Warning to Person Executing This Document

This is an important legal document. It creates a durable power of attorney. Before executing this document, you should know these facts:

1. This document may provide the person you designate as your attorney in fact with broad powers to dispose, sell, convey and encumber your real and personal property.

2. These powers will exist for an indefinite period of time unless you limit their duration in this document. These powers will continue to exist notwithstanding your subsequent disability or incapacity.

3. You have the right to revoke or terminate this durable power of attorney any time.

Durable Power of Attorney

1. Creation of Durable Power of Attorney

By signing this document, I, Jonathan Chen, intend to create a durable power of attorney. This durable power of attorney shall not be affected by my subsequent disability or incapacity, and shall remain effective until my death, or until revoked by me in writing.

2. Effective Date

This durable power of attorney shall become effective only in the event that I become incapacitated or disabled so that I'm not able to handle my own financial affairs and decisions. That determination shall be made in writing by a licensed physician, and the writing shall be

3. Designation of Attorney in Fact

I, Jonathan Chen, hereby appoint Lucas Wilkes, of 147 Iris Street, Lansing, Michigan, as my attorney in fact, to act for me and in my name and for my use and benefit. Should Lucas Wilkes for any reason fail to serve or cease to serve as my attorney in fact, I appoint Edward Chen of 9433 5th Avenue, East Lansing, Michigan to be my attorney in fact.

4. Authority of Attorney in Fact

I grant my attorney in fact full power and authority over all my property, real and personal, and authorize him to do and perform all and every act which I, as owner of the property, could do or perform, and I hereby ratify and confirm all that my attorney in fact shall do or cause to be done under this durable power of attorney.

[Special Provisions Or Limitations. Add to this Section 4 any specific limitation(s), restriction(s), direction(s), etc. you want.]

5. Reliance by Third Parties

The powers conferred on my attorney in fact by this durable power of attorney may be exercised by my attorney in fact alone, and my attorney in fact's signature may be accepted by any third person or organization as fully authorized by me and with the same force and effect as if I were personally present, competent and acting on my own behalf.

No person or organization who relies on this durable power of attorney or any representation my attorney in fact makes regarding his authority, including but not limited to:

(i) the fact that this durable power of attorney hasn't been revoked:

(ii) that I, Jonathan Chen, was competent to execute this power of attorney;

(iii) the authority of my attorney in fact under this durable power of attorney

shall incur any liability to me, my estate, heirs, successors or assigns because of such reliance on this durable power of attorney or on any such representation by my attorney in fact.

Executed this 19th day of October, 1989, at Lansing, Michigan.

_____

Jonathan Chen

Witnesses

_____   of 712 Oak Street, Lansing, Michigan

Randy Viceroy

_____   of 38 Blossom Village, East Lansing, Michigan

Laura Elliot

Notarization

State of Michigan

County of _____

On this 19th day of October in the year 1989, before me a Notary Public, State of Michigan, duly commissioned and sworn, personally appeared Jonathan Chen, personally known to me (or proved to me on the basis of satisfactory evidence) to be the person whose name is subscribed to in the within instrument, and acknowledged to me that he executed the same.

IN WITNESS WHEREOF, I have hereunto set my hand and affixed my official seal in the _____ County of Michigan on the date set forth above in this certificate.

_____

Notary Public

State of Michigan

My commission expires June 1, 1992

Clause for Creating a Durable Power of Attorney, Effective Immediately

As we've discussed, most people want their durable powers of attorney to be implemented only if they become incapacitated (the "springing" kind). Some others, however, will want them to take immediate effect (they're already ill). If this applies to you, substitute the following for clause 2 in the above durable power of attorney:

> *The durable power of attorney shall be effective as of the date of my signing it.*

Note: The appendix contains a form for a "springing" durable power of attorney for finances.

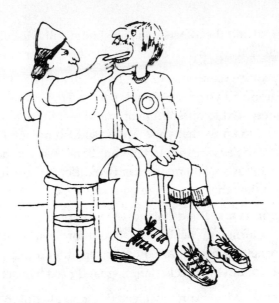

C. AUTHORITY FOR MEDICAL DECISIONS

In a medical emergency, there's a need for someone to have clear, legal authority to make medical decisions for an ill person unable to make his or her own decisions. Vital issues come up: choice of hospitals or treating doctors, types of medication, methods of treatment, use of "experimental" medicine, use of life support equipment, decisions to discontinue treatment and hospital visitation rights.

As we've discussed, if a person is unable to make his or her own medical decisions, a hospital or doctor will, without clear legal authority to the contrary, generally turn to a spouse, a parent, an adult child or a sibling. This can, and has, resulted in lovers or close friends being completely shut off from making decisions and sometimes being denied the right to visit the ill person in the hospital. To avoid such tragedies, a non-family member must establish clear legal authority to make decisions and visit in a medical emergency.

Generally, the best way to handle the authorization to make medical decisions in an emergency is by use of a durable power of attorney for health care. (Read Section B of this chapter, if you haven't already, for general information on durable powers of attorney.) The principal (the person executing the document) authorizes whoever she chooses to be her "attorney in fact" to make medical decisions for her. The principal can also specify any particular desires she has regarding treatment. A durable power of attorney for health care can take immediate effect, or it can take effect only if the principal becomes incapacitated. The latter type is called a "springing durable power of attorney."

Obviously, the principal and the attorney in fact should fully discuss the principal's desires before the principal signs the durable power of attorney.

Although some people create one durable power of attorney for health care and finances, we recommend you keep them separate. They are very different documents and are presented to different people and institutions. There's no reason for your hospital to know that your rent is paid from your Tyco Bank checking account and there's no reason to tell your bank that you don't want to use life support systems.[3] Also, you may select two different attorneys in fact— one for health care and the other to manage your finances.

Two states—California and Rhode Island—have expressly authorized the use of a durable power of attorney for health care. In California and Rhode Island, a durable power of attorney for health care must be separate from any other power of attorney, and must contain the precise language required by each state's law.

Although no other state has expressly created a separate durable power of attorney for health care, they are accepted because states allow attorneys in fact to make health care decisions using general durable powers of attorney. In some states, however, the scope and authority of the attorney in fact may be limited. If you live in one of the following states, be sure to have a knowledgeable lawyer review your durable power of attorney for health care:

Connecticut	Louisiana	Oklahoma
Florida[4]	Mississippi	South Carolina
Georgia	New Hampshire	Texas
Idaho	New York	Virginia
Illinois		

Even if you don't live in one of those states, if you fear that a biological family member will challenge your selection of the attorney in fact, have a lawyer review your durable power of attorney for health care.

Remember, an attorney in fact may have to make extremely difficult decisions, often based largely on information provided by the doctors. For this reason, ask the doctor to put all facts relating to the attorney in fact's decision into your medical records. Should any questions later arise, this will allow the attorney in fact to show how he or she made the decisions.

---

[3]Again, we recommend Clifford, *The Power of Attorney Book* (Nolo Press) if you want more information on powers of attorney.

[4]If you live in Florida, however, you won't be able to name your lover as the "attorney in fact." Florida law, Section 709.08 of the Florida Annotated Code, limits the attorney in fact to "spouse, parent, child, sibling, niece or nephew of the principal."

Note: Be sure a copy of your durable power of attorney for health care is placed in your hospital records if hospital care is anticipated. Hospital bureaucracies sometimes take weeks to transfer documents to the appropriate place, so ask the doctor or nurse to place the form directly in your medical records. And introduce the attorney in fact to the attending doctor as soon as is practical in the given situation.[5]

SPRINGING DURABLE POWER OF ATTORNEY FOR HEALTH CARE [NOT VALID IN CALIFORNIA OR RHODE ISLAND]

Durable Power of Attorney for Health Care

1. Creation of Durable Power of Attorney

    To my family, relatives, friends and my physicians, health care providers, community care facilities and any other person who may have an interest or duty in my medical care or treatment: I, Jonathan Chen, being of sound mind, willfully and voluntarily intend to create by this document a durable power of attorney for my health care by appointing the person designated as my attorney in fact to make health care decisions for me in the event I become incapacitated and am unable to make health care decisions for myself. This power of attorney shall not be affected by my subsequent incapacity.

2. Designation of Attorney in Fact

    The person designated to be my attorney in fact for health care in the event I become incapacitated is Lucas Wilkes of 147 Iris Street, Lansing Michigan.

    If Lucas Wilkes for any reason shall fail to serve or ceases to serve as my attorney in fact for health care, Edward Chen of 9433 5th Avenue, East Lansing, Michigan shall be my attorney in fact for health care.

3. Effective on Incapacity

    This durable power of attorney shall become effective in the event I become incapacitated and am unable to make health care decisions for myself, in which case it shall become effective as of the date of the written statement by a physician, as provided in Paragraph 4.

4. Determination of Incapacity

---

[5]We dislike repeating ourselves, but we really must emphasize that this discussion on durable powers of attorney for health care is just an overview. If any of your questions are unanswered, consult Nolo's *The Power of Attorney Book.*

(a) The determination that I have become incapacitated and am unable to make health care decisions shall be made in writing by a licensed physician. If possible, the determination shall be made by Dr. Rosemary Carson, Oslo Medical Center, Lansing, Michigan.

(b) In the event that a licensed physician has made a written determination that I have become incapacitated and am not able to make health care decisions for myself, that written statement shall be attached to the original document of this durable power of attorney.

5. Authority of My Attorney in Fact

My attorney in fact shall have all lawful authority permissible to make health care decisions for me, including the authority to consent, or withdraw consent or refuse consent to any care, treatment, service or procedure to maintain, diagnose or treat my physical or mental condition, except

[add any exceptions here]

6. Inspection and Disclosure of Information Relating to My Physical or Mental Health

Subject to any limitations in this document, my attorney in fact has the power and authority to do all of the following:

(a) Request, review, and receive any information, verbal or written, regarding my physical or mental health, including, but not limited to, medical and hospital records.

(b) Execute on my behalf any releases or other documents that may be required in order to obtain this information.

(c) Consent to or prohibit the disclosure of this information.

7. Signing Documents, Waivers and Releases

Where necessary to implement the health care decisions that my attorney in fact is authorized by this document to make, my attorney in fact has the power and authority to execute on my behalf all of the following:

(a) Documents titled or purporting to be a "Refusal to Permit Treatment" and "Leaving Hospital Against Medical Advice."

(b) Any necessary waiver or release from liability required by a hospital or physician.

8. I authorize my attorney in fact to make all permitted decisions regarding who shall be permitted to visit me in the hospital.

9. Duration

I intend that this Durable Power of Attorney remain effective until my death, or until revoked by me in writing.

Executed this 19th day of October, 1989 at Lansing, Michigan.

_____

Jonathan Chen

Witnesses

I declare that the principal is personally known to me, that the principal signed or acknowledged this durable power of attorney in my presence, that the principal appears to be of sound mind and under no duress, fraud or undue influence.

I further declare that I'm not related to the principal by blood, marriage or adoption, and to the best of my knowledge, I'm not entitled to any part of the estate of the principal upon the death of the principal under a Will now existing or by operation of law.

Witnesses

_____ of 712 Oak Street, Lansing, Michigan

Randy Viceroy

_____ of 38 Blossom Village, East Lansing, Michigan

Laura Elliot

Notarization

State of Michigan

County of _____

On this 19th day of October in the year 1989, before me a Notary Public, State of Michigan, duly commissioned and sworn, personally appeared Jonathan Chen, personally known to me (or proved to me on the basis of satisfactory evidence) to be the person whose name is subscribed to in the within instrument, and acknowledged to me that he executed the same.

IN WITNESS WHEREOF, I have hereunto set my hand and affixed my official seal in the _____ County of Michigan on the date set forth above in this certificate.

_____

Notary Public

State of Michigan

My commission expires June 1, 1992

Statement of Permissible Authority of Attorney in Fact (optional)

If you have any specific desires or directions regarding your medical treatment, especially concerning the use of life-support procedures, specify them in item 5 above.

Example #1

I don't want my life to be artificially prolonged by the use of life-support or life-sustaining machinery or procedures. I desire to have a natural death, and if I'm in a terminal condition, I direct that no life-support or life-sustaining machinery or procedures be used.

Example #2

If at any time I should have an incurable injury, disease or illness which is a terminal condition, and the application of life-sustaining procedures or machinery would serve only to artificially prolong the moment of my death, I direct that such procedures or machinery not be used, and that I be permitted to die naturally and I further direct that my attorney in fact take all actions necessary to allow me to die such a natural death.

The *Power of Attorney Book* contains a detailed discussion of options and clauses concerning the right to a natural death, and terminating life support systems.

The California Durable Power of Attorney for Health Care

This statutory durable power of attorney form complies with the requirements of California law. The warnings must be included in any California health care durable power of attorney, unless it has been prepared by an attorney who includes the certificate set forth at the end of the form.

STATUTORY FORM DURABLE POWER OF ATTORNEY FOR HEALTH CARE
(CALIFORNIA CIVIL CODE SECTION 2500)

Warning To Person Executing This Document

This is an important legal document which is authorized by the Keene Health Care Agent Act. Before executing this document, you should know these important facts:

This document gives the person you designate as your agent (the attorney in fact) the power to make health care decisions for you. Your agent must act consistently with your desires as stated in this document or otherwise made known.

Except as you otherwise specify in this document, this document gives your agent the power to consent to your doctor not giving treatment or stopping treatment necessary to keep you alive.

Notwithstanding this document, you have the right to make medical and other health care decisions for yourself so long as you can give informed consent with respect to the particular decision. In addition, no treatment may be given to you over your objection at the time, and health care necessary to keep you alive may not be stopped or withheld if you object at the time.

This document gives your agent authority to consent, to refuse to consent, or to withdraw consent to any care, treatment, service, or procedure to maintain, diagnose, or treat a physical or mental condition. This power is subject to any statement of your desires and any limitations that you include in this document. You may state in this document any types of treatment that you don't desire. In addition, a court can take away the power of your agent to make health care decisions for you if your agent (1) authorizes anything that is illegal, (2) acts contrary to your known desires, or (3) where your desires aren't known, does anything that is clearly contrary to your best interests.

Unless you specify a shorter period in this document, this power will exist for seven years from the date you execute this document and, if you are unable to make health care decisions for yourself at the time when this seven-year period ends, the power will continue to exist until the time when you become able to make health care decisions for yourself.

You have the right to revoke the authority of your agent by notifying your agent or your treating doctor, hospital or other health care provider orally or in writing of the revocation.

Your agent has the right to examine your medical records and to consent to their disclosure unless you limit this right in this document.

Unless you otherwise specify in this document, this document gives your agent the power after you die to (1) authorize an autopsy, (2) donate your body or parts thereof for transplant or therapeutic or educational or scientific purposes, and (3) direct the disposition of your remains.

This document revokes any prior durable power of attorney for health care.

You should carefully read and follow the witnessing procedure described at the end of this form. This document won't be valid unless you comply with the witnessing procedure.

If there's anything in this document that you don't understand, you should ask a lawyer to explain it to you.

Your agent may need this document immediately in case of an emergency that requires a decision concerning your health care. Either keep this document where it's immediately available to your agent and alternate agents or give each of them an executed copy of this document. You may also want to give your doctor an executed copy of this document.

Don't use this form if you are a conservatee under the Lanterman-Petris-Short Act and you want to appoint your conservator as your agent. You can do that only if the appointment document includes a certificate of your attorney.

1. Designation of Health Care Agent.[6] I, Marlene O'Goughal, 717 Lake Street, Bolinas, California, do hereby designate and appoint Sharon Weiss, 717 Lake Street, Bolinas California (415) 555-9696, [Insert name, address, and telephone number of one individual only as your agent to make health care decisions for you. None of the following may be designated as your agent: (1) your treating health care provider, (2) a non-relative employee of your treating health care provider, (3) an operator of a community care facility, or (4) a non-relative employer of any operator of a community care facility] as my attorney in fact (agent) to make health are decisions for me as authorized in this document. For the purposes of this document, "health care decision" means consent, refusal to consent, or withdrawal of consent to any care, treatment, service, or procedure to maintain, diagnose, or treat an individual's physical or mental condition.

2. Creation of Durable Power of Attorney for Health Care. By this document I intend to create a durable power of attorney for health care under Sections 2430 to 2443, inclusive, of the California Civil Code. This power of attorney is authorized by the Keene Health Care Agent Act and shall be construed in accordance with the provisions of Sections 2500 to 2506, inclusive, of the California Civil Code. This power of attorney shall not be affected by my

---

[6]"Health Care Agent" is another term for the attorney in fact (the person you name to have authority to make decisions).

subsequent incapacity.

3. General Statement of Authority Granted. Subject to any limitation in this document, I hereby grant to my agent full power and authority to make health care decisions for me to the same extent that I could make such decisions for myself if I had the capacity to do so. In exercising this authority, my agent shall make health care decisions that are consistent with my desires as stated in this document or otherwise made known to my agent, including, but not limited to, my desires concerning obtaining or refusing or withdrawing life-prolonging care, treatment, services and procedures.

(If you want to limit the authority of your agent to make health care decisions for you, you can state the limitation in paragraph 4 ("Statement of Desires, Special Provisions, and Limitations") below. You can indicate your desires by including a statement of your desires in the same paragraph.)

4. Statement of Desires, Special Provisions, and Limitations. (Your agent must make health care decisions that are consistent with your known desires. You can, but aren't required to, state your desires in the space provided below. You should consider whether you want to include a statement of your desires concerning life-prolonging care, treatment, services, and procedures. You can also include a statement of your desires concerning other matters relating to your health care. You can also make your desires known to your agent by discussing your desires with your agent or by some other means. If there are any types of treatment that you don't want to be used, you should state them in the space below. If you want to limit in any other way the authority given your agent by this document, you should state the limits in the space below. If you don't state any limits, your agent will have broad powers to make health care decisions for you, except to the extent that there are limits provided by laws.)

In exercising the authority under this durable power of attorney for health care, my agent shall act consistently with my desire as stated below and is subject to the special provisions and limitations stated below:

(a) Statement of desire concerning life-prolonging care, treatment, service, and procedures:

I want my life to be prolonged and I want life-sustaining treatment to be provided unless I'm in a coma which my doctors reasonably believe to be irreversible. Once my doctors have reasonably concluded I'm in an irreversible coma, I don't want life-sustaining treatment to be provided.[7]

(b) Additional statement of desires, special provisions, and limitations:

---

[7]Obviously, if you don't want life support systems, or if you want them even if you're in a coma, modify this paragraph. If you don't want life support systems, substitute: "I don't want my life to be artificially prolonged by the use of life-support or life-sustaining machinery or procedures. I desire to have a natural death, and if I'm in a terminal condition, I direct that no life-support or life-sustaining machinery or procedures be used."

_____

_____

_____

(You may attach additional pages if you need more space to complete your statement. If you attach additional pages, you must date and sign each of the additional pages at the same time you date and sign this document).

5. Inspection and Disclosure of Information Relating To My Physical Or Mental Health. Subject to any limitation in this document, my agent has the power and authority to do all of the following:

(a) Request, review, and receive any information, verbal or written, regarding my physical or mental health, including, but not limited to, medical and hospital records.

(b) Execute on my behalf any releases or other documents that may be required in order to obtain this information.

(c) Consent to the disclosure of this information. (If you want to limit the authority of your agent to receive and disclose information relating to your health, you must state the limitations in paragraph 4 ("Statement of Desires, Special Provisions, and Limitations") above).

6. Signing Documents, Waivers, and Releases. Where necessary to implement the health care decisions that my agent is authorized by this document to make, my agent has the power and authority to execute on my behalf all of the following:

(a) Documents titled or purporting to be a "Refusal to Permit Treatment" and "Leaving Hospital Against Medical Advice."

(b) Any necessary waiver or release from liability required by a hospital or physician.

7. Autopsy; Anatomical Gifts; Disposition of Remains. Subject to any limitations in this document, my agent has the power and authority to do all of the following:

(a) Authorize an autopsy under Section 7113 of the Health and Safety Code.

(b) Make disposition of a part or parts of my body under the Uniform Anatomical Gift Act (Chapter 3.5 (commencing in Section 7150) of Part 1 of Division 7 of the Health and Safety Code).

(c) Direct the disposition of my remains under Section 7100 of the Health and Safety Code. (If you want to limit the authority of your agent to consent to an autopsy, make an anatomical gift, or direct the disposition of your remains, you must state the limitations in paragraph 4 ("Statement of Desires, Special Provisions, and Limitations") above.)

8. Duration. (Unless you specify a shorter period in the space below, this power of attorney will exist for seven years from the date you execute this

MEDICAL EMERGENCIES • 8:19

document and, if you are unable to make health care decisions for yourself at the time when this seven-year period ends, the power will continue to exist until the time when you become able to make health care decisions for yourself.)

This durable power of attorney for health care expires on

_____

[Fill in this space only if you want the authority of your agent to end earlier than the seven-year period described above.]

9. Designation of Alternate Agents. (You aren't required to designated any alternate agent, but you may do so. Any alternate agent you designate will be able to make the same health care decisions as the agent you designated in paragraph 1, above, in the event that agent is unable or ineligible to act as your agent. If the agent you designate is your spouse, he or she becomes ineligible to act as your agent if your marriage is dissolved.)

If the person designated as my agent in paragraph 1 isn't available or becomes ineligible to act as my agent to make a health care decision for me or loses the mental capacity to make health care decisions for me, or if I revoke that person's appointment or authority to act as my agent to make health care decisions for me, then I designate and appoint the following person to serve as my agent to make health care decisions for me as authorized in this document, such persons to serve in the order listed below:

A. First Alternate Agent: Roberta Shay, 404 Rose Terrace, Santa Rosa, California (707) 555-9480. [Insert name, address, and telephone number of first alternate agent]

B. Second Alternate Agent: Wilfred O'Goughal, 1106 Mountain View Lane, Fresno, California (209) 555-0311. [Insert name, address and telephone number of second alternate agent]

10. Nomination of Conservator of Person. (A conservator of the person may be appointed for you if a court decides that one should be appointed. The conservator is responsible for your physical care, which under some circumstances includes making health care decisions for you. You aren't required to nominate a conservator but you may do so. The court will appoint the person you nominate unless that would be contrary to your best interest. You may, but aren't required to, nominate as your conservator the same person you named in paragraph 1 as your health care agent. You can nominate an individual as your conservator by completing the space below.)

If a conservator of the person is to be appointed for me, I nominate the following individual to serve as conservator of the person Sharon Weiss, 717 Lake Street, Bolinas, California. [Insert name and address of person nominated as conservator of the person]

11. Prior Designations Revoked. I revoke any prior durable power of attorney for health care.

Date and Signature of Principal
(You must date and sign this power of attorney)

I sign my name to this Statutory Form Durable Power of Attorney for Health Care on August 4, 1989 at Bolinas, California

_____

[Marlene O'Goughal]

(This power of attorney won't be valid unless it's signed by two qualified witnesses who are present when you sign or acknowledge your signature if you have attached any additional pages to this form. You must date and sign each of the additional pages at the same time you date and sign this power of attorney.)

Statement of Witnesses

(This document must be witnessed by two qualified adult witnesses. None of the following may be used as a witness: (1) a person you designated as your agent or alternate agent, (2) a health care provider, (3) an employee of a health care provider, (4) the operator of a community care facility, (5) an employee of an operator of a community care facility. At least one of the witnesses must make the additional declaration set out following the place where the witnesses sign.)

[Read Carefully Before Signing. You can sign as a witness only if you personally know the principal or the identity of the principal is proved to you by convincing evidence.]

(To have convincing evidence of the identity of the principal, you must be presented with and reasonably rely on any one or more of the following:

(1) An identification card or driver's license issued by the California Department of Motor Vehicles that's current or has been issued within five years.

(2) A passport issued by the Department of State of the United States that's current or has been issued within five years.

(3) Any of the following documents if the document is current or has been issued within five years and contains a photograph and description of the person named on it, is signed by the person, and bears a serial or other identifying number:

(a) A passport issued by a foreign government that has been stamped by the United States Immigration and Naturalization Service.

(b) A drivers' license issued by a state other than California or by a Canadian or Mexican public agency authorized to issues drivers' licenses.

(c) An identification card issued by a state other than California.

(d) An identification card issued by any branch of the armed forces of the United States.

(Other kinds of proof of identity aren't allowed.)

I declare under penalty of perjury under the laws of California that the person who signed or acknowledged this document is personally known to me (or proved to me on the basis of convincing evidence) to be the principal, that the principal signed or acknowledged this durable power of attorney in my presence, that the principal appears to be of sound mind and under no duress, fraud, or undue influence, that I'm not the person appointed as attorney in fact by this document, and that I'm not a health care provider, an employee of a health care provider, the operator of a community care facility, or an employee of an operator of a community care facility.

Signature: _____
Resident Address: 758 Lake St., Bolinas, California
Print Name:
Date: August 4, 1989

Signature: _____
Resident Address: 913 Tiffany Street, Alameda, California
Print Name:
Date: August 4, 1989
(At least one of the above witnesses must also sign the following declaration.)

I further declare under penalty of perjury under the laws of California that I'm not related to the principal by blood, marriage, or adoption, and, to the best of my knowledge, I'm not entitled to any part of the estate of the principal upon the death of the principal under a will now existing or by operation of law.

Signature: _____
Signature: _____

Statement of Patient Advocate or Ombudsman

(If you are a patient in a skilled nursing facility, one of the witnesses must be a patient advocate or ombudsman. The following statement is required only if you are a patient in a skilled nursing facility—a health care facility that provides the following basic services: skilled nursing care and supportive care to patients whose primary need is for availability of skilled nursing care on an extended basis. The patient advocate or ombudsman must sign both parts of the

"Statement of Witnesses" above and must also sign the following statement.)

I further declare under penalty of perjury under the laws of California that I'm a patient advocate or ombudsman as designated by the State Department of Aging and that I'm serving as a witness as required by subdivision (f) of Section 2432 of the Civil Code.

Signature: _____

Attorney Certificate

In California, the durable power of attorney for health care warnings aren't required to be included if the durable power of attorney has been prepared by an attorney, and the attorney signs the following certificate as part of the document:

> *I have advised my client concerning his [or her] rights in connection with this durable power of attorney and the law applicable thereto, including, but not limited to, the matters listed in subdivision (a) of Section 2433 of the Civil Code, and the consequences of signing or not signing this durable power of attorney, and my client, after being so advised, has executed this durable power of attorney.*
>
> *Date* _____
>
> *Attorney at Law* _____

Even if an attorney prepares a durable power of attorney for health care, we suggest that the warnings be kept in. There's no harm in including the warnings, and hospitals and other health care providers may look for them.

D. SELF-DELIVERANCE AND THE RIGHT TO A NATURAL DEATH

As we discussed above, you may include a clause allowing the termination of, or refusal to use, life support systems in a durable power of attorney. In addition, many states authorize a "right to a natural death" by use of a "living will" or "directive to physicians." These legal tools don't allow euthanasia or mercy killing. They do, however, allow critically ill people to decline "artificially prolonging life by use of mechanical means." In other words, ill people can choose to live, and die, by natural means, and cannot be forced to use life-preserving machines—such as artificial lungs, heart pumps or dialysis (kidney) machines.

We know of people with AIDS who have wanted to obtain information about "self-deliverance" or suicide as a means of regaining control over the last part of their lives. Attempting suicide is illegal in most states; similarly, it's illegal for friends, family or medical personnel to aid a suicide attempt. So, practical information about self-deliverance is hard to come by. The best source of information we know of is "Let Me Die Before I Wake," the Hemlock's Society's Book of Self-Deliverance For the Dying, by Derek Humphrey (available from The Hemlock Society, P.O. Box 66218, Los Angeles, CA 90044).

We believe it's preferable to handle life support and natural death issues in a durable power of attorney, rather than a living will. A durable power of attorney is valid in all states, and it legally appoints someone to enforce your stated desires. By contrast, a living will is a directive from you to your doctors, and covers only the right to a natural death, not other medical matters. In addition, even in some states where living wills are valid, unless the patient has learned that he or she has a terminal illness, a living will is only a "guide" for a doctor, and your wishes may be ignored.

There's no harm in signing a living will, however, in addition to a durable power of attorney (as long as the two are consistent.) Ask your doctor and hospital to each put a copy in your files, as well as keeping copies for yourself.

Living wills statutes usually contain various restrictions. Check your state's laws, and make sure the document you sign complies with your state's requirements (see Chapter 12 on doing your own legal research). For example, the protections and requirements for a "Directive to Physicians" in California are:

1. Unless the directive has been signed at least 14 days after the patient has been diagnosed and notified as having a terminal condition, it's only advisory and the physician isn't required to comply.

2. The directive must be witnessed by two persons. The witnesses may *not* be

- related to the patient by blood
- beneficiaries to the patient's estate
- persons with a claim on the patient's estate
- the patient's physician
- employees of either the patient's physician or of the facility in which patient is receiving care

If the patient is in a nursing facility, one witness *must* be a "patient advocate" or "ombudsman" designated by the State Department of Aging.

The following is a California Directive to Physicians:

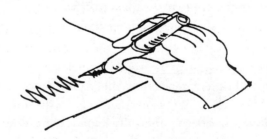

DIRECTIVE TO PHYSICIANS

Directive made this 8th day of March, 1989.

I, Theodore Matthews, being of sound mind, willfully and voluntarily make known my desire that my life shall not be artificially prolonged in the circumstances set forth below, do hereby declare.

1. If at any time I should have an incurable injury, disease, or illness certified to be a terminal condition by two physicians, and where the application of life-sustaining procedures would serve only to artificially prolong the moment of my death and where my physician determines that my death is imminent whether or not life-sustaining procedures are used, I direct that such procedures be withheld or withdrawn, and that I be permitted to die naturally.

2. In the absence of my ability to give directions regarding the use of such life-sustaining procedures, it's my intention that this directive shall be honored by my family and physician(s) as the final expression of my legal right to refuse medical or surgical treatment and accept the consequences of such refusal.

3. If I have been diagnosed as pregnant and that diagnosis is known to my physician, this directive shall have no force or effect during the course of my pregnancy.

4. I have been diagnosed and notified at least 14 days ago as having a terminal condition by Lawrence Daniels, M.D., whose address is 4506 Market Street, Sausalito, California, and whose telephone number is (415) 555-8300. I understand that if I haven't filled in the physician's name and address, it shall be presumed that I didn't have a terminal condition when I made out this directive.

5. I understand the full import of this directive and I am emotionally and mentally competent to make this directive.

6. This directive shall have no force or effect five years from the date filled in below.

Signed: _____

City, county, and state of residence: Mill Valley, Marin County, California

The declarant has been personally known to me and I believe him or her to be of sound mind.

Dated: _____   Witness _____
                                            Andrew Jones

Dated: _____   Witness _____
                                            Marcia Montgomery

E. ESTATE PLANNING NOTE

In preparing for a possible medical emergency, consider what will happen to your property after you die. This is what lawyers call "estate planning," and it's particularly important for seriously ill people. After someone dies, his property is transferred either by his "estate planning documents," e.g., a will, living trust, etc., or by-laws imposed by his state. No other method is possible. A durable power of attorney ceases to be effective after the principal dies, so the attorney in fact can't transfer the property, and even while the principal is alive, an "attorney in fact" doesn't have the power to make a will or estate plan for the principal.

In addition, without estate planning documents, your lover has no rights concerning your affairs after you die. Your lover can't receive any of your property, decide how it's disposed of, or arrange for your burial and body disposition (unless you've made written instructions).

All these dire consequences can be avoided by proper estate planning, which we discuss in Chapter 9. Here we want to stress how important estate planning can be. If you do nothing else, at least prepare a will, so you, not your state's laws, determine who gets your property.

F. BURIAL AND BODY DISPOSITION

Burial and body disposition is another potential problem for the survivors of someone whose medical emergency results in death. We know of a biological family who claimed the body of a person who died from AIDS and refused to give the service and disposition the deceased wanted. Instead, they gave their own, which conflicted drastically with the deceased's spiritual values. We even know a surviving lover who was excluded entirely from a burial service. These tragedies can be avoided by proper planning and advance discussions, so lovers, friends and biological families know what's wanted.

Written Instructions: After death, a body must be disposed of quickly. If you haven't left written instructions, nearly every state gives control to your blood relatives—your lover or friend can be frozen out if your family is hostile. Your durable power of attorney is of no help because it terminates when you die. In most states, however, written body disposition instructions are binding. (But do check your state's laws if this concerns you.) Written instructions allow you to state your wishes and name someone to carry them out. Your will is a standard place to include these instructions, but you can also make a separate document, or do both. Either way, the instructions aren't complicated. Here are two examples:

- I have made arrangements with the Tri-City Funeral Society regarding my funeral and burial. I appoint Alfred Gwynne to be responsible for implementing these arrangements regarding my death.
- I've made the following arrangements regarding my death:

1. I've made an agreement under the Uniform Anatomical Gift Act with Hillman Hospital, San Francisco, California, to donate any of my organs or body parts needed by the hospital;

2. After any such donation, I direct that my remains be cremated, and my ashes scattered at sea. I have made written arrangements with the Nicean Society regarding my cremation.

3. I direct that Anna Rodriguez, my good friend and executor, be solely responsible for insuring that these instructions are carried out.

If you anticipate objections from your family, make sure your instructions are in your will and that any separate document has been notarized.

Choices Regarding Disposition of the Body: You have a number of choices, including esoteric ones like cryonics (body-freezing with the hope of being brought back to life sometime later). The major ones are:

- A traditional funeral by a commercial funeral parlor, which often includes embalming and open-casket viewing of the body.
- A funeral through a funeral society cooperative. These exist in many states and are devoted to low-cost funerals/burials and simple, dignified memorial services.
- Cremation, either through a specialized cremation company (irreverently dubbed "burn and scatter outfits" in the trade), or a commercial funeral parlor or funeral society.
- Donation of your body to a medical school.
- Donation of body parts and organs to hospitals or organ banks.

Note: People with AIDS cannot donate body parts and organs to hospitals and organ banks. They can often, however, donate their bodies to a medical school.

For decades, funerals and burials were controlled by commercial funeral parlors, which were both secretive and expensive. The business of funerals first came under attack in the 1960s, especially through Jessica Mitford's fine book *The American Way of Death*.[8] Since then, reforms have been instituted in most states. Today it's usually possible to find good funeral services at a reasonable price if you ask knowledgeable friends for recommendations, and monitor costs closely.

---

[8]Other good books on the subject are Harmer, *The High Cost of Dying*, and Consumer Reports, *Funerals: Americans' Last Rights*.

In our opinion, there's something unnecessary—both in cost and dignity—about embalming and open-casket viewing. We subscribe to the beliefs of funeral societies that funeral/burial costs should be kept low, and that a "memorial service" is more meaningful than looking at an embalmed body. But we certainly know people who believe that viewing an embalmed body helps them emotionally. The choice is yours. What's important is to consider your options and make a deliberate decision.

We don't have space to give you an exhaustive rundown on each alternative, but here are a few significant points:

- Embalming is generally not legally required.
- Commercial funerals can easily cost many thousands of dollars. Price competition, however, has come to the commercial funeral business, after years of effective price fixing. So, again, find out who does a good job in your area, and don't be afraid to compare prices. Compare the services offered too, and check the prices non-profit funeral societies charge for similar services.
- Funeral societies are cooperatives run (at least theoretically) by their members. They exist in most major urban areas. Membership fees are minimal, about $15 to $25. Most funeral societies don't handle funerals or burials themselves, but have contractual arrangements with cooperating local funeral parlors to provide inexpensive services to their members.
- Donation of your body to medical school requires an arrangement with a specific medical school or coordinator. In many areas, there's no pressing need for bodies. In all of California, for example, only about 1,000 bodies are needed a year.
- Donation of body parts is a much more pressing need. Thousands of people in this country are kept alive by dialysis machines while waiting months or years for a kidney transplant. Other organs are needed—eyes, heart tissues, even knee parts have been transplanted. Some states have adopted the "Uniform Anatomical Gift Act." It allows you to authorize the donation of body parts simply by carrying a short, signed donor's card with you. It's useful, though, to arrange with a hospital or organ bank to receive, and use, your donation. Incidentally, bodies donated to medical schools are normally not returned for funerals. Bodies from which organs have been transplanted normally are.
- Cremations have increased over the past few years. Cremation—as we imagine most people known—is the burning of the body, followed by the inurnment or scattering of the ashes. The details vary depending upon state law. Some states allow ashes to be scattered over private land; other states forbid it. Cremations are offered by many

commercial funeral parlors, funeral societies and by organizations such as the Neptune Society or Telephase, which specialize in providing low-cost cremations.

• Many funeral/burial businesses have couple rates, allowing a couple to pay for services in advance. We know of a business which refused to give its couple rate to a gay couple. This is another form of discrimination that's still legal. Otherwise, we haven't heard of discrimination against lesbian/gays in the funeral business, though some funeral parlors have refused to handle the bodies of people who died from AIDS. (Support your local gay undertaker!)

-9-

LOOKING (WAY) AHEAD: ESTATE[1] PLANNING

A. INTRODUCTION[2]

No one looks forward to the day when they will depart this earth; actually making plans for that inevitable time can seem dull, even macabre. But it's vitally important that lesbians and gays—especially those who are coupled—plan what they want to happen to their property after they die. Generally, if you die without a will (or any of the other legal means for disposing of your property, such as establishing a living trust or placing your property in joint tenancy), your property will be distributed under your state's "intestacy" laws. These laws require that *all* your property pass to certain specified relatives, namely a spouse, children, parents, and siblings.

We've heard quite a few horror stories involving people's families suddenly swooping down on the surviving lover to claim all the deceased person's property. An article in Christopher Street Magazine described the plight of one gay man whose lover died and left no will. The deceased's family quickly appeared and started removing property from the couple's apartment. "His

---

[1]Estate in this context refers generally to all your property.
[2]Much of the information in this chapter has been adopted from *Plan Your Estate: Wills, Probate Avoidance, Trusts and Taxes* (Nolo Press) by Denis Clifford.

mother took the pillows and pillowcases off the bed," the lover said. "I ended up having to fight for my own clothes. We wore the same size."

Because state death laws don't recognize lesbian or gay "marriages" or relationships, estate planning is particularly important for lesbian and gay couples. If you want to be sure that certain property will actually, and legally, be transferred to your lover, you must arrange that transfer by a proper legal device (will, living trust, etc.). A living together contract, by itself, is not enough. Why? Because the function of a living together contract is to define how a couple owns property while both partners are alive. It's not a safe substitute for a will or living trust, documents which validly and legally specify what happens to each person's property after he or she dies.

If no estate planning has been done, a surviving member of a lesbian or gay couple can try to obtain her deceased lover's property by arguing—or litigating— that a living together agreement, even an oral agreement, gives her rights in that property. But it's far from certain that this kind of claim would succeed. You might well have to sue, which will be time-consuming, expensive and nasty. The safe path is for each partner to specify, in an appropriate legal document, what happens to his or her property after death. If there could be any uncertainty regarding what property each partner owns, that, of course, should be resolved in a clearly-defined living together contract.

Deciding what you want done with your property after you die isn't the only benefit of estate planning. If you're a single parent, you can nominate a guardian for your child. Further, you can appoint the person you want to be responsible for supervising the distribution of your property. You can also summarize your funeral/body disposition wishes, or specify that the arrangements are to be made by your lover; if you do neither, your blood relatives have legal authority to make that decision.

This chapter presents two approaches to estate planning for lesbian and gay couples. Section C discusses wills, and contains a sample form you can use or adapt for drafting your own. At a minimum, we advise every reader of this book to prepare a will; this will ensure that your property is legally transferred to whomever you want to have it after you die.

Section D presents information on more extensive estate planning. Transferring all your property by a will can have drawbacks, principally probate. Probate is a legal proceeding where your will is filed with a court, your assets identified, your debts paid, and then your property distributed to your inheritors. Probate usually involves substantial attorney's and other fees, and long delay. By planning ahead, you can often eliminate the need for probate, and sometimes save on death taxes as well. Section D should help you to decide whether your estate planning can sensibly end with a will, or whether more is warranted. For now, it's enough for you to know that if you have a "small" estate (roughly, under $50,000) it may not be worth the bother to do more than prepare a will.

Before we plunge into particulars of wills and financial estate planning, let us acknowledge that giving attention to the practical consequences of death, while important, seems quite minor when compared to the misery, grief and tragedy of the death of a loved one. We share the thoughts of a friend who lost his lover of nearly three decades.

B. Reflections on the Death of a Mate

Recognizing that one individual's reactions to death are no basis for generalization, I offer the following only as a personal response to a question about the feelings a survivor experiences when an abiding homosexual relationship is ended by the death of one of the partners. My only qualification for doing so lies in being such a survivor after a mutual love of nearly thirty years. From what I perceive through observation, through literature, or by intuition, I strongly suspect that, except for easier distribution of property in a legally binding relationship, there may not be great differences of impact for the survivor whether the love has been homosexual or heterosexual. The death of a mate obviously leaves one emotionally and, in the case of a long illness, physically spent. What are the significant feelings that survive after the initial shock of finality has exhausted itself in the busy-work that ensues around the affairs of the decedent? Despair isn't quite one of them, for if a close relationship has endured two or three decades, each partner has already recognized and yielded to the necessity for mutual independence and steadfast self-reliance. Nonetheless, there's a transient sense of cosmic inquiry: "What am I doing here?" which may easily deteriorate to, "What am I doing anywhere?" But the daily business of living—and it may seem a business without profit—does supersede such disorientation.

The feelings that continue, and which most poignantly harbor the pain, can be identified, I believe, as essentially two. The first of these is the piercing loneliness of having no focus for one's affection after so long a time. The emptiness of not loving is an infinite void, and it summons the most painful recognition of loss. Such feelings, however, though perpetual, aren't near the surface and reveal themselves most forcefully in what seems to be the dullness of leisure or in the sadness of reflection.

Lying nearer the surface are the daily—sometimes hourly, for a little while perhaps constant—reminders that feed the second and more persistent pain, one that will never be totally consumed. Couples inevitably develop their own language, visual as well as verbal, based on shared experiences, shared jokes, mutual acceptance of difficulty, shared joys and sorrows, reciprocal devotion. Layers are thereby added to the relationship much as alluvial deposits are washed down to enrich life's texture in a less psychologically ornamented environment. The survivor continues to use that language, for it's a part of him, although he now lacks an auditor who grasps its overtones, undertones, and essential meanings. When those symbols, and the figure in the carpet which they represent, appear—whether verbally, cerebrally, or viscerally—and no one's there to recognize an allusion, to be counted on for sympathetic amusement at one's own folly, to recognize an earlier situation now cryptically cited to give sharpened meaning to the present, the vacancy is felt as the ebbing away of an adult lifetime.

For those of us who aren't artists, the structure which houses those symbols may be the closest we shall ever come to the creation of poetry. Like poetry, the form of communication and its underlying history make up an economical construct of imagery that distills experience. To borrow a verb from Gerard Manley Hopkins, the distillation "explodes" as mutual recognition, as ineffable joy, as reciprocal contemplativeness—in short, as the impact of art. The irreversible decay of the only context in which the construct obtained, and in which a man's life has been elevated out of the limitations of self-concern into felicitous union, is what I perceive to be the basis of grief. Although the "grief returns with the revolving year," it is, in the fullness of time, merged into a sense of one's own good fortune, into the joyful remembrances of things past, and into an appreciation for what the relationship still contributes to one's future.

C. Wills

Most all of us know what a will is—a document where you specify who gets your property when you die. The main advantages of a will are that it's relatively easy to make, and that you can leave your property to anyone you wish. No laws prohibit you from leaving your property to a gay or lesbian lover (or anyone else, for that matter). Also, it's easy to change or revoke your will; you're not stuck with it once you make it. Furthermore, your will is your own business. Discussing it with your lover is probably a good idea, but you're not required to reveal its contents to anyone.

As we stated in the introduction, the one considerable drawback to using a will is probate.[3] So, after reading Section D, you may decide to arrange to avoid probate. Even if you come to that conclusion, you should still make a will. First, you may have property at your death that you hadn't thought of, or known of, when planning your estate, such as a suddenly-inherited house, a gift of an expensive stereo or computer from your lover, big winnings at the races, a personal injury lawsuit recovery, etc. If you have a will, you can simply pass all "newly acquired" property to your lover (or whomever you choose). And, as we've said, a will is the place to name who will supervise your property and to specify funeral arrangements and nominate a guardian for your minor child, or children, if you have them.

Once you decide what property you want to transfer by will, prepare the paperwork promptly. There are no benefits to postponing the drafting of your will, and doing so risks the consequences of an untimely death, i.e., your property going to your blood relatives, as defined by your state legislature, rather than going to the person(s) you would have chosen.

Now let's look at some concerns of lesbians and gays about wills. Afterwards, we present a sample will with accompanying explanations so you can prepare your own.

1. Can I Make a Legally Binding Will?

Yes. Anyone who's legally an adult[4] and "of sound mind" can make a valid will. The will form in this book can be used by residents of all states except Louisiana, which has a different legal system (one derived from French law) than those of the other states. If you live in Louisiana, you'll need to see a lawyer to prepare your will.

A person has to be pretty far gone before an otherwise valid will can be upset on the grounds that the maker wasn't "of sound mind." If you're reading this book, you're competent to draft your will. And we firmly believe that basic wills, sufficient for many people's situations, can readily be prepared without the assistance, and cost, of a lawyer. If you have a large estate and desire extensive estate planning (complicated trusts, "pour-over" wills—that sort of thing), you'll need to have your will prepared by a lawyer. But if you have a moderate estate

---

[3]One possible exception: many states provide simplified probate, or require no probate at all, for small estates, often between $5,000 and $60,000. These laws are summarized in *Plan Your Estate: Wills, Probate Avoidance, Trusts and Taxes.*

[4]As defined by state law. It is 18 or younger in all states, except Georgia, where you must be 19 to leave real estate in a will.

and envision a straightforward distribution, you can very likely prepare your own will. Lawyers try to scare people into buying their expensive services by claiming that each will requires "expert, professional attention," then routinely have their secretaries use the same formbook wills, over and over and over again.

Caution: If you have relatives who vehemently object to your being lesbian or gay (and especially if you have a considerable amount of money), it's possible, though not likely, that if you leave your property to your lover (or, say, a gay freedom foundation), those relatives will challenge your will on grounds that you were incompetent, or under "undue influence," when you made your will. Although will contests are rare, there have been a number of legal challenges to AIDS patients' wills. Anyone diagnosed with AIDS should promptly prepare a will, to minimize the chances that the will could be successfully challenged on the grounds the will writer wasn't mentally competent when the will was signed.

In general, it's wise to be careful and cautious about your will. If you think there's any reasonable possibility that some relation will challenge your will, take action now to establish that you are competent and not under undue influence when you signed your will. If worse comes to worst, this evidence can be used in court after your death.

One possibility is to have your will prepared and signed in a "respectable" lawyer's office, before a lawyer who can testify that you were obviously competent. Another possibility is to write your will yourself and then pay a lawyer only for review and the final, ceremonial signing. If you're truly concerned about a challenge, explore various possibilities. Consult a lesbian/gay attorney service which can provide lawyers experienced with will contests. (In some cities, including San Francisco and Los Angeles, there's even a "Wills on Wheels" service, which sends lawyers to hospitals in emergencies); or consider using a lawyer who's familiar with videotaping, so when you sign your will, you can look into the camera and tell the world how sane you are; or follow the approach of a lawyer with a large lesbian and gay clientele who advises her clients to insert a clause like the following which shows you considered leaving your property to your relatives:

> *I don't make my gifts to Ben Tymons out of any lack of love for my parents, sister, brother, Aunt Susan, Uncle Jonathan, cousin Cynthia, cousin Harold or other relatives, but rather because I specifically wish to benefit my friend, Ben, who has been a source of great love and comfort to me over many years.*

If you're caring for someone with AIDS dimentia, have a doctor document (in his file) that he was competent on the day he signed his will.

2. Can I Really Do What I Want With My Property in My Will?

Yes. Some of the important things you can accomplish in a will include:

- leaving property to any beneficiaries you name; you have great freedom in leaving property to beneficiaries. You can leave anything you own to anyone[5] or any institution you choose. You can leave money, book royalties, clothes or your cat. And you never have to state your relationship to the beneficiary—it's no one's business.

You're not required to hold onto property while you're alive just because it's left to someone in your will. If in your will you left your Renoir painting to your friend Bob, but sell the painting before you die, Bob's out of luck.

- forgiving debts owed to you.
- disinheriting anyone you want.[6] Just as you may leave anything to anyone, you can leave nothing to anyone. You can disinherit anyone you want to, simply by not mentioning them in your will, except there are different rules for your children (or children of a deceased child) and a spouse (in common law states). You must take more affirmative steps to disinherit a child (or children of a deceased child). There are two ways to do this. One, you can state the disinheritance expressly in your will. For example, "I disinherit my son William Jones and direct

---

[5]There are a few exceptions. For example, some states don't allow certain felons to inherit property.

[6]Except in some states, you can't completely disinherit a spouse—a problem few of our readers should face. If that issue does concern you, see *Plan Your Estate: Wills, Probate Avoidance, Trusts and Taxes.*

that he receive nothing from my estate." Two, you can leave a child a minimal sum by your will, which works as a functional disinheritance.

There are state laws designed to prevent the accidental disinheritance of children, called "pretermitted heirs." These laws provide that if you fail to mention a child (or child of a deceased child) in your will, that child receives a set percentage of your estate. To be sure you haven't violated these laws, the will forms in this chapter ask you to name each of your children (and children of a deceased child), and then specifies that you leave each of them $1.00, in addition to any other property you leave them. So, if you want to disinherit a child (or child of a deceased child) using a will prepared from the form in this book, simply leave that child $1.00, and no more. If you want to use an express disinheritance clause, you'll find samples in *Nolo's Simple Will Book*.

- suggesting a personal guardian for your minor children.
- naming a property guardian to manage your minor children's property.
- setting up simple trusts to delay when a beneficiary gets the property (this can be wise if you have young kids).
- naming the person who will supervise the distribution of your property left by your will; this person is called your "executor," or, in some states, your "personal representative." You can name your lover, or anyone you trust, to be your executor. Some states require that a bond be posted if your executor doesn't live in the state; so it is a good idea to name an executor who lives in the same state you do.

3. What Are the Technical Requirements to Prepare a Valid Will?

There are few technical requirements you must comply with in preparing a valid will. If you do all of the following, your will is valid in every state except Louisiana. (As we previously stated, because Louisiana law is derived from French law, it functions differently than the laws of the other states. To prepare a will in Louisiana, you'll need to see a lawyer.) Your will:

- must be typed (or partially typed and partially printed)
- must state that it's your will ("this is the will of (your name)" suffices)
- must be signed and dated by the will writer, who must declare to three witnesses[7] at the time of the signing that it's his or her will.

---

[7] In many states, only two witnesses are required. Using a third, however, can't hurt and means the will is valid in all states.

(Some authorities recommend the will writer say, "This is my will," and the witnesses answer, "He says it's his will." It sounds like Gilbert and Sullivan.) The witnesses have to know the document is a will, but aren't expected (or required) to read it.

- must be witnessed by three witnesses who won't receive anything under the will. The witnesses sign and date the will after watching you, the will writer, sign and date it.

4. What About Handwritten Wills?

In some states, "holographic" (handwritten) wills are valid. In others, they're not. Whatever your state's rule, it's preferable to have your will typed and witnessed, rather than handwritten (and unwitnessed). Even in states which allow holographic wills, they often receive suspicious treatment by courts; they must be letter-perfect and can't have any cross-outs, machine-printed dates, etc. If you're trapped in the woods and the wolves are coming to get you, write out a will (if you haven't previously prepared a valid one) and say your prayers. Under normal circumstances, prepare a formal (typed) will, and have it properly signed and witnessed.

5. What About Joint Wills?

A joint will is one document through which two people leave their property. After the first person dies, the joint will specifies what happens to the property of the second person when she dies. We don't recommend joint wills; the survivor, we believe, should have the freedom to dispose of his or her property. If you're thinking of using a joint will (despite our recommendation), see a lawyer. This type of will can be tricky.

6. What Happens If I Move to a New State After I've Made My Will?

If you use the form in this book, your will is valid in any state, except, as we said, in Louisiana. You might want to draft a new will after a permanent move, however, if your executor now resides in a different state and you have a good candidate (perhaps your lover) who resides in your new state of residence. To accomplish this change, you can revoke your will and write a new one, or add a "codicil" changing your executor (see "Changing Your Will," later in this chapter).

7. Will Clauses For a Basic Will

The clauses found in the form that follows can be used by most lesbians or gay men with a moderate-sized estate to prepare a basic will. The actual will clauses are printed on left-hand pages; explanatory comments are on right-hand pages. The comments correspond to the will provisions by clause number.

Prepare and Type Your Will Neatly and Carefully: After you've read this chapter and have formed your overall estate plan, prepare a rough draft of your will, using or adapting the will form we provide. Once you're satisfied you've covered everything, type the will carefully on 8 1/2" x 11" white typing paper. Get your witnesses together and date and sign the will at the end—you don't have to sign each page. Store the original (signed) will in a safe place you share with your lover. You can make copies of the will, but *don't* sign them. If you do, they become additional "originals;" if you later decide to change your will, you will have to change each original.

It's legal, though never advisable, to make alterations on the face of your will prior to your and the witness' signing by crossing something out and initialing the change. Don't do this. Instead, type a new will. Once your will has been witnessed, you can't cross out a provision or add a new one. You must amend or revoke your will in a formal manner (see the next section).

Important: If your will doesn't comply with the technical requirements (for example, you have only one witness), the court will toss it out and your property will pass to your blood relatives. A will's not hard to do correctly. But check and double-check to be sure you do!

When preparing your will, complete only the sections of the form that pertain to you. For instance, if you were never married and have no children, delete Clause II, "Prior Marriage and Children." Then you have to renumber the remaining clauses. Thus, clause "III: Gifts" would become "II: Gifts." And, in general, use plain language and common sense. If you write "I leave my car to my sister Sue," she will receive whatever car you own when you die. If you write, "I leave my Toyota to my sister Sue," and sell it before you die and buy a Porsche, Sue gets no car. Courts try to give effect to the "intent" of the will writer, but they can't contradict clear words.

Note on More Complex Wills: The will form here is basic; you can leave your property to whomever you want to have it and name a guardian for your minor children. Many complexities are not covered. For example, there are no provisions for stating how you want death taxes paid.[8] Nor can you establish a

---

[8]We discuss death taxes in Section C.

children's trust to delay the age when minor children inherit past 18. If your situation warrants a more complex will than what we provide, consult a lawyer, or Nolo's other will-preparation resources, *Nolo's Simple Will Book* or *WillMaker*, a computer program which allows you to write your own will (good in all states but Louisiana) on many Apple, IBM, IBM-compatible and Commodore personal computers. For more information, see the back of this book.

WILL OF [YOUR NAME]

I, [your name], a resident of [your county] County, [your state], declare that this is my will.

I. Revocation

I revoke all wills and codicils that I have previously made.

II. Prior Marriages and Children

A. I was married to [name of former spouse] and am now divorced.

B. I have [number] children now living, whose names and dates of birth are:

Name	Date of Birth

(repeat as often as needed)

I have the following children of my deceased child ____(name)____ .

Name	Date of Birth

(repeat as often as needed)

The terms "my children" as used in this will shall include any other children hereafter born to or adopted by me.

C. If at my death any of my children are minors, and a guardian is needed, I recommend that ____(name)____ be appointed guardian of the persons of my minor children, and I appoint ____(name)____ as property guardian of my minor children.

III. Gifts

A. I make the following gifts of money or personal property:

1. I give every child or grandchild listed in Clause II $1.00 (one dollar) in addition to any other property I may give them elsewhere in this will, or otherwise.

2. I give the sum of $ [amount] to [name] if [he/she/it] survives me by 60 days; if [he/she/it] doesn't, this gift shall be made to [name].

(repeat as often as needed)

3. I give [identify item of property] to [name] if [he/she/it] survives me by 60 days; if [he/she/it] doesn't, the gift shall be made to [name].

(repeat as often as needed)

4. I forgive and cancel the debt of $ [amount] owed to me by [name].

(repeat as often as needed)

B. I make the following gifts of real estate:

1. I give my real estate in [county] [state], commonly known as [address and street], to [name] if [he/she/it] survives me for 60 days. If [he/she/it] doesn't survive me for 60 days, that property shall be given to [name.]

(repeat as often as needed)

IV. Residue

I give the residue of my property subject to this will as follows:

A. To [name], if [he/she/it] survives me by 60 days;

B. If not, to [name] if [he/she/it] survives me by 60 days;

C. If neither [name in 1] nor [name in 2] survives me by 60 days, then to [name].

V. Executor

A. I nominate [name] as executor of this will, to serve without bond. If [name] shall for any reason fail to qualify or cease to act as executor, I nominate [name] to serve without bond.

B. I grant to my executor the right to place my obituary of [her/his] choosing in the papers [she/he] thinks appropriate.

VI. No Contest

If any person or persons named to receive any of my property under my will, in any manner contests or attacks this will or any of its provisions, that person or persons shall be disinherited and shall receive none of my property, and my property shall be disposed of as if that contesting beneficiary had died before me leaving no children.

VII. Funeral/Burial Arrangements

I have made funeral arrangements with [name of organization]. I also direct that _____

_____.

and I direct my executor to take all steps necessary to carry out my funeral/burial arrangements.

VIII. Simultaneous Death

If [name of lover] and I should die simultaneously, or under such circumstances as to render it difficult or impossible to determine who predeceased the other, I shall be conclusively presumed to have survived [name] for purposes of this will.

I subscribe my name to this will this [day] of [month], [year], at [city, county], [state].

[your full name]

IX. Signature and Witnessing

On this [day] of [month], [year], [your full name] declared to us, the undersigned, that this instrument was [his/her] will, and requested us to act as witnesses to it. [He/she] thereupon signed this will in our presence, all of us being present at the time. We now, at [his/her] request, in [his/her] presence, and in the presence of each other, subscribe our names as witnesses and declare we understand this to be [his/her] will, and that to the best of our knowledge the testator is competent to make a will, and under no constraint or undue influence.

_____   _____
Witness's Signature   Address

_____   _____
Witness's Signature   Address

_____   _____
Witness's Signature   Address

Your Name and Address

Use your full name and use it the same way throughout the will.

If you had connections with two states, each may try to impose state estate taxes. Giving your residence will help minimize this, and should help establish in which county your will is to be probated. (It's probated in the county where you made your home.) If you have real ties to these states, see a lawyer to be sure both won't try to impose death taxes.

I. Revocation

This clause applies to and covers all prior wills, including any hand written document that could possibly be construed as a will.

II. Prior Marriages and Children

Fill in this section only if you've ever been married, or have children. If you've been married, mention the marriage(s) and that it ended (obviously, we're assuming it has). In referring to your children, list all of them, and include children of any child of yours who is deceased (i.e., your grandchildren by a deceased child). As previously mentioned, if you wish to "disinherit" a child using this will form, name that child and leave him or her only the $1.00 given in Clause III(A)(1).

If you have custody of minor children, you can nominate a personal guardian for those children in Section II(C). Also, in this section, you can name a property guardian for your minor children; this property guardian will supervise any property you leave your children and can supervise any other property they acquire before they become 18.

Lesbian and gay parents are usually very concerned with who will get custody of their minor children when they die. State laws strongly favor granting custody to a surviving natural parent over everyone else. Many divorced gay parents want their lovers, not their ex-spouses, to have custody. But the law is clear. Parents cannot "will" their children. When there is no surviving competent parent, custody of a child whose parent dies is decided by a judge. However, a parent can nominate a person in their will to take custody, and if there is no competent natural parent in the picture, the person nominated as guardian has a very good chance of obtaining custody. Or, to say this same thing slightly differently, while you can't "will" your child, your wishes will usually be accorded considerable respect by a court if the other legal parent doesn't take custody. For more information on wills and custody of minor children, see *Nolo's Simple Will Book.*

Minor's Trusts: Many parents want to delay their children's inheritance until they reach an age older than 18, the age when they become legal adults and are normally entitled to receive outright property left them by will. Usually, the best way to delay the age minors receive property is by use of a minor's trust. In the trust document, the parent specifies the age the minor must reach before she receives the trust property, and names the trustee, the adult who will manage the trust property until the minor reaches that age. The trust document also sets forth the terms of the trust, e.g., that trust income can be used for the minor's education, etc. Nolo's *WillMaker* software allows you to create a will with a children's trust on your home computer, and *Nolo's Simple Will Book* includes children's trusts in its will forms.

III A. Gifts of Money or Personal Property

Section A allows you to name your beneficiaries for your money and personal property (i.e., everything but real estate which you give away in Section B). This clause is appropriate for direct, unconditional gifts to a single beneficiary, either a person or organization. If you want to make a gift to be shared by two or more beneficiaries, see Nolo's other will resources, or a lawyer. And, if you want to place conditions on a gift, you'll need to see a lawyer.

If you give monetary gifts, you might want to add to the bequest "but in no event more than [number] percent of my (net or probate) estate" just in case there's not as much there as you'd planned.

You can also state what happens to property if the beneficiary for it doesn't survive you by naming an alternate beneficiary. If you don't provide for that, and the beneficiary predeceases you, this will form provides that the property becomes part of the "residue" (see clause IV).

Many people don't want to leave something to someone who will never benefit from it, so they require the beneficiary to survive them by some specified period of time. This will form requires the beneficiary to survive you by 60 days in order to receive the property. You can specify any other reasonable period you want, such as 30 or 100 days (two years isn't reasonable).

If you're giving specific items of property, especially major items, describe them with sufficient detail so that there can be no question as to what property is meant. If you also have a lot of minor personal items, however, and don't want to list them all, you can state, for example, that I give "all my furniture (or my tools or my records) to [name]." Or, for minor pieces of personal property, you can insert an additional clause stating that these items "are to be distributed as my executor deems proper."

In Section III(A)(4), you can also forgive debts owed you. Forgiving a debt is one way to make a gift, to the debtor.

III B. Gifts of Real Estate

Here, as with other gifts, you name a beneficiary. You can also name an alternate beneficiary if you wish to. And, if the beneficiary (and alternate beneficiary, if you name one) doesn't survive you, the real estate goes to your residuary beneficiary).

If you want to give real estate free of a mortgage, see one of Nolo's other will resources.

Again, it's wise to include a survivorship period, and to name an alternate beneficiary to take if the primary beneficiary doesn't survive the 60-day period.

IV. Residue

The "residue" in your will is exactly what it sounds like—all property subject to your will that remains after all the specific gifts made in paragraph III have been distributed. Again, you can select any person or organization you want to receive the "residue" of your estate. It's prudent to name two separate back-ups as alternate beneficiaries for your residue. Some people leave the bulk of their estate to their residuary beneficiary.

V. Executor

As discussed, your executor should be someone you trust and can rely on, and who will be available and competent when you die. You should name at least one successor executor in case your original choice dies before you, declines to serve or is incompetent when you die. (If a will names no executor, the probate court appoints one.)

If you don't state that the executor is "to serve without bond," the probate court will probably require the executor to post a bond (a sum of money). This means that either a large amount of cash from the estate is tied up, or the estate must pay a bondsman's fee (usually 10% of the amount of the bond).

If you name an out-of-state executor, the court may require a bond, even if you stated "to serve without bond."

VI. No Contest

Clearly, this clause is designed to discourage will contests. We have not included any general disinheritance clause, or a clause giving $1 to all nieces and nephews, etc. As discussed, child(ren) are special cases and can be disinherited specifically if that's your wish. There's no need to specifically exclude other people; most will drafters and contemporary will formbooks omit a general disinheritance clause.

VII. Funeral/Burial Arrangements

In most states, a will provision declaring what's to be done with the body is given immediate effect, even if the will isn't otherwise valid. You should insert any specific directions you have regarding your funeral/burial. For example, if you've made a provision for your body, or parts, to be given to a scientific or medical institution, specify that here.

VIII. Simultaneous Death

People often wonder what happens if they die at the same time as their lover or other beneficiary. Most states have adopted the Uniform Simultaneous Death Act. This law presumes that when two people die together (e.g., car crash or plane wreck) and it's impossible to know who died first, the beneficiary is presumed to have died first. This way, the will writer's property passes to his or her alternate beneficiaries, and not to the briefly surviving lover and then to the lover's beneficiaries. If you name alternate beneficiaries with survivorship periods, this shouldn't be a problem, But in any case, it doesn't hurt to include this provision in your will, even if your state has adopted the Uniform Simultaneous Death Act, and you have named alternate beneficiaries.

If you own property in joint tenancy, and you and the other joint tenant died simultaneously, you're presumed to have died last. Thus your share passes through your will (in this will, through your residuary clause) and the other joint tenant's share passes in her/his will.

If you own insurance, and you and the beneficiary die simultaneously, the proceeds of the policy are distributed as if the beneficiary had died before you.

IX. Signature and Witnessing

Sign and date your will in front of your three witnesses, who then sign the witness clause in front of each other. (Please re-read the material in Section C(1) of this chapter about the will-signing ceremony.)

In many states, wills can be witnessed by what's called a "self-proving affidavit," which can simplify or even eliminate witnesses' need to go to court after the will writer dies. Explanations of self-proving affidavits and sample forms are set forth in *Nolo's Simple Will Book* and *WillMaker*.

8. Storing and Copying Your Will

Store your will in a safe place, one that your executor has ready access to. If you want to store your will in a safety deposit box, be sure your executor will have ready access to your will when you die. Check to be sure the bank will allow him or her access, and that there are no state laws requiring safety deposit boxes to be sealed upon death of an owner.

You can make copies of your will for any person you want to have one. But do not sign any copies directly (photocopies made of your signature on your original will are okay). The reason for this is to prevent any possibility of duplicate wills, which can cause trouble later, especially if you subsequently amend your will.

9. After Your Will Is Drafted

Changing Your Will: Suppose you want to make a minor change in your will. For example, Mary died, and your library of lesbian fiction that you were going to leave her you now want to leave to Martha. Do you have to redo your entire will? Or suppose you make a drastic change (you and your lover just split up). How can you change or revoke your will? Does this require an entirely new will? Do you have to have the original witnesses present? Obviously, anyone who drafts a will should know how to change or revoke it.

When you should change your will is a matter of common sense. Impromptu changes are obviously not desirable. You can't just ink out a provision or a gift in your will. Changes must be made formally, as we discuss below.

The term describing the form used to make legal changes to a will is "codicil." A codicil is an addition, amendment or alteration to a will after the will has been drafted, signed and witnessed. A codicil is a sort of legal "P.S." to a will and must be executed with the same formalities of a will. Practically, this means that it should be typed on the last page of the will itself, or on an additional page or pages. The codicil must be dated and signed by the will writer and three witnesses.[9] Codicils are usually used for minor matters, like the change of the beneficiary for the lesbian fiction library in the example above. For major revisions, a codicil isn't advisable. Why? Because a will that has been substantially rewritten by a codicil is confusing, awkward to read, and may not clearly state the relationship of the codicil to the original will. For major revisions, draft a new will; the first provision "I revoke all wills and codicils that I have previously made," will revoke your earlier will and any codicils to it.

A codicil should be titled—e.g., "First Codicil of the Will of [your name], dated [date of your will]." The following is a sample you can use or adapt to make a codicil:

A copy of your codicil should be added to each copy of your will. This may be a nuisance, but can prevent confusion and conflict later.

---

[9]They don't have to be the ones who witnessed the will, but try to use them if they're available.

First Codicil to the Will of [your name], dated [date of your will]

I, [your name], a resident of [name of county] County, [name of state], declare this to be the first codicil to my will dated [date of your will].

First: I revoke Section [number] of Paragraph [roman numeral], and substitute the following: (Add whatever new provision is desired.)

Second: I add the following new Section [number] to Paragraph [roman numeral]: (Add whatever is desired.)

Third: In all other respects I confirm and republish my will dated date of your will], this [day] day of [month], [year], at [county], [state].

_____

[your full name]

On the date written below, [your full name] declared to us, the undersigned, that this instrument, consisting of [number] pages, including this page signed by us as witnesses, was the first codicil to [his/her] will and requested us to act as witnesses to it. [He/she] thereupon signed this codicil in our presence, all of us being present at the same time. We now, at [his/her] request, in [his/her] presence, and in the presence of each other, subscribe our names as witnesses, and declare we understand this to be [his/her] will, and that to the best of our knowledge the testator is competent to make a will, and under no constraint or undue influence.

Executed on [date], at [county], [state].

We declare under penalty of perjury that the foregoing is true and correct.

_____   _____
Witness's Signature   Address

_____   _____
Witness's Signature   Address

_____   _____
Witness's Signature   Address

10. Revoking Your Will

Wills can be revoked easily. A will writer who wants to revoke her will or codicil should do so by: 1) writing a new will, expressly stating that she's revoking all previous wills, or 2) destroying the old will (i.e., burn, tear, conceal, deface, obliterate or otherwise destroy it with the intent to revoke it). If you destroy your will, do it before witnesses; otherwise, after you die, it may be difficult to determine what your intent was.

D. FINANCIAL ESTATE PLANNING

Lesbians and gays who own substantial amounts of property can often obtain significant benefits for their surviving beneficiaries—i.e., their lover and other friends or family they want to receive their property—by more extensive estate planning than simply writing a will. If you have little property, planning beyond a will is probably not necessary. Our rough rule of thumb is that anyone owning more than $50,000 in assets can probably benefit from comprehensive estate planning, which means determining and setting up the least expensive and most efficient method(s) of transferring property. Remember—probate can be expensive. The probate fees on a $100,000 estate can be $6,000 or more. These fees are taken out of the deceased's property and obviously reduce the amount finally received by the beneficiaries. If property is transferred by an estate planning device which avoids probate, you can eliminate probate fees.

Here we provide you with a broad overview of the primary financial estate planning methods. If you decide to investigate the subject further, be assured you that estate planning needn't be as forbidding as many "professionals" would have you believe it is. After all, they have a financial interest in making what they do seem as complicated (expensive) as possible. People with moderate estates (roughly, under $600,000) can normally do most of the planning themselves, if they have good information.[10]

1. Estimating the Value of Your Property

Your first step is to estimate the net value of what you own. Create a list of estimated amounts of your assets and debts. This is useful for your planning

---

[10]To repeat it once more, we suggest those interested in extensive estate planning start with Clifford, *Plan Your Estate: Wills, Probate Avoidance, Trusts and Taxes* (Nolo Press).

process, especially to determine if you'll be liable for federal estate taxes, which are assessed for estates worth more than $600,000. Also, it should be a help to your survivors, giving them the identity and location of all your property. Here's an example:

Net Estate of Leslie Grayson

Personal Property	Value	Location or Description
Cash	$500	Safe Deposit Box
Savings accounts	$2,500	Tyson Bank
Checking accounts	$1,500	Tyson Bank
Government bonds	$0	
Listed (private corporation) stocks and bonds	$5,000 $2,000	Matco Corporation Break-Monopoly Company
Unlisted stocks and bonds	$0	
Money owed you including promissory notes and accounts receivable (including mortgages owed you, leases, etc.)	$5,000	Jason Michaels (sold him my car)
Vested interest in profit-sharing plan, pension rights, stock options, etc.	$7,000	Death benefit from Invento Corporation Pension
Automobile and other vehicles (include boats and recreation vehicles; deduct any amounts owed)	$3,000 $7,000	Honda Motorcycle Toyota
Household goods, net total	$10,000	In my house
Art works and jewelry	$1,000	3 lithographs in my bedroom
Miscellaneous	$3,000	Silver set
Real estate (do separately for each piece owned)		
Current market value	$175,000	1807 Saturn Drive Newkirk, Delaware

Mortgages and other liens that you owe on the property	$85,000
Equity (current market value less money owed)	$90,000
Your share of that equity if you have less than sole ownership	$45,000

Business/property interests
(including patents & copyrights)

Name and type of business	Invento Corporation; patenter of small telephone related inventions
Percentage you own	33%
When acquired	1980
Estimate of present (market) value of your interest	$250,000

Life insurance
(for each policy list)

Company and type (or number) of policy		AETCO
Name of insured		Leslie Grayson
Owner of policy		Leslie Grayson
Beneficiary of policy		Robin Anderson
Amount Collectible	$50,000	
Cash surrender value, if any	$1,000	
Total value of assets	**$392,500**	
Debts (not already calculated —i.e., excluding mortgage on real estate)	$3,000	
Taxes (excluding estate taxes)	$12,000	
Total (other) liabilities	$15,000	
Total net worth	**$377,500**	

2. Probate Avoidance

As we discussed in the introduction, probate is a court proceeding where your will[11] is filed, assets gathered, debts and taxes paid, and remaining property distributed to your beneficiaries. Probate is expensive. Lawyers and executors receive fees,[12] often substantial fees, for what's usually routine, albeit tedious, paperwork. Probate also takes considerable time, normally a minimum of several months. By contrast, property transferred outside of probate can usually be received by the beneficiaries within a few days of the deceased's death.

Probate has acquired a rather notorious aura. Most people may not know exactly what it involves, but they sense it's a lawyer's rip-off. There's a lot of truth in that. Probate is largely an institutionalized racket. No European country has the expensive, form-filled probate process America has. Even in England, where our probate system got its start in feudal times, probate was simplified in 1926; now, only if there's an actual conflict do courts and lawyers get involved.

There seems to be little likelihood that our probate system will be reformed soon; it's too lucrative for too many lawyers. The best you can do is keep your own probate costs down by transferring all, or most, of your property outside of probate. Maybe if everyone does that, lawyers (and legislators) will come to realize that probate doesn't have to be as complicated and costly as they've made it.

There are several well-established methods of transferring property that avoid probate. These include:

- revocable living trusts
- informal bank account trusts
- joint tenancy
- life insurance

Each method has advantages and drawbacks, which we briefly discuss below.

---

[11]Or your property transferred under "intestate" proceedings, if you wrote no will or other valid transfer device.

[12]Fees are usually set by state law. Although the computation methods vary from state to state, fees are often based on the size of the estate. Rest assured that they are generous, no matter how calculated. For example, the fees for both attorney and executor in California for a probate estate of $200,000 are roughly $10,300; court filing fees and appraisals can raise the total a good bit. If $100,000 is removed from the probate estate, the total attorney and executor fees are $6,300, so $4,000 or more is saved.

a. Revocable Living Trusts

A revocable living or "inter vivos" (Latin for "among the living") trust is usually the best way for a lesbian or gay person to avoid probate. A revocable living trust is created by establishing a trust document[13] and giving the trust a name (e.g., "The R.P. Payne Trust"). It's revocable because you have the right to revoke or change it at any time before your death. In the trust document, you name yourself as both the settlor (the person setting up the trust) and the initial trustee (the person who manages the trust property). You also name your beneficiary or beneficiaries—that is, the people you want to receive the trust property after you die. Next, you name a successor trustee to manage the trust after you die or become incapacitated. The successor trustee can be a beneficiary. You must sign the trust document and have it notarized. It doesn't have to be witnessed or recorded. Finally, you must transfer all documents of title of trust property into the trust's name. For example, if you place your house in the trust, you must execute and record a deed transferring the house from you to the trust.

When you die, your successor trustee transfers the trust property to your beneficiaries without the necessity of any court proceedings. While you are still alive, the living trust is essentially a paper transaction, with no real world effects. You maintain full control over the property in the trust (e.g., you can spend, sell or give it away) and can end the trust whenever you want. Also, all trust transactions are reported as part of your regular income tax return, and require no extra tax forms. The only downside is that property with a legal document title, such as real estate and securities, must actually be transferred into the trust's name.

Example: Wayne creates a living trust, with his lover Mark as successor trustee. In the trust, Wayne makes several small gifts to friends, and names Mark as the beneficiary of Wayne's principle assets, a house and an apartment house. Wayne then executes and records deeds transferring title to the house and apartment house into the name of the trust. When Wayne dies, Mark, acting as successor trustee, distributes the small gift to Wayne's friends, and executes new deeds transferring the house and apartment house to the beneficiary, i.e., himself.

---

[13]We've put a sample basic living trust form in the Appendix. We urge anyone who wants to prepare a living trust, however, to read the extensive discussion on it in *Plan Your Estate: Wills, Probate Avoidance, Trusts and Taxes* before actually preparing one.

b. Informal Bank Account Trusts

An informal bank trust account, sometimes called a "pay-on-death" account or "Totten trust" is a type of account which avoids probate. You manage the account as you would any other bank or savings and loan account. The only difference is that you name whomever you want—your lover or anyone else—as beneficiary of the account, to receive whatever money is in it, without probate, after you die. During your life, you retain full and exclusive control over the account—you can remove any funds in the account for any reason, make deposits, close the account, etc.

There are no drawbacks to an informal bank account trust. Most banks have standard forms allowing you to create this type of trust—either by opening a new account, or transferring an existing account. And bank account trust fees are normally no higher than the fees for other types of bank accounts.

c. Joint Tenancy

We discussed joint tenancy in Chapter 5 (Real Estate). As we said, joint tenancy is a form of shared property ownership. What sets joint tenancy apart from other forms of joint ownership is what is known as the "right of survivorship." This means that when one joint tenant dies, his or her share in the joint property automatically passes to the surviving joint tenants.[14] Indeed, it's not possible to leave your share of joint tenancy property to someone other than the joint tenant(s) when you die. If you attempt to leave joint tenancy property in a will, the will provision will be ignored.

---

[14]If there's more than one survivor, each acquires an equal share of the deceased tenant's original interest.

Any property can be bought and owned in joint tenancy, although it's most commonly used with real estate. Joint tenancy can be a good probate avoidance device for property you acquire, 50-50, with your lover—assuming that each of you wants his share of the property to pass to the other after death. You can also create joint tenancy ownership in property you own alone by transferring title of the property from yourself to yourself and someone else as joint tenants. (Again, see Chapter 5.) A gift tax may be assessed, however, if you give property worth more than $10,000 to the new joint tenant. Also, there are unfavorable tax consequences if one owner transfers into joint tenancy, property, which has appreciated in value since it was purchased, or is likely to appreciate in value. Usually, a living trust is a better probate avoidance device than a transfer into joint tenancy for solely-owned property.

There can be other significant drawbacks to joint tenancy. Any joint tenant can sell his or her interest in the joint tenancy at any time. This means that the joint tenancy can be destroyed by any joint tenant. If a joint tenant sells (or gives away) his or her share, the new owner and the remaining owner(s) are called "tenants in common." Tenants in common don't have rights of survivorship; if a tenant in common dies, his or her share passes by the will, or by the state's law, if she or he died without a will. Another drawback of joint tenancy is that joint tenants must own equal shares of the property. If you own unequal shares, joint tenancy won't work.

d. Life Insurance

Normally, life insurance proceeds are paid to the policy's beneficiary directly, without going through probate. The proceeds of a life insurance policy are subject to probate, and included in the value of the probate estate, *only* if the proceeds are payable to the "estate," as opposed to a specific beneficiary. Only in the rare case of a large estate with no other assets to pay the death taxes and probate costs is there any reason to name the estate as the beneficiary.

3. Death Taxes

All property owned at the time of death is subject to federal estate (death) taxes. Also, many states impose state death taxes. Death taxes are imposed whether the property is transferred by will (through probate) or by another device (outside of probate). Death taxes are harder to reduce or avoid than are probate fees, but there are some ways to achieve savings.

a. Federal Estate Taxes

Federal estate taxes are assessed against the net worth of the estate (called the "taxable estate") of a person who died. There's an exemption for "moderate" estates. Property worth up to $600,000[15] (net) can be transferred free of federal estate taxes. This means many gays and lesbians don't have to worry about federal taxes being paid from their estate.

Federal law exempts some other items from federal estate taxes, including:[16]

- The expenses of your last illness, burial costs and probate fees and expenses.
- Certain debts, in particular any state death taxes assessed.
- All bequests made to tax-exempt charities.

Keep in mind these rules:

- All property you legally own will be included in your federal taxable estate.
- The worth of a house, or any other property, is your equity in it (we discuss equity in real estate in Chapter 5), not (necessarily) the full market value.
- *All* the value of property held in joint tenancy will be included in your taxable estate, minus the portion the surviving joint tenant can prove he or she contributed. The government presumes that the deceased person contributed 100% of any joint tenancy property, and the survivors contributed nothing. If the survivors can prove they contributed all or some of the money for joint tenancy property, the taxable portion will be reduced accordingly.

Example: Eighteen years ago, Joe and Ben bought a lemon-yellow Jaguar XKE together, and have preserved it in mint condition. It's always been owned in joint tenancy, but the records proving that each person contributed half the purchase price have long since been lost. Joe dies. The government will include the current market value of the entire car in Joe's taxable estate unless Ben can somehow prove that he contributed half the cost.

Example: The same facts, except Ben contributed *all* the money used to buy the car, and kept the records. Joe dies. Even though the car was owned in joint

---

[15]Assuming none of the federal "tax credit" has been previously used for taxable gifts. We discuss how gifts relate to estate taxes in Section 4 below.

[16]There's also a "marital deduction," exempting all property left to a surviving spouse. This is one major reason lesbian and gay couples want to be allowed to marry.

tenancy, *none* of its value is included in his taxable estate because Ben can prove that Joe didn't contribute any of the purchase price.[17]

The mathematics of federal estate taxes work as follows: Determine the net worth of the estate. The first $600,000 is exempt from tax. This exemption works by means of a tax credit. The first $192,800 of tax assessed is forgiven because of the tax credit. $192,800 is the tax due on $600,000. Property over $600,000 is taxed according to the table below:

Example: Willie has a net estate which amounts to $520,000. This is below the taxable amount (to repeat, $600,000), so no federal tax is assessed.

Example: Marty's net estate amounts to $700,000, $100,000 above the exemption limit. Marty needs to look at the following table to figure out the tax:

UNIFIED FEDERAL ESTATE TAX RATE SCHEDULE			
Column A	Column B	Column C	Column D
total net taxable estate over	but not over	tax on amount in Column A	rate of tax on excess over amount in Column A (percent)
$0	$10,000	$0	18
10,000	10,000	1,800	20
20,000	40,000	3,800	22
40,000	60,000	8,200	24
60,000	80,000	13,000	26
80,000	100,000	18,200	28
100,000	150,000	23,800	30
150,000	250,000	38,800	32
250,000	500,000	70,800	34
500,000	750,000	155,800	37
750,000	1,000,000	248,300	39
1,000,000	1,250,000	345,800	41
1,250,000	1,500,000	448,300	43
1,500,000	2,000,000	555,800	45
2,000,000	2,500,000	780,800	49
2,500,000	infinity	1,025,800	50

---

[17]Both of these examples ignore complexities introduced by mutual contributions to upkeep on the car.

Note: An astute reader will notice that the beginning part of the chart doesn't apply. (Estates subject to tax must be over $600,000, and the tenth line begins at $500,000). This top part of the chart is the Federal tax on gifts, which we discuss in Section 4.

HOW TO READ THE CHART

1. Locate the numbers in Column A and Column B between which the anticipated value of your estate falls.

Estate	= $700,000
Column A	= $500,000
Column B	= $750,000

2. Subtract the number in Column A from the number in Column B.

$750,000
- $500,000
$250,000

3. Multiply the difference by the percentage in Column D.

$250,000
x____.37
$92,500

4. Add the product of Step 3 to the tax in Column C.

$92,500
+ $155,800
$248,300

5. Subtract the federal estate tax credit ($192,800) from the total in Step 4. The difference is your federal estate tax liability. The federal estate tax credit is the tax on $600,000, which, as we've discussed, is not taxed.

Estate Tax Liability:
$248,300
- $192,800
$55,500

---

b. State Death Taxes

The states listed below impose no effective death taxes. If you live in one of these states, you don't need to worry about state death taxes:

STATES WITH DEATH TAXES

Alabama	Georgia	Texas
Alaska	Hawaii	Utah
Arizona	Illinois	Vermont
Arkansas	Maine	Virginia
California	Missouri	Washington
Colorado	New Mexico	Wyoming
Florida	North Dakota	

If you live in any other state, your estate will be subject to state death taxes. Worse, many states' death tax rules discriminate against property left to anyone other than legal family. Here's how that works. A number of states laws provide different classes of death tax exemptions. The amount of exemption varies, depending on the legal relationship of the deceased person to the beneficiary. Usually, the largest exemption is for property left to a spouse, the next largest for property left to minor children, then for property given to other blood relatives, and finally to "strangers" (all others, including a lover). A few states, North Carolina, for one, don't provide any exemption at all for property left to "strangers." Finally, some states vary the tax rate itself, depending on whom the property is left to. Generally, the rate is lowest for property left to a spouse, highest for property left to "strangers."

What this means is that if you live in a state with death taxes and want to know their impact on your estate, you'll have to check your state's laws to determine the precise rules. (There's a state-by-state breakdown of death tax rules in *Plan Your Estate: Wills, Probate Avoidance, Trusts and Taxes*). The tax rate will be substantively less than the federal tax rate, but, because "strangers" are taxed the most, the taxes will be much higher on property you leave your lover than would be if you were married—one more inequity resulting from the law's insistence that love and marriage be synonymous.

The state of your "domicile"—where you reside (generally, where your address is) when you die is the state that imposes death taxes. If you own real property (land, real estate) in another state, however, that state will impose its death taxes on the property in that state.

A Word Of Advice: "Domicile" is a legal term of art, which refers to your principal residence, i.e., your home. Usually, this is easy to ascertain from voting records, driver's license and all the other permission slips that you carry about. If you move around a lot, however, you risk having your estate subjected to more than one state death tax. Pick one place and declare that your legal home. If you're very wealthy, get some legal advice on this point.

c. Avoiding or Reducing Federal and State Death Taxes

Estate tax planning is often thought to be a form of lawyer's magic, or chicanery, to escape death taxes. Certainly there's some gimmickry in many schemes of the rich used to escape or reduce death taxes, although not as much as there used to be. The sad truth, however, is that for most folks, death taxes aren't easy to escape, or even reduce. But there are a few ways to reduce death taxes, such as:

- Making gifts
- Establishing trusts—trusts established in wills are usually desirable only for large estates (over $600,000) and are commonly used to save on taxes. Because of the complex nature of trusts, a serious discussion is beyond the scope of this book. But if you have a substantial estate, you may save considerable death taxes by using trusts, particularly if you're in either of the following situations:[18]

Δ where the bulk of your estate will be left to a person who's old or ill and likely to die soon. When that person dies, the property you left him or her will be taxed again. If you set up a trust in your will leaving the old or ill person only the income from the trust, with the principal eventually going to someone else, this "second tax" can be avoided.

Δ If you leave all your property to your children, it'll be taxed when you die and then taxed again when the children die. For years, one of the death tax dodges of the very rich was to leave their wealth in trust for their grandchildren, escaping taxation on the middle generation. Tax law changes curtailed this by introducing a "generation-skipping transfer tax." You can now leave up to $1,000,000 in a trust for your grandchildren and escape estate taxes on the middle generation. Any

---

[18]If so, see a tax accountant.

amount over this $1,000,000 is subject to federal estate taxes in each generation. So if you have children, grandchildren and a hunk of money, consider establishing a generation-skipping trust. If so, you'll need to see a lawyer.

- Transferring ownership of certain property, particularly life insurance, before death

Life insurance proceeds are not included in the federal taxable estate of the person who died if she was not the legal owner of the policy for at least three years before death. By contrast, if the deceased "owned" the policy, the proceeds are included in the taxable estate. The IRS presumes you're trying to avoid taxes if you give the gift within three years of your death, and assesses taxes anyway. The IRS is strict in determining ownership. If the deceased had significant powers over an insurance policy (called, in insurance lingo, "maintaining incidents of ownership") within three years of death, she will be held to be the owner. Significant powers include:

Δ The right to change, or name, the beneficiaries of the policy

Δ The right to borrow against the policy, pledge any cash reserve it has or cash it in

Δ The right to surrender, convert or cancel the policy

Δ The right to select a payment option, e.g., to decide to pay the beneficiary in a lump sum, in installments, etc.

Δ The right to make payments on the policy

There are two basic ways an insurance policy can be owned by someone other than the insured. First, a person having what's called an "insurable interest" can take out, and pay for, a policy on the insured's life. Second, the insured can buy a policy and transfer ownership to another who doesn't have to have an "insurable interest in the insured." For technical (and discriminatory) reasons, some insurance companies don't allow lesbians and gays to have an "insurable interest" in their lovers; they require marriage, or a business (economic) relationship. Anyone, however, has an "insurable interest" in his or her own life. So, you can buy a policy and assign it to anyone else (including your lover)—even if he or she would have no "insurable interest" to start with. Life insurance policies are usually transferred by making a gift to the new owner.[19] It's the new owner who is now responsible for paying the premiums.

Warning: Once you give a gift of a life insurance policy, that's it. Gifts are final. If you break up later, your ex-lover has the right to continue to own the policy. You couldn't compel him to cancel it. Thus, you can retain control over your life insurance policy, or reduce your taxable estate. But you can't do both.

---

[19]We've included a sample transfer form in the Appendix.

4. Gifts and Gift Taxes

At first hearing, the concept of gift taxes may not sound fair. (You mean the feds even tax generosity?) Well, sort of. But think of it this way. If a rich person could "give" away all his property tax-free just before death, there wouldn't be any purpose for death taxes. So Congress has defined the point at which giving gifts becomes a matter for the tax collector. The rule, stated simply, is that *gifts of up to $10,000 per person per year are tax-free*. If Adrian gives $13,000 to Justin, gift taxes are assessed on $3,000; if Adrian gives $10,000 to Justin and $10,000 to Jack, no gift taxes are assessed. Also, if Adrian gives $10,00 to Justin each year for three years, no gift taxes are assessed.

The same tax rates and dollar exemptions apply to gift taxes as apply to estate taxes. (Remember the chart a few pages back?) This means the $600,000 federal exemption can be used for gift taxes as well as estate taxes. For example, if Adrian gives Justin $60,000 in one year, $50,000 is subject to a gift tax. But Adrian can use up $50,000 of his Gift/Estate tax credit and avoid actually paying tax. Indeed, the IRS position is that Adrian must use up this part of his credit to "pay" this tax. When Adrian dies, $50,000 less of his estate will exempt. So, if he'd made no other taxable gifts, he could give $550,000 free of federal estate tax.

The $10,000 annual assessed gift tax exemption can be used to lower the eventual value of one's estate with estate planning.

Example: Sarah and Louise, both in their sixties, want their trusted young friend Marcy to have their co-owned summer house after they both die. The house is worth $200,000. They transfer title to Marcy for a "loan" of $100,000 each, at 10% interest. Payments are $10,000 a year. Marcy signs two promissory notes, secured by two mortgages. Each year, Sarah and Louise each make a "gift" of $10,000 to Marcy by forgiving the loan payment due, and continue to do this until the property is fully owned by Marcy with no tax liability.[20]

Note: Suppose you make an interest-free loan of $50,000 to a close friend. Is there a gift of the interest you didn't charge? Probably. Under a Supreme Court case, you're obligated to charge reasonable interest—or to be taxed as if you did.

If you're wealthy, other options are available that involve gifts. These include "pooled income" funds, transfers to charitable pools, and charitable remainder annuity trusts. These devices aren't available for people with average incomes or estates, and so we don't cover them. Anyone making, or contemplating making, a substantial gift should check it out with a tax attorney or tax accountant.

---

[20]Obviously, this takes a lot of trust. Also, if either Sarah or Louise died, her estate might insist that the remaining loan payments be paid—although the debt could be forgiven in a will.

-10-

Potpourri

In this chapter we discuss three subjects often of concern to lesbian and gay couples—changing your name, immigration and welfare. Each subject merits an entire book; the information presented here is informational and clearly not exhaustive.

A. Changing Your Name to Suit Your Style

When Reverend Jim Dykes and his lover affirmed their commitment, they decided to symbolize that commitment by sharing the same last name. They agreed that hyphenated names were ungainly; Jim chose to take his lover's last name. "We decided I would change my name to Dykes," he told us, "because my lover comes from a wonderful Southern family with a proud and historic name." As Dykes went on to explain, the process of legally changing his name was easy and didn't require hiring a lawyer.

There are a lot of reasons why a gay person might want to change her or his last name, including:

- wanting to assume your lover's last name
- wanting to return to a pre-marital name
- never having liked your last name and wanting one that better fits your identity.

How do you legally change your name? There are two methods. The first is by "usage." The second is by receiving a court order changing your name. There are a few important restrictions. You cannot legally change your name to defraud creditors, for any illegal purpose or if the name you want to adopt invades another person's privacy (e.g., you can't become "Bette Midler" or "Gore Vidal"). Otherwise, you can change your name for any reason and assume any name you wish.

Caveat: Each state has its own law governing the court petition method. While they are all similar, if you're serious about changing your name, and want to use the court procedure, check your state laws, available at any law library. In California, *How To Change Your Name,* by David Loeb & David Brown, will help you do the job quickly and efficiently.

1. Change of Name By Usage

You can change your name simply by using a new one. Last week you were Steve Nurd; this week you decide you're Steve Savage. If you use Savage consistently and insist it's your name, it is. The obvious example of usage name change is marriage. There's no legal proceeding (aside from the marriage itself) when a woman changes her name to her husband's. She simply does it—and it's perfectly legal. Anyone can accomplish a similar name change.

The keys to changing your name by usage are consistency and stubbornness. You must use your new name in all aspects of your life—socially, professionally, on all your identity cards and on all personal documents such as credit cards, driver's license and social security card. Getting these documents changed can be quite a hassle. It's not hard for married women because clerks and bureaucrats are so familiar with the custom that they quite agreeably change the last names on request. Many bureaucracies have a specific form for changing your name on their documents. Even the Passport Office will allow a change of name on a passport if you can establish that you have already changed your name on other documents and present proof that you've used your new name for two years.[1]

---

[1] When you go to the passport office, you'll have to bring two witnesses who can say that they've known you under the new name for two years, and public documents that show you've used the new name for two years. You'll also have to bring any previous passport issued to you within the past eight years. The passport office will issue you a new passport in both names if you've been using the new name from two to five years. If you've been using it more than five years, the passport will contain only your new name.

2. Change of Name By Court Order

The second way to change your name is by court proceeding. The proceeding is usually pretty simple: You file a petition, publish a legal notice of your intention to change your name in a local legal newspaper (which no one reads) and attend a routine court hearing. In many states you're supposed to give a reason for the change. If you're changing your name for a personal reason, such as adopting your lover's name, you need not tell the judge. You can simply state that your new name will make it more convenient for business, etc. The entire procedure is easy enough in most states for you to do the legal work yourself.[2]

Once you obtain the court order changing your name, you must still change your records, identity cards, etc. This will now be quite easy (unlike change of name by usage), however, because you can show the various bureaucrats the judge's order.

B. IMMIGRATION: CAN MY FOREIGN LOVER COME VISIT OR LIVE WITH ME?

Suppose a fantasy comes true: You take a trip abroad and meet a magical, loving person in some distant land. How can you arrange for your dream person to come visit you in America? Further, if you two wish to stay together here—then what? Well, you have problems. That's what. Short-term visits can be impossible if the immigration authorities learn that your visitor is gay or lesbian. And relocating in a new country has almost always been difficult, whether one is gay or straight. These days, when seemingly half the world wants to live in North America, it's quite difficult for any foreigner to move permanently to the United States.

The laws governing immigration to the United States are very complex. In addition, many critical decisions are made by immigration officers—either when granting visas or at the place of entry—so subjective factors can come into play. Anyone with a serious immigration problem should consult a knowledgeable counselor or lawyer for current rulings, practices, and for information on dealing with the whims of local immigration officers. Most attorneys know nothing about immigration, so be sure to ask about their qualifications. In many large cities, especially coastal ones, agencies and groups specialize in helping with

---

[2]To repeat, in California, see *How to Change Your Name* (Nolo Press), by Loeb & Brown.

immigration problems. (We know. One helped us out tremendously in handling immigration problems of some of our clients.)

1. Gaining Entry into the United States

A 1983 gay rights court victory[3] prohibits the Immigration and Naturalization Service (INS) from barring gay visitors to the United States. Carl Hill came from England to cover the San Francisco Gay Freedom Day Parade for a London gay newspaper. He wore a gay pride button at the San Francisco airport and candidly admitted to the immigration officer that he was gay. Hill was arrested, detained, questioned and ordered to undergo a psychiatric examination to determine his eligibility for entry, because immigration laws prohibit foreigners afflicted with a "psychopathic personality, sexual deviation or a mental defect" to be admitted into the U.S, and these laws have been interpreted to include gay people. Hill's attorneys fought his arrest and threatened expulsion. That's when the battle began.

Under the immigration law, the psychiatric test was administered by the Public Health Service (PHS). But as a result of the publicity from Hill's case, the Surgeon General declared homosexuality no longer a "mental disorder," and the PHS doctors would no longer administer the psychiatric test to gay people. The INS therefore had no way of conducting their psychiatric examination of Hill, or other lesbian and gay visitors. But the INS still fought to enforce their discriminatory law on the ground that because Hill self declared that he's gay, no test was necessary.[4] In 1983, a federal appellate court for California (Nevada, Arizona, Idaho, Montana, Washington, Oregon, Alaska and Hawaii, too) ruled that the INS was required to get a medical ruling from the PHS to exclude someone for being gay; an admission by that person wasn't sufficient. But because the PHS refuses to administer the psychiatric tests, the INS regulations, although still on the books, are effectively inoperative in the western states.[5]

---

[3] *Hill v. INS*, 714 F.2d 1470 (9th Cir. 1983).

[4] In fact, two days after Hill was allowed to enter the U.S., the INS detained two Mexicans at the border on suspicion of being gay. There is no way of knowing how many lesbian and gay visitors to the U.S. are stopped by INS officials, choose not to fight, and turn around and go home.

[5] The INS continues to assert that lesbians and gay men are excludable on their own declaration in all other parts of the country. This position was upheld in a Texas case, *Matter of Longstaff*, 716 F.2d 1439 (5th Cir. 1983).

2. Becoming a U.S. Resident or Citizen

Suppose you and your foreign lover decide you want to live together forever? Visitor and student visas are good for only relatively short stays. Moreover, foreigners cannot legally work on visitor or student visas. A foreigner can apply for immigration visas, but the U.S. strictly limits the numbers given. Using this method, it normally takes years (at best) for a person to gain entry into the U.S. and become a citizen. It certainly didn't offer much hope to Jane, who wrote her sister the following letter from Venice, where she'd been traveling:

> *I met a woman near the Bridge of Sighs whose hair smells of apples. She dresses in feathers and taffeta; her eyes are filled with magic and her heart with tenderness. She knows strange songs. I think I'm in love.*

Jane was determined that theirs was one travel romance that wouldn't die after a few letters. Her lover, Sophie, came over on a tourist visa a few weeks after Jane returned. But soon the visa would expire. Then what? If Jane and Sophie could have married, the problem would have been solved. Marriage to a U.S. citizen entitles the foreign spouse to remain in the U.S., obtain a permanent visa and gain priority for citizenship. But, of course, this isn't an alternative for lesbian and gay couples who are denied the right to marry. Even the one case in which a gay couple was actually granted a marriage license came out badly. Once married, the foreign partner applied for immigration as the spouse of an American citizen. The INS refused to recognize the marriage as legitimate for immigration purpose, denied the application and deported the foreigner.

Attempting to bring her lover in by adoption was, Jane learned, equally hopeless. Although a child of an American citizen is given preferential status for immigration, the child must be under 14 and must have lived with the adoptive parent for two years in order to qualify for the preferential status.

When Jane and Sophie talked to us, all we could tell them was that legally, their future together in the U.S. looked bleak. That was the last we saw of them for over a year. When we met again, they were arm-in-arm, and all smiles. Jane told us that they proceeded on a course that would have been illegal for us, as attorneys, to suggest, but which worked. She and Sophie had found a gay American man who wanted to get married to appease his parents. They arranged a marriage, along with a tidy prenuptial agreement keeping all their property separate. Sophie moved some clothing and a toothbrush to her husband's apartment and even lived with him until after the grueling INS post-marriage interview (they try to weed out "fraudulent" marriages) but then moved in with Jane. We mentioned that we knew other couples forced to adopt the same subterfuge, but that we also knew the INS's high priority on discovering these "fraudulent" marriages. Jane responded that they were familiar with the INS practices and in consequence had been scrupulously discreet, telling absolutely no one about the arrangement who didn't need to know. We wished them good luck.

C. WELFARE—WILL LIVING WITH YOUR LOVER MEAN A CUT-OFF?

We've been asked several times whether a welfare recipient will have her or his payments terminated if a lover moves in. The answer is, "Be careful." The rules vary from state to state, but in many places, having a lover move in can cause problems, especially if you're receiving general welfare or Aid to Families with Dependent Children (AFDC). If you're receiving welfare on some other basis (Aid to the Aged, Blind or Disabled), there shouldn't be any problem. These welfare programs usually function like social security—once you qualify, you're pretty much left alone. General welfare and AFDC are different. They are the largest welfare programs, and the most subject to attack politically. As a result, numerous rules, allegedly designed to prevent welfare cheating, can and do cause hardship to welfare recipients.

In the early 1970's, in many states, if an AFDC recipient lived with a sexual partner, the recipient's grant could be terminated, basically for "living in sin." The law has changed and grants can no longer be terminated on moral grounds. But there still may be serious problems. First, an AFDC or general welfare recipient is legally required to tell the Welfare Department of all changes in her circumstances that could affect her grant. This includes the fact that she's living with a lover (in welfare departmentese, an "URAW"—unrelated, adult woman) who may be paying some bills. If the department discovers an unreported lover's presence, the recipient can be penalized, or even have her grant terminated, on ground of "noncooperation" with the Welfare Department. If the recipient reports that she's living with her lover, she'll face other problems.

If the Welfare Department determines that the lover is contributing money or aid to the welfare recipient, her grant will be reduced, normally by the amount contributed. A person is considered to be "contributing" whether they give $20 a month cash, pay $20 of the rent, pay for food or buy the kids $20 worth of clothing. Moreover, some state regulations "presume" that a live-in lover contributes a set amount per month to the recipient's family, whether or not she does. And here's the Catch 22: If the lover moves in with a recipient and doesn't contribute toward rent and utilities (or claims she doesn't), she's committing a federal crime of living off a welfare grant she doesn't qualify for.

So the best advice, as far as the Welfare Department goes, is to treat your lover as a roommate. In the peculiar logic of our social work establishment, a roommate is okay—she's not presumed to contribute anything to a welfare family. For once, the system's blindness and prejudices can work to favor lesbians. Most welfare departments are concerned with nabbing men who move in with female AFDC recipients. If a woman moves in with another woman, caseworkers are willing to accept that she's just a roommate, so the grant shouldn't be affected except to the extent the roommate pay some rent and utilities.

To be safe, keep all finances separate. Avoid letting the recipient have any access or control over any of her lover's money or the welfare department will conclude the lover is "contributing" to the family. Avoid letting the lover have access to the recipient's money or the welfare department will conclude the lover is living off the recipient's grant.

Keep food separate, at least in theory; be able to show the Welfare Department you buy your food separately. Be prepared to prove it's stored separately at home. Certain welfare rights groups suggest keeping cupboards marked with each woman's name in case of a home visit by the social worker. They even suggest, to be safe, that you at least say you eat most meals separately and that each does her own cooking. Also, it's a good idea to establish records, such as a receipt book or ledger, showing that your lover pays her share, and only her share, of household expenses, such as rent and utilities. To determine this share, go to the Welfare Department and pick up the schedule that calculates these shares in detail. Your lover should keep the car registered in her name only, and state that you don't have permission to use it. One welfare rights group suggests that the couple not live together in the recipient's old place because the rent grant would be reduced, but rather move into a new place together (preferably with a small, separate room for the nonrecipient).

Another AFDC concern can be for a woman who has a child by artificial insemination. If you apply for AFDC, and your state doesn't automatically terminate the donor's parental rights and obligations, the welfare department might look for the donor, bring a paternity action to have him declared the father and request that he support the child. Before applying for AFDC, consult a legal aid attorney to best assist you in how not to reveal the donor's identity.

All of this sounds technical, we know. But technical or not, it can be very important. If possible, try to find a sympathetic welfare or eligibility worker to discuss your situation with before you set up housekeeping or apply for benefits. We have found that the welfare department can be dealt a bit easier with a little advance planning.

-11-

Going Separate Ways

A. Introduction

Splitting up with a lover is usually a difficult, emotionally traumatic experience. Obviously, no lawyer can assist someone with the grief, pain, anger and sense of loss that accompany a separation. Arguments over who owns what are rarely the real core of separating, although fights over property can become a way for an ex-couple to take out their frustrations against each other. But once started, property disputes often take on a life of their own and degenerate into bitterness that poisons a relationship for years to come, and prevents the ex-couple from maintaining any friendly relationship. To avoid this sort of warfare, we offer practical advice on the settlement of your economic matters. But first, here are some observations about what's really involved.

A breakup, especially of a couple that's been together for a while, often strikes friends as sad, though it may be quite healthy for the people involved. The very language that's used to describe the end of a relationship often gets in the way of arriving at a positive understanding of what's happening. Breaking up is often described as a "failure" while a relationship that lasts is called "successful." To us, it seems a peculiar notion that the endurance of a relationship determines its worth. In fact, the very idea that "success" and "failure" can be applied to love strikes us as crazy. We subscribe to the views of E.M. Forster when he discussed a man who sees experience in terms of winning, losing and imposing his will on the world:

> *He fails with a completeness which no artist and no lover can experience, because with them the process of creation is itself an achievement, whereas with him the only possible achievement is success.*[1]

Love is complete in itself; it isn't an effort toward some later result. What matters in a breakup isn't "what do I have to show for my one—five—or fifteen years with you?" but rather the preservation of whatever good remains from living and loving together during those years. Even if in retrospect your time together looks bleak and insincere, you can't salvage anything good from it by being mean or nasty during the separation. We know this sounds obvious, and that it's much easier to state it than live it. Still, it's worth remembering and helps put property disputes in perspective.

Sympathetic people, or organizations, can help a separating couple hold onto their humanity and regard for each other. For instance, Jim Dykes, formerly pastor of the San Francisco Metropolitan Community Church, provided a ritual to encourage a couple to reach a measure of peace regarding their separation. First, he met with the couple and asked them to go through the painful but cathartic process of talking about why they got together in the first place and reviewing the positive and creative aspects of their relationship. Next he asked them to discuss why they could no longer live together; finally, he asked that they say what they gained from being together. Dykes stated:

> *If after this discussion the couple still felt they must separate, then the most important goal was to achieve closure of the relationship—an ending so that each understood that it was over. Each could grieve over the passing of an era, and then be open to a new relationship. I hate to see a gay man or lesbian woman bring the ghost of an old relationship to a new one.*

To achieve "closure," Dykes asked the couple to come before the church congregation and perform a "ritual of separation" in which they express their love for each other and announce their "separateness." If they exchanged rings or any other symbols of unity earlier, they give the items back. Dykes reported that the ritual seemed to assist a couple in coming to terms with their emotions and move on without bitterness.

---

[1]E.M. Forster, "What I believe," in *Two Cheers for Democracy.*

B. ANOTHER PLUG FOR A LIVING-TOGETHER CONTRACT

Once more, let us urge those of you who plan to stay together to prepare living-together contracts. If you don't have a contract, and it looks like you're separating, you have two choices:

- You can be reasonable and reach a compromise over property distribution or
- You can engage in all-out, legal warfare.

A full-scale court battle between former lovers over property will be expensive. There can be research, depositions, interrogatories, motions and a trial—and all the while the lawyer's meter runs at $100 to $200 an hour. Also, to make things worse, you're litigating in a relatively new area of the law; no one can predict results with certainty. Some judges will be hostile to the mere existence of lesbian and gay couples; others won't be and will find the legal issues of your case interesting. Whichever, you and your former lover will lose money, time and what remains of your good feelings. Avoid this craziness if at all possible. Of course, there are extreme situations where going to court is necessary. If you're not the recorded owner of valuable property (e.g., you're not named on a deed for a house), but you put up money for it or worked on it, and your former lover refuses to give you *any* interest in the property or settle the dispute, you might have to sue to get your fair share.

As more evidence of the undesirability of lawsuits, here are two examples based on cases in which we were involved:

Example: In the first dispute, an emotionally disturbed former lover (Sonia) sued our client (Virginia), claiming a partnership interest in Virginia's thriving business. In the carefree days of initial romance, Virginia allowed Sonia to meander through the business and use company credit cards and paid Sonia quite well for occasional jobs. When they split, Sonia asked a court to restrain Virginia from continuing her own business until Sonia received her claimed half-interest. The litigation became protracted and nasty. Aside from paying considerable legal fees, Virginia had to stand up to threats of "exposure," "ruining her image" and the like. Finally, after several courtroom defeats, it became apparent to Sonia—and particularly to her lawyer—that no evidence supported the claim of a partnership; the case settled for a minimal amount.

Example: In the second case, our client's lover (Ed) bought a house, putting only his money down and took title in his name alone. Ed and our client, Raymond, lived in the house for years and acted as if both owned the house in some vague undefined way. Raymond contributed to the monthly mortgage payments and did extensive work on the place, spending two weeks of one vacation painting it, etc. When they separated, after nine years of living together in the house, Raymond suddenly realized he had no legal ownership of the property whatsoever. Initially Ed denied that Raymond had contributed anything, and maintained he had no interest in the house.

Surprise! This is a story with a happy ending. After calming down, both men were willing to talk, and Ed soon acknowledged that Raymond had made important contributions. Although the two men couldn't agree how to calculate their respective interests, neither took an intransigent position and they agreed to go to mediation to reach a fair settlement. In the process of compromising, they reconciled. But they also had the good sense to change the recorded ownership of the house to reflect their agreement.

The moral of these two tales is that legal disputes over property division don't have to be expensive and destructive, but that they often are. There's a risk you'll end up in a lawsuit if you don't design a living-together contract. Remember, nobody anticipates being dragged into court until it's too late.

1. Practical Steps Upon Splitting Up

As we discussed in Chapter 4, it's sometimes advisable to maintain separate bank and credit card accounts. But there are occasions to have joint accounts—to pay household bills, to plan vacations together, etc. After you separate, you must untwine your finances as soon as possible. Creditors need to be notified of your "single" status.

First terminate all joint charge accounts. We've heard of horror stories where people were stuck with large bills when their ex-lovers charged a fortune on joint credit card accounts. Notify not only credit card companies, but also any store or business who might extend credit to you jointly—the grocer, the hardware store, the lumberyard, etc. Cancellation of joint credit accounts usually must be in writing; and keep a copy of the letter you send.

A Reminder: You are responsible for your lover's debts only if you co-signed for it, she used a joint credit card or credit was extended in reliance that you'd both be responsible for payment. If you have joint or shared debts (e.g., a refrigerator bill from Sears), the creditor can come to either of you for the whole debt—even if only one of you ends up with the refrigerator. As soon as possible, allocate joint debts between you. You could then ask each creditor to put each debt in the name of persons taking responsibility for the debt. Creditors probably won't do it, however, as good business sense dictates that it's better to have two people responsible for a debt than one. So, realistically, you're probably stuck having to trust your ex-lover to pay her share. If you end up paying the ones she said she'd pay, you can sue her, but that doesn't help much if she's living in the south of France.

2. Separation—Who Owns What?

If you haven't made a living-together agreement, a separation agreement is essential if you've been living together for a long time and have accumulated a lot of property. And even if you have a contract, a separation agreement is useful to pin down details of who gets what, who pays for what, etc. The sooner you make a separation agreement, the less chance there is for misunderstanding. This doesn't mean that "cooling off" time isn't helpful if pain or anger make communication difficult initially. Also, your friends can help you start making a separation agreement. And when feelings are raw, a little generosity and a calm attitude often work wonders. As the Bible says, "A soft answer turneth away wrath."

But however you start, resolve questions of property; don't just hope they'll go away.

Note: That you're separating doesn't mean you can't continue to own property or do business together. If you plan to, however, writing out a new agreement is essential.

Let's assume you're splitting up and we've convinced you and your mate to make a separation agreement. How do you start? Our approach is to list all the property you two own. Identify each item as shared property, your separate property, your (ex) lover's separate property or property whose ownership is disputed. Make a similar list for your debts. Here are worksheets to make the lists, and examples as to how to use them.

PROPERTY DIVISION - WORKSHEET

Separate Property

1. Owned by [your name]:

_____

_____

_____

2. Owned by [your lover's name]:

_____

_____

_____

Separate Debts

1. Owed by [your name]:

_____

_____

_____

2. Owed by [your lover's name]:

_____

_____

_____

Shared Property

Item	Market Value	(Less) Amt Owed	(Equals) Equity[2]

Total
Equity $_____

---

[2]Equity is the market value minus what you owe. Remember to add the percentage of each person's equity if property is owned in unequal shares.

Shared Debts

Amount   Owed to

_____

_____

_____

Total owed: $ _____

Disputed Property

Item   Value   Owed   Equity   Reason disputed

_____

_____

_____

_____

_____

Disputed Debts

Amount Owed   Owed to   Reason Disputed

_____

_____

_____

_____

_____

_____

_____

_____

To best use these worksheets, concentrate on what you agree to, and put off the areas of dispute until later. When you disagree as to who owns or owes something, list it under Disputed Property or Disputed Debts and go on.

EXAMPLE:

Disputed Property

Item	Value	Owed	Equity	Reason disputed
Silverware	$800	-0-	$800	Mike says his mother gave it to him and he should have it all. Al says it was a joint gift so he should get half.
Truck	$1,400	$400	$1,000	Al says he paid the $400 down payment to buy the truck, so he should get it. Mike says he contributed to half the insurance and half of ten payments, so he wants a two-fifths interest.
Garbo, the cat				Mike and Al both love her and want her.

Disputed Debts

Amount Owed	Owed to	Reason Disputed
$1,700	Vacation land	Mike says Al paid the entire vacation as a gift to Mike; Al says they agreed to share it.

If you've been able to put all your property and debts in either one of the separate property/debts entries or the shared property/debts category, you are ready for the distribution. Each person keeps his or her separate property and pays his or her debts. Your shared property and debts are divided 50-50, unless there's unequal ownership of some, or any of them. Obviously, don't chop your oak table in half. By 50-50, we mean each keeps half the value of all the shared property and pays half of the shared debts. Negotiate and compromise. If disputes remain over how to divide joint property or over whether an item of property or a debt is joint or separate, we urge you to resolve them by arbitration or mediation.

3. Drafting Your Separation Agreement

Once you've divided your property, it's time to draft a separation agreement. This is no more than writing out the division you've just reached. Here's a sample form that can be used, or adapted:

SEPARATION AGREEMENT

We, Alice Hobbs and Michele Watson, have agreed to go our separate ways, and to divide our property as specified in this agreement. This is a final division of all our property and can only be changed or amended by both of us, in writing.

Property

We have agreed to divide all of our property as follows:

1. We agree that the following is the separate property of Alice Hobbs and she has the full right to ownership of each item.

    a. Platform bed

    b. Hockney lithograph

    c. Handblown glass collection

    etc.

2. We agreed that the following property is the separate property of Michele Watson and she has the full right to ownership of each item:

    a. Fold out couch

    b. Dresser

    c. Goya print

    etc.

3. We agreed that we will both retain (share) ownership of the following property:

a. 1988 Toyota (we will trade off use until one of us buys it from the other or until we sell it)

etc.

Debts

We have divided our debts so that each person will be solely responsible for the debts listed below under her name. Should the person listed fail to make a payment on a debt, and the other person end up making the payment, that (other) person may sue the person listed as responsible, for all costs and expenses incurred, including the reasonable legal fees necessary to enforce this agreement.

Debts assumed by Alice Hobbs:

Creditor	Amount owed
a. Vacation spot	$1,000
b. Sears	$ 350
etc.	

Debts assumed by Michele Watson:

Creditor	Amount owed
a. Vacation spot	$700
b. Visa	$400
etc.	

Dated: _____   Signature: _____
                                           Alice Hobbs

Dated: _____   Signature: _____
                                           Michele Watson

Note: You can add as many additional clauses to your separation agreement as you need or desire. Our preference is to keep these agreements short and succinct, but at the same time, to cover all financial affairs. If you are going to continue shared ownership in some property, specify the exact terms you've agreed on. If one of you will buy out the other (common in the case of shared real estate), specify all the terms and conditions of the buy-out (see Chapter 5).

4. Support Agreements

It's conceivable, though not likely, that if one member of a separating lesbian or gay couple sued the other for support, claiming that there was agreement for support in the event of separation, a court would award it. If the couple has a written agreement explicitly providing for support, most courts will enforce it. Without an express provision, if one member of the couple was a homemaker—economically dependent, cooking, cleaning, caring for children—and the other member was the sole economic provider, some support for the economically dependent person seems fair. In this situation, the couple can include a support provision in their separation agreement. Here's a sample:

SAMPLE SUPPORT AGREEMENT

Alfred Gwynne and Mark Jones have decided to separate and live apart from this time on. For the past seven years they have lived together; Mark hasn't been employed outside the home during that time and has provided many household services for Alfred.

Alfred and Mark agree that Alfred will pay Mark the sum of $400 a month for one year, commencing December 1, 1990 with the payments to be made on the first of each month; these payments are to help Mark during his transition following the parties' separation, and to assist him while he seeks gainful employment. In exchange, Mark relinquishes all claims he may have against Alfred for money or support for his services to Alfred during the time they lived together.[3]

Dated:_____   Signature: _____
                                          Alfred Gwynne

Dated: _____   Signature: _____
                                          Mark Jones

Note: Support payments for divorced couples are treated like income—they're deductible for the payor and taxable to the recipient. The tax status of support payments for lesbian and gay couples is uncertain. The payments might be treated as a gift and taxed accordingly (if over $10,000 per year) or regarded as

---

[3]The contract is phrased in terms of each person relinquishing all claims not because we're encouraging paranoia about lawsuits but because of the technical rules of contracts. They're not important to get into, but you need to include the language.

compensation for previous work, treated as income and taxed the same way as for married couples.

C. MEDIATION AND ARBITRATION

Disputing separating couples have alternatives to litigation: mediation and arbitration. These methods of resolving disputes are almost invariably preferable to court battles. As we discussed in Chapter 3, mediation involves a neutral third party (or parties) assisting the couple in reaching an agreement. In arbitration, the neutral third party issues a binding decision of the disputes submitted to him. Mediation's strength is that neither person feels "they wuz robbed" because the couple discusses, compromises and reaches the agreement. Arbitration's strength is that it's quick and final, as someone else imposes a decision. In almost all states, if the losing party to arbitration challenges the decision in court, it won't be overturned unless the arbitrator was bribed, clearly biased, etc.

In many ways, mediation and arbitration are similar. Both are speedy, informal and economical. Both provide a forum for you to express your views and anger, and be heard by an independent person. In both, the couple voluntarily chooses to participate. If you refuse, you can't be compelled to participate unless you've previously agreed to arbitration or mediation in a living-together contract. You select the mediator or arbitrator yourselves. The issues resolved are determined by you; the mediator or arbitrator can't consider an issue you haven't asked them to consider.

Mediation and arbitration can range from costly and formal to inexpensive and down-home. Professional mediators and arbitrators are found in all major cities. The American Arbitration Association (AAA) provides trained, professional arbitrators; we recommend against using them, however. They are costly—often hundreds of dollars per day. Moreover, there's no certainty that an AAA arbitrator would be knowledgeable or sympathetic about lesbian and gay issues. It's wiser and cheaper to select mediators or arbitrators who will understand your situation.

With arbitration, it's common for each person to select one arbitrator, and then to have the two arbitrators select a third. Mediation is commonly done with one mediator, but more can be used. We hope someday that mediators and arbitrators will be chosen from panels within the lesbian/gay community. Several gay and lesbian lawyers who've handled property disputes, are working on the creation of a panel in San Francisco. Not all, perhaps not a majority, of the panelists will be lawyers. Psychiatrists, social workers—even just a wise human being or two—will be included.

In addition to selecting the mediator or arbitrator, you decide what issues they are to resolve. You also decide the rules of the proceeding. This is usually done with help from the arbitrator or mediator. Here are a few things to determine:

- When and where is the proceeding to take place?
- If using mediation, will you limit the number of sessions?
- Will you be allowed to submit a written statement?
- Will attorneys or other representatives be allowed, or will each represent himself or herself?
- Is cross-examination allowed?

If it's arbitration, other issues to resolve are:

- Can the arbitrator(s) order you to produce evidence? (Normally they have this power.)
- Must the decision be explained (that is, how and why the arbitrator(s) reached it)?
- Is there a time limit within which the decision must be rendered?

Once you answer these questions, write down your agreement. Here's a sample "Agreement to Arbitrate" that can be used, or adapted:

AGREEMENT TO ARBITRATE

1. This agreement is made on April 21, 1990, between Robert Trion and Martin Auberge, of 1 Paris Way, Macon, Georgia.

2. We have chosen to separate, and in order to resolve certain conflicts between us, submit the following issues to arbitration.

    a) Which party is entitled to remain in the apartment shared by us at 1 Paris Way?

    b) Which party is entitled to ownership of the Ford Mustang automobile we own in joint tenancy, and what's fair compensation for the other party?

    etc.

3. Each of us will select one arbitrator within *15* days of the date of this agreement. The two arbitrators will jointly agree on a third arbitrator within 15 days.[4] Each party will pay the expenses he incurs, and will bear the expenses, if any, of the arbitrators equally. A decision by a majority of the arbitrators will be binding.

4. The arbitrators will determine the time and place of the arbitration hearing, and the procedures to be followed, except that at least three day's notice shall be required if the arbitrators or either party requests to see books, records, etc. (Add any other limitation, procedure, etc. you want.)

Dated: _____   Signature: _____
                                    Robert Trion

Dated: _____   Signature: _____
                                    Martin Auberge

---

[4]If you want to be cautious, you can add, "If the two arbitrators cannot agree within 15 days, the selection will be made by _____" (whomever you choose—a minister, a wise man or woman, a judge, etc.).

LAWYERS AND DOING
YOUR OWN RESEARCH

We hope you never need a lawyer. If you follow our urgings and create your own contracts, durable powers of attorneys and wills, you may escape their clutches. Still, there may come a time when you'll need one, so a few words on the subject seem pertinent.

A. HAVING A LAWYER REVIEW YOUR WORK

For one or more reasons, you may want a lawyer to review the documents you've prepared using this book: you may want to check your state laws, or you may need more complex forms than we've provided, or you may simply want the security you feel a lawyer's review provides. By now, you're aware that we're leery of much of the legal profession. Still, we know there are situations when a lesbian or gay couple needs the advice or service of a lawyer.

Finding a lawyer these days isn't a problem; there's a growing surplus. But finding a good lawyer can be difficult. Make sure any lawyer you hire is aware of the issues you bring to him or her (e.g., don't hire a bankruptcy lawyer to review your buying-a-house contract) and sympathetic to lesbians and gay men. In addition, many lawyers—gay or straight—have as their main goal living well, and you can guess who pays for the Porsches and plumage. So, check fees at the start. Remember, too, that lawyers are to provide a service to you—not intimidate you. Decide what type of attorney you want—female or male, gay, lesbian, or straight—and whether you want to pay the high fees of a prestigious law firm. Don't just set out to hire a "lawyer." Instead, hire one who fits your needs.

A lawyer-client relationship should be one of trust and confidence. You should feel comfortable coming out to your attorney, and in fact, should do so. If your attorney doesn't meet your initial expectations, you can fire him. Tell your lawyer you expect to be told of all developments in your legal affairs and expect to make all major decisions, with his advice. The best way to find an attorney is to ask around and choose someone a friend used and liked. If that doesn't work, call a lesbian and gay legal referral (in many major cities), or consult the list of Lesbian and Gay Legal Resources provided in Section E of this chapter.

For intelligent consumers, consulting with a lawyer doesn't mean hiring one and turning your affairs over to her carte blanche. At a minimum, understand your needs and prepare a rough draft of your own document before going to see a lawyer. Most readers of this book who hire lawyers will probably want their attorneys to do little more than answer specific questions and review the finished product. Be clear with yourself and the lawyer. Don't let any lawyer cast you in the role of a passive "client." If she tries, hire someone else.

B. Fighting in Court

Despite your (and our) intentions, you may find yourself in litigation. If you do, whether it's a lawsuit for breach of a living-together contract, a relative contesting your lover's will or a custody proceeding, you need a lawyer. While the saying "a person who represents himself has a fool for a client" has been perpetuated by self-interested lawyers, in court you're on their turf and you need to hire one so you can play their game.

Judge Learned Hand said it the best: "As a litigant, I should dread a lawsuit beyond almost anything short of sickness and death..." But if you're in court with a lawyer, don't turn your case, or your life, over to her. Learn to do much of the legal work yourself, and insist on understanding all of it. If your lawyer can't explain what's going on, you need another lawyer. It's your life, and you should be the one(s) making the decisions.

A Reminder: Recall what happened to Oscar Wilde in the 1890s, when he sought to use the legal system. Wilde, it seems accurate to say, was "seeing" Lord Alfred Douglas, son of the Marquis of Queensbury. Queensbury heard rumors of the relationship and chose to fight Wilde. (Queensbury was a notorious pugilist, remembered also for the "Queensbury Rules" of boxing.) He left a visiting card at

Wilde's apartment, adding the words "To Oscar Wilde posing as a sodomite." Wilde, naive, bold or mad, sued for libel. The court proceedings lead to Wilde's physical, economic and professional ruin. After the third day of the trial, Queensbury's counsel made it clear that they were going to call witnesses of Wilde's sexual relations with males: Wilde was forced to drop his case. Queensbury, however, was far from finished. His lawyers sent their prospective witnesses' statements to the Director of Public Prosecution. Wilde was arrested and charged, essentially, with being a homosexual. While he was awaiting trial, his creditors took his house and possessions, his publisher refused to publish his works, he was socially disgraced and many friends deserted him. He was tried, found guilty and sentenced to two years of hard labor. He was eventually released and died shortly thereafter. The law of the 1980's isn't as brutal and primitive as the 1890's, but the moral hasn't changed much: Beware of the law.

C. BRINGING POLITICAL CASES

Whenever a lesbian or gay person is involved in a lawsuit because of her or his sexual orientation, there's the possibility of making the suit a political forum for lesbian and gay legal rights. By treating your case as a "gay rights" case and seeking media coverage, you can turn an ordinary lawsuit into a political cause. This strategy can be seductive to you, and even more so to your attorney who can gain a great deal of publicity and notoriety with little at stake but ego. Consider carefully whether making your case a political one is likely to achieve your goals or help other lesbians and gays. If your attorney raises the possibility, ask if he's putting your interest, or his, first.

One example we can offer involves Perry Watkins, a gay man who fought for lesbian and gay rights. After a 17-year career with the army as an open gay man, Watkins was discharged for being gay. He chose to fight the Army through the court system, and although one court ruled in his favor, stating that the Army's policy of discharging gays is unconstitutional, that decision was vacated (i.e., erased) by that same court in order to reconsider its decision, and Watkins' fate is currently unknown.

Some cases are most effectively battled in the press, as well as in court. A good example was Carl Hill's struggle with the United States Immigration and Naturalization Service (INS), that we discussed in Chapter 10. Fortunately, after choosing to fight the INS, Hill found Gay Rights Advocates, a public interest law firm in San Francisco. Hill and his attorney Don Knutson sought to allow Hill to visit San Francisco, and to attack the regulation used to try to prevent his entry into the United States. They sought publicity in the press, and questioned the constitutionality of the law in the courts. Their strategy turned out to be very effective. A federal court allowed Hill to stay for the parade. The publicity drew the attention of the world-wide gay community, and provided impetus toward a change in the regulations.

In other situations, however, publicity and politicizing may be the worst possible strategy. In most child custody cases, a low profile is the best approach. And remember, being a party to a political case isn't the same as being a guest speaker at a sunny, friendly gay rights rally. Political cases are often expensive and always exhausting; you run the risk of injuring your personal interests. We admire people who stand and fight injustice (who doesn't), but we urge you to avoid litigation if possible and, if not possible, to carefully consider before you embark on a political case. But if you do—more power to you!

D. Doing Your Own Research

There's an alternative to hiring a lawyer, especially if you are not involved in contested litigation: learn to do your own legal research. This book gives you a good start toward solving most of your legal problems, but many questions (especially peculiarities of state law) may not be answered. Why not research the subject yourself? It'll take time and diligence, and you may conclude it isn't worth the effort, but because lawyers charge $100 to $200 per hour, why not give it a try. Often the work is really not difficult.

If you decide to do your own research, you need to have a research aid. If you can't hire your own law librarian (they're usually not for hire), the best book explaining how to do legal work is Elias, *Legal Research: How to Find and Understand the Law* (Nolo Press). Other good research sources are publications of the National Gay and Lesbian Task Force (1517 "U" St., N.W., Washington, D.C. 20009) and *Partners, The Newsletter for Gay and Lesbian Couples* (Box 9685, Seattle, Washington 98109).

Next, locate a law library (or a public library with a good law collection). There's usually one in your main county courthouse. These law libraries are supported by tax dollars or fees paid when filing legal papers, and are usually open to the public. The county law librarians are generally helpful and courteous to nonlawyers doing their own legal research. Ask them how to locate your state's statutes (called "codes," "laws" or "statutes," depending on the state). You'll want the "annotated version," which contains the statutes, excerpts from relevant cases and cross references to related articles.

Once you find the statutes, check the index for the subject of your concern. State statutes are usually divided into sections. The major section is the Civil Code, which usually contains laws relating to contracts, living together, divorce, custody, adoption and credit. The Probate Code contains laws relating to wills. There are other codes as well—some states have insurance codes, real property codes and welfare codes. Each code is numbered sequentially, and once you get the code number from the index, it's easy to find the statute you need. If you have trouble, ask the law librarian for help.

Once you look at the statute in the hardcover volume, check the pocket part at the back of the book for any amendments. Then skim the summaries of recent court decisions contained in the "Annotation" section immediately following the statute itself. If the summary looks helpful, you'll want to read the entire case from which the summary was taken.

Judicial cases are printed in books called Reports. In this book, we've included several citations to important legal cases, in the event you want to read the entire text. Interpreting a case citation is easy once you learn the code. For instance, the citation to the "Gay Olympics" case is *San Francisco Arts and Athletics, Inc. v. United States Olympic Committee,* 107 S.Ct. 2971 (1987). What does this mean? The first part is the names of the parties. San Francisco Arts and Athletics is the group sponsoring the gay games. "S.Ct." means the Supreme Court Reports, the Report series publishing the case. The volume in which the case appears is the number before the name of the series; here you want Volume 107. The number after the series name is the page on which the case starts: here it's page 2971. The last number is the year. This may seem a little confusing (it did to us in law school), but any law librarian can quickly explain it to you.

Another important tool is legal encyclopedias that explain the state laws. These are indexed by subject (such as custody, child support, homosexuality, guardianship, etc) and provide a synopsis of your state's law on the subject. Also, ask the law librarian to show you form books. These are collections of sample legal forms lawyers use in dealing with common legal tasks. Finally, ask if your state has any books designed to keep lawyers up to date. Most larger states have these "how-to" books for lawyers. These books are fairly easy to use. (They never teach this practical stuff in law school.)

E. LESBIAN AND GAY LEGAL REFERRALS

American Civil Liberties Union (ACLU)
132 West 43rd Street
New York, NY 10036
212- 944-9800

American Civil Liberties Union (ACLU)
National Gay Rights Project
633 South Shatto Place
Los Angeles, CA 90005

Bay Area Lawyers for Individual Freedom (BALIF)
Legal Referral Panel
P.O. Box 1983
San Francisco, CA 94101
415-431-1444

Custody Action for Lesbian Mothers
P.O. Box 281
Narbeth, PA 19072
215-667-7508

Gay & Lesbian Advocates & Defenders
P.O. Box 218
Boston, MA 02112
617-426-1350

Gay Rights National Lobby
P.O. Box 1892
Washington, DC 20013
202-546-1801

Lambda Legal Defense & Education Fund
666 Broadway
New York, NY 10012
212-995-8585

Lesbian Mothers' National Defense Fund
P.O. Box 21567
Seattle, WA 98111
206-325-2643

Lesbian Rights Project
1370 Mission Street, 4th Floor
San Francisco, CA 94103
415-621-0674

National Gay & Lesbian Task Force
1517 "U" Street NW
Washington, DC 20009
202-332-6483

National Gay Rights Advocates
540 Castro Street
San Francisco, CA 94114
415-863-3224

APPENDIX
TABLE OF CONTENTS

Document

Living Together Agreement—Keeping Things Separate

Living Together Agreement—Sharing Most Property

Certificates

Durable Power of Attorney for Finances

Durable Power of Attorney for Health Care
(Not Valid in California or Rhode Island)

Durable Power of Attorney for Health Care
(California Only)

Conventional Power of Attorney

Revocable Living Trust

Revocation of Living Trust

Joint Tenancy Documents—Personal Property

Joint Tenancy for Real Property—Grant Deed

Assignment of Life Insurance

AIDS Referral List

Living-Together Agreement:
Keeping Things Separate

We, _____ and _____,
agree as follows:

1. This contract sets forth our rights and obligations toward each other, which we intend to abide by in the spirit of joy, cooperation and good faith.

2. We agree that all property owned by either one of us as of the date of this agreement shall remain separate property and cannot be transferred to the other unless done by writing. We have attached a list of our major items of separate property.

3. The income of each person, as well as any accumulations of property from that income, belongs absolutely to the person who earns the money.

4. We shall keep our own bank accounts, credit accounts, etc., and neither is in any responsible for the debts of the other.

5. Living expenses, which include groceries, utilities, rent, day-to-day expenses, shall be equally divided.

6. We may from time to time decide to keep a joint checking or savings account for some specific purpose, or to own some property jointly. Any joint ownership shall be reflected in writing or shall be reflected on the ownership document of the property. If we fail to otherwise provide in writing for the disposition of our jointly owned property should we separate, we agree to divide the jointly held property equally. Such agreements aren't to be interpreted as creating an implication that other property is jointly owned.

7. Should either of us receive real or personal property by gift or inheritance, the property belongs absolutely to the person receiving the gift or inheritance and cannot be transferred to the other except by writing.

8. We agree that neither of us shall have any rights to, or financial interest in, any separate real property of the other, whether obtained before or after the date of this contract, unless that right or interest is in writing.

9. Either one of us may terminate this contract by giving the other a one-week written notice. In the event either of us is seriously considering leaving or ending the relationship, that person shall take at least a three-day vacation from the relationship. We also agree to at least one counseling session if either one of us requests it.

10. In the event that we separate, all jointly owned property shall be divided equally, and neither of us shall have any claim for support or for any other money or property from the other.

11. We agree that any dispute arising out of this contract shall be mediated by a third person mutually acceptable to both of us. The mediator's role shall be to help us arrive at our solution, not to impose one on us. If good faith efforts to arrive at our own solution to all issues in dispute with the help of a mediation prove to be fruitless, either of us may:

(1) initiate arbitration by making a written demand for arbitration, defining the dispute and naming one arbitrator; (2) within five days from receipt of this notice, the other shall name the second arbitrator; (3) the two named arbitrators shall within ten days name a third arbitrator; (4) within seven days an arbitration meeting will be held. Each of us may have counsel if we choose, and may present evidence and witnesses pertinent; (5) the arbitrators shall make their decision within five days after the hearing. Their decision shall be in writing and shall be binding upon us; (6) if the person to whom the demand for arbitration is directed fails to respond within five days, the other must give an additional five days' written notice of his or her intent to proceed. If there's no response, the person initiating the arbitration may proceed with the arbitration before the arbitrator he or she has designated, and his/her award shall have the same force as if it had been settled by all three arbitrators.

12. This agreement represents our complete understanding regarding our living together and replaces any and all prior agreements, written or oral. It can be amended, but only in writing, and must be signed by both of us.

13. We agree that if a court finds any portion of this contract to be illegal or otherwise unenforceable, the remainder of the contract is still in full force and effect.

Signed this _____ day of _____ at _____.

_____   _____
(Signature)   (Signature)

EXHIBIT A:

Separate personal property of _____:

Exhibit A

EXHIBIT B:

Separate personal property of _____:

Exhibit C:

Jointly owned property:

LIVING TOGETHER AGREEMENT: SHARING MOST PROPERTY

We, _____ and _____,
agree as follows:

1. This contract sets forth our rights and obligations toward each other, which we intend to abide by in a spirit of joy, cooperation, and good faith.

2. All property earned or accumulated prior to this date belongs absolutely to the person who earned or accumulated it and cannot be transferred to the other except in writing. Attached is a list of the major items of property we own separately.

3. All income earned by either of us while we are living together and all property accumulated from that income belongs in equal shares to both of us, and should we separate, all accumulated property shall be divided equally.

4. Should either of us receive real or personal property by gift or inheritance, the property belongs absolutely to the person receiving the gift or inheritance and cannot be transferred to the other except by writing.

5. We agree that neither of us has any rights to, or financial interest in, any separate real property of the other, whether obtained before or after the date of this contract, unless that right or interest is in writing.

6. Either one of us may terminate this contract by giving the other a one-week written notice. In the event either of us is seriously considering leaving or ending the relationship, that person shall take at least a three-day vacation from the relationship. We also agree to at least one counseling session if either one of us requests it.

7. In the event we separate, all jointly owned property shall be divided equally, and neither of us shall have any claim for support or for any other money or property from the other.

8. We agree that any dispute arising out of this contract shall be arbitrated under the terms of this clause. If we both choose, we shall first try to resolve the dispute with the help of mutually agreeable mediator(s). Otherwise, either one of us may: (1) initiate arbitration by making a written demand for arbitration, defining the dispute and naming one arbitrator; (2) within five days from receipt of this notice, the other shall name the second arbitrator; (3) the two named arbitrators shall within ten days name a third arbitrator; (4) within seven days an arbitration meeting will be held. Each of us may have counsel if we choose, and

may present evidence and witnesses pertinent; (5) the arbitrators shall make their decision within five days after the hearing. Their decision shall be in writing and shall be binding upon us; (6) if the person to whom the demand for arbitration is directed fails to respond within five days, the other must give an additional five days' written notice of his or her intent to proceed. If there's no response, the person initiating the arbitration may proceed with the arbitration before the arbitrator he or she has designated, and his/her award shall have the same force as if it had been settled by all three arbitrators.

9. This agreement represents our complete understanding regarding our living together and replaces any and all prior agreements, written or oral. It can be amended, but only in writing, and must be signed by both of us.

10. We agree that if the court finds any portion of this contract to be illegal or otherwise unenforceable, that the remainder of the contract is still in full force and effect.

Signed this _____ day of _____ at _____.

_____   _____
(Signature)   (Signature)

EXHIBIT A:

Separate personal property of _____:

Exhibit B:

Separate personal property of _____:

EXHIBIT C:

Jointly owned property:

CERTIFICATE

We _____

hereby commit ourselves to sharing
our lives and love with one another
and joyfully proclaim ourselves a
couple. We will venture forth into
the sunshine and rainstorms, the
lightning and rainbows, in the years
ahead with kindness, commitment,
compassion, and a sense of humor.

AT _____

_____
SIGNATURE

_____
SIGNATURE

_____
DATE

_____
DATE

This is to Certify

That we _____ and _____

do hereby commit ourselves each to the other.

    Intreat me not to leave you
    Or to return from following after you:
    For whither you go, I will go,
    And where you lodge, I will lodge.
    Your people will be my people
    And your life my life:
    Where you die, I will die,
    And there will be buried
    May only death part us.

from Ruth 1: 16

On this day of _____
in the company of _____

    signed _____

_____

DURABLE POWER OF ATTORNEY
FOR FINANCES

Recording requested by and when recorded mail to:

_____

_____

_____

Warning To Person Executing This Document

This is an important legal document. It creates a durable power of attorney. Before executing this document, you should know these facts:

1. This document may provide the person you designate as your attorney in fact with broad powers to dispose, sell, convey and encumber your real and personal property.

2. These powers will exist for an indefinite period of time unless you limit their duration in this document. These powers will continue to exist notwithstanding your subsequent disability or incapacity.

3. You have the right to revoke or terminate this durable power of attorney at any time.

Durable Power of Attorney

1. Creation of Durable Power of Attorney

By signing this document, I, _____,
intend to create a durable power of attorney. This durable power of attorney shall not be affected by my subsequent disability or incapacity, and shall remain effective until my death, or until revoked by me in writing.

2. Effective Date

This durable power of attorney shall become effective only in the event that I become incapacitated or disabled so that I'm not able to handle my own financial affairs and decisions. That determination shall be made in writing by a licensed physician, and the writing shall be attached to this durable power of attorney.

3. Designation of Attorney in Fact

I, _____, hereby appoint

_____ of _____

_____, as my attorney in fact, to act for me
in my name and for my use and benefit. Should

_____ for any reason fail to serve or
cease to serve as my attorney in fact, I appoint _____
of_____
to be my attorney in fact.

4. Authority of Attorney in Fact

I grant my attorney in fact full power and authority over all my property, real
and personal, and authorize _____ to do and perform all and every act
which I as owner of that property could do or perform and I hereby ratify and
confirm all that my attorney in fact shall do or cause to be done under this
durable power of attorney.

[SPECIAL PROVISIONS OR LIMITATIONS. Add to this section any specific
limitation(s), restriction(s), direction(s), etc. you want.]

_____

_____

_____

5. Reliance by Third Parties

The powers conferred on my attorney in fact by this durable power of
attorney may be exercisable by my attorney in fact alone, and my attorney in
fact's signature or act under the authority granted in this durable power of
attorney may be accepted by any third person or organization as fully authorized
by me and with the same force and effect as if I were personally present,
competent and acting on my own behalf.

No person or organization who relies on this durable power of attorney or
any representation my attorney in fact makes regarding [his/her] authority,
including but not limited to:

(i) the fact that this durable power of attorney hasn't been revoked;

(ii) that I, _____, was competent to execute this
power of attorney;

(iii) the authority of my attorney in fact under this durable power of attorney shall incur any liability to me, my estate, heirs, successors or assigns because of such reliance on this durable power of attorney or on any such representation by my attorney in fact.

Executed this _____ day of _____, 19 __, at _____

_____.

_____

Principal

Witnesses

_____ of _____

_____

_____ of _____

_____

Notarization

State of _____

County of _____

   On this _____ day of _____ in the year 19__, before me a Notary Public, State of _____, duly commissioned and sworn, personally appeared_____ , personally known to me (or proved to me on the basis of satisfactory evidence) to be the person whose name is subscribed to in the within instrument, and acknowledged to me that _____ executed the same.

   IN WITNESS WHEREOF, I have hereunto set my hand and affixed my official seal in the _____ County of _____ on the date set forth above in this certificate.

_____

Notary Public

State of_____

My commission expires _____

Durable Power of Attorney
for Health Care

1. Creation of Durable Power of Attorney

To my family, relatives, friends and my physicians, health care providers, community care facilities and any other person who may have an interest or duty in my medical care or treatment: I,_____, being of sound mind, willfully and voluntarily intend to create by this document a durable power of attorney for my health care by appointing the person designated as my attorney in fact to make health care decisions for me in the event I become incapacitated and am unable to make health care decisions for myself. This power of attorney shall not be affected by my subsequent incapacity.

2. Designation of Attorney in Fact

The person designated to be my attorney in fact for health care in the event I become incapacitated is_____ of
_____. If
_____ for any reason shall fail to serve or ceases to serve as my attorney in fact for health care, _____
of _____ shall be my attorney in fact for health care.

3. Effective on Incapacity

This durable power of attorney shall become effective in the event I become incapacitated and am unable to make health care decisions for myself, in which case it shall become effective as of the date of the written statement by a physician, as provided in Paragraph 4.

4. Determination of Incapacity

(a) The determination that I have become incapacitated and am unable to make health care decisions shall be made in writing by a licensed physician. If possible, the determination shall be made by _____,
_____.

(b) In the event that a licensed physician has made a written determination that I have become incapacitated and am not able to make health care decisions for myself, that written statement shall be attached to the original document of this durable power of attorney.

5. Authority of My Attorney in Fact

My attorney in fact shall have all lawful authority permissible to make health care decisions for me, including the authority to consent, or withdraw consent or refuse consent to any care, treatment, service or procedure to maintain, diagnose or treat my physical or mental condition, **EXCEPT**

[add any exceptions here]

_____

_____

_____

6. Inspection and Disclosure of Information Relating to My Physical or Mental Health

Subject to any limitations in this document, my attorney in fact has the power and authority to do all of the following:

(a) Request, review, and receive any information, verbal or written, regarding my physical or mental health, including, but not limited to, medical and hospital records.

(b) Execute on my behalf any releases or other documents that may be required in order to obtain this information.

(c) Consent to, or prohibit, the disclosure of this information.

7. Signing Documents, Waivers and Releases

Where necessary to implement the health care decisions that my attorney in fact is authorized by this document to make, my attorney in fact has the power and authority to execute on my behalf all of the following:

(a) Documents titled or purporting to be a "Refusal to Permit Treatment" and "Leaving Hospital Against Medical Advice."

(b) Any necessary waiver or release from liability required by a hospital or physician.

8. Duration

I authorize this Durable Power of Attorney remain effective until my death, or until revoked by me in writing.

Executed this ___ day of _____, 19__ at_____
_____.

_____
Principal

Witnesses

I declare that the principal is personally known to me, that the principal signed or acknowledged this durable power of attorney in my presence, that the principal appears to be of sound mind and under no duress, fraud or undue influence.

I further declare that I'm not related to the principal by blood, marriage or adoption, and to the best of my knowledge, I'm not entitled to any part of the estate of the principal upon the death of the principal under a Will now existing or by operation of law.

_____ of _____

_____

_____ of _____

_____

Notarization

State of _____

County of _____

On this _____ day of _____ in the year 19__, before me a Notary Public, State of _____, duly commissioned and sworn, personally appeared_____ , personally known to me (or proved to me on the basis of satisfactory evidence) to be the person whose name is subscribed to in the within instrument, and acknowledged to me that _____ executed the same.

IN WITNESS WHEREOF, I have hereunto set my hand and affixed my official seal in the _____ County of _____ on the date set forth above in this certificate.

_____

Notary Public

State of_____

My commission expires _____

STATUTORY FORM DURABLE POWER OF ATTORNEY FOR HEALTH CARE

(California Civil Code Section 2500)

Warning To Person Executing This Document

This is an important legal document which is authorized by the Keene Health Care Agent Act. Before executing this document, you should know these important facts:

This document gives the person you designate as your agent (the attorney in fact) the power to make health care decisions for you. Your agent must act consistently with your desires as stated in this document or otherwise made known.

Except as you otherwise specify in this document, this document gives your agent the power to consent to your doctor not giving treatment or stopping treatment necessary to keep you alive.

Notwithstanding this document, you have the right to make medical and other health care decisions for yourself so long as you can give informed consent with respect to the particular decision. In addition, no treatment may be given to you over your objection at the time, and health care necessary to keep you alive may not be stopped or withheld if you object at the time.

This document gives your agent authority to consent, to refuse to consent, or to withdraw consent to any care, treatment, service, or procedure to maintain, diagnose, or treat a physical or mental condition. This power is subject to any statement of your desires and any limitations that you include in this document. You may state in this document any types of treatment that you don't desire. In addition, a court can take away the power of your agent to make health care decisions for you if your agent (1) authorizes anything that's illegal, (2) acts contrary to your known desires, or (3) where your desires aren't known, does anything that's clearly contrary to your best interests.

Unless you specify a shorter period in this document, this power will exist for seven years from the date you execute this document and, if you're unable to make health care decisions for yourself at the time when this seven-year period ends, the power will continue to exist until the time when you become able to make health care decisions for yourself.

You have the right to revoke the authority of your agent by notifying your agent or your treating doctor, hospital or other health care provider orally or in writing of the revocation.

Your agent has the right to examine your medical records and to consent to their disclosure unless you limit this right in this document.

Unless you otherwise specify in this document, this document gives your agent the power after you die to (1) authorize an autopsy, (2) donate your body or parts thereof for transplant or therapeutic or educational or scientific purposes, and (3) direct the disposition of your remains.

This document revokes any prior durable power of attorney for health care.

You should carefully read and follow the witnessing procedure described at the end of this form. This document won't be valid unless you comply with the witnessing procedure.

If there's anything in this document that you don't understand, you should ask a lawyer to explain it to you.

Your agent may need this document immediately in case of an emergency that requires a decision concerning your health care. Either keep this document where it's immediately available to your agent and alternate agents or give each of them an executed copy of this document. You may also want to give your doctor an executed copy of this document.

Don't use this form if you're a conservatee under the Lanterman-Petris-Short Act and you want to appoint your conservator as your agent. You can do that only if the appointment document includes a certificate of your attorney.

1. Designation of Health Care Agent

I, _____ of _____
_____, do hereby designate and appoint
_____ of _____.
[Insert name, address, and telephone number of one individual only as your agent to make health care decisions for you. None of the following may be designated as your agent: (1) your treating health care provider, (2) a non-relative employee of your treating health care provider, (3) an operator of a community care facility, or (4) a non-relative employer of any operator of a community care facility.] as my attorney in fact (agent) to make health care decisions for me as authorized in this document. For the purposes of this document, "health care decision" means consent, refusal to consent, or withdrawal of consent to any care, treatment, service, or procedure to maintain, diagnose, or treat an individual's physical or mental condition.

2. Creation of Durable Power of Attorney for Health Care

By this document I intend to create a durable power of attorney for health care under Sections 2430 to 2443, inclusive, of the California Civil Code. This power of attorney is authorized by the Keene Health Care Agent Act and shall be construed in accordance with the provisions of Sections 2500 to 2506, inclusive, of

2. Creation of Durable Power of Attorney for Health Care

By this document I intend to create a durable power of attorney for health care under Sections 2430 to 2443, inclusive, of the California Civil Code. This power of attorney is authorized by the Keene Health Care Agent Act and shall be construed in accordance with the provisions of Sections 2500 to 2506, inclusive, of the California Civil Code. This power of attorney shall not be affected by my subsequent incapacity.

3. General Statement of Authority Granted

Subject to any limitation in this document, I hereby grant to my agent full power and authority to make health care decisions for me to the same extent that I could make such decisions for myself if I had the capacity to do so. In exercising this authority, my agent shall make health care decisions that are consistent with my desires as stated in this document or otherwise made known to my agent, including, but not limited to, my desires concerning obtaining or refusing or withdrawing life-prolonging care, treatment, services and procedures.

(If you want to limit the authority of your agent to make health care decisions for you, you can state the limitation in paragraph 4 ("Statement of Desires, Special Provisions, and Limitations") below. You can indicate your desires by including a statement of your desires in the same paragraph.)

4. Statement of Desires, Special Provisions, and Limitations

(Your agent must make health care decisions that are consistent with your known desires. You can, but aren't required to, state your desires in the space provided below. You should consider whether you want to include a statement of your desires concerning life-prolonging care, treatment, services, and procedures. You can also include a statement of your desires concerning other matters relating to your health care. You can also make your desires known to your agent by discussing your desires with your agent or by some other means. If there are any types of treatment that you don't want to be used, you should state them in the space below. If you want to limit in any other way the authority given your agent by this document, you should state the limits in the space below. If you don't state any limits, your agent will have broad powers to make health care decisions for you, except to the extent that there are limits provided by laws.)

In exercising the authority under this durable power of attorney for health care, my agent shall act consistently with my desire as stated below and is subject to the special provisions and limitations stated below:

(a) Statement of desire concerning life-prolonging care, treatment, service, and procedures:

_____

_____

_____

(b) Additional statement of desires, special provisions, and limitations:

_____

_____

_____

(You may attach additional pages if you need more space to complete your statement. If you attach additional pages, you must date and sign each of the additional pages at the same time you date and sign this document).

5. Inspection and Disclosure of Information Relating to My Physical or Mental Health

Subject to any limitation in this document, my agent has the power and authority to do all of the following:

(a) Request, review, and receive any information, verbal or written, regarding my physical or mental health, including, but not limited to, medical and hospital records.

(b) Execute on my behalf any releases or other documents that may be required in order to obtain this information.

(c) Consent to the disclosure of this information. (If you want to limit the authority of your agent to receive and disclose information relating to your health, you must state the limitations in paragraph 4 ("Statement of Desires, Special Provisions, and Limitations") above).

6. Signing Documents, Waivers, and Releases

Where necessary to implement the health care decisions that my agent is authorized by this document to make, my agent has the power and authority to execute on my behalf all of the following:

(a) Documents titled or purporting to be a "Refusal to Permit Treatment" and "Leaving Hospital Against Medical Advice."

(b) Any necessary waiver or release from liability required by a hospital or physician.

7. Autopsy; Anatomical Gifts; Disposition of Remains

Subject to any limitations in this document, my agent has the power and authority to do all of the following:

(a) Authorize an autopsy under Section 7113 of the Health and Safety Code.

(b) Make disposition of a part or parts of my body under the Uniform Anatomical Gift Act (Chapter 3.5 (commencing in Section 7150) of Part 1 of Division 7 of the Health and Safety Code).

(c) Direct the disposition of my remains under Section 7100 of the Health and Safety Code. (If you want to limit the authority of your agent to consent to an autopsy, make an anatomical gift, or direct the disposition of your remains, you must state the limitations in paragraph 4 ("Statement of Desires, Special Provisions, and Limitations") above.)

8. Duration

(Unless you specify a shorter period in the space below, this power of attorney will exist for seven years from the date you execute this document and, if you're unable to make health care decisions for yourself at the time when this seven-year period ends, the power will continue to exist until the time when you become able to make health care decisions for yourself.)

This durable power of attorney for health care expires on

_____

[Fill in this space only if you want the authority of your agent to end earlier than the seven-year period described above.]

9. Designation of Alternate Agents

(You aren't required to designate any alternate agent, but you may do so. Any alternate agent you designate will be able to make the same health care decisions as the agent you designated in paragraph 1, above, in the event that agent is unable or ineligible to act as your agent. If the agent you designate is your spouse, he or she becomes ineligible to act as your agent if your marriage is dissolved.)

If the person designated as my agent in paragraph 1 isn't available or becomes ineligible to act as my agent to make a health care decision for me or loses the mental capacity to make health care decisions for me, or if I revoke that person's appointment or authority to act as my agent to make health care decisions for me, then I designate and appoint the following person to serve as my agent to make health care decisions for me as authorized in this document, such persons to serve in the order listed below:

A. First Alternate Agent _____

_____

[Insert name, address, and telephone number of first alternate agent]

B. Second Alternate Agent _____

_____

[Insert name, address and telephone number of second alternate agent]

10.   Nomination of Conservator of Person

(A conservator of the person may be appointed for you if a court decides that one should be appointed. The conservator is responsible for your physical care, which under some circumstances includes making health care decisions for you. You aren't required to nominate a conservator but you may do so. The court will appoint the person you nominate unless that would be contrary to your best interest. You may, but aren't required to, nominate as your conservator the same person you named in paragraph 1 as your health care agent. You can nominate an individual as your conservator by completing the space below.)

If a conservator of the person is to be appointed for me, I nominate the following individual to serve as conservator of the person

_____

_____.

[Insert name and address of person nominated as conservator of the person]

11. Prior Designations Revoked

I revoke any prior durable power of attorney for health care.

Date and Signature of Principal

(You must date and sign this power of attorney)

I sign my name to this Statutory Form Durable Power of Attorney for Health Care on

_____ at

_____   _____

_____

(This power of attorney won't be valid unless it's signed by two qualified witnesses who are present when you sign or acknowledge your signature if you have attached any additional pages to this form. You must date and sign each of the additional pages at the same time you date and sign this power of attorney.)

Statement of Witnesses

(This document must be witnessed by two qualified adult witnesses. None of the following may be used as a witness: (1) a person you designated as your agent or alternate agent, (2) a health care provider, (3) an employee of a health care provider, (4) the operator of a community care facility, (5) an employee of an operator of a community care facility. At least one of the witnesses must make the additional declaration set out following the place where the witnesses sign.)

[READ CAREFULLY BEFORE SIGNING. You can sign as a witness only if you personally know the principal or the identity of the principal is proved to you by convincing evidence.]

(To have convincing evidence of the identity of the principal, you must be presented with and reasonably rely on any one or more of the following:

(1) An identification card or driver's license issued by the California Department of Motor Vehicles that's current or has been issued within five years.

(2) A passport issued by the Department of State of the United States that's current or has been issued within five years.

(3) Any of the following documents if the document is current or has been issued within five years and contains a photograph and description of the person named on it, is signed by the person, and bears a serial or other identifying number:

(a) A passport issued by a foreign government that has been stamped by the United States Immigration and Naturalization Service.

(b) A drivers' license issued by a state other than California or by a Canadian or Mexican public agency authorized to issues drivers' licenses.

(c) An identification card issued by a state other than California.

(d) An identification card issued by any branch of the armed forces of the United States.

(Other kinds of proof of identity aren't allowed.)

I declare under penalty of perjury under the laws of California that the person who signed or acknowledged this document is personally known to me (or proved to me on the basis of convincing evidence) to be the principal, that the principal signed or acknowledged this durable power of attorney in my presence, that the principal appears to be of sound mind and under no duress, fraud, or undue influence, that I'm not the person appointed as attorney in fact by this document, and that I'm not a health care provider, an employee of a health care provider, the operator of a community care facility, or an employee of an operator of a community care facility.

Signature: _____

Resident Address: _____

_____

Print Name: _____

Date: _____

Signature: _____

Resident Address: _____

_____

Print Name: _____

Date: _____

(At least one of the above witnesses must also sign the following declaration.)

I further declare under penalty of perjury under the laws of California that I'm not related to the principal by blood, marriage, or adoption, and, to the best of my knowledge, I'm not entitled to any part of the estate of the principal upon the death of the principal under a will now existing or by operation of law.

Signature: _____

Signature: _____

Statement Of Patient Advocate Or Ombudsman

(If you're a patient in a skilled nursing facility, one of the witnesses must be a patient advocate or ombudsman. The following statement is required only if you're a patient in a skilled nursing facility—a health care facility that provides the following basic services: skilled nursing care and supportive care to patients whose primary need is for availability of skilled nursing care on an extended basis. The patient advocate or ombudsman must sign both parts of the "Statement of Witnesses" above and must also sign the following statement.)

I further declare under penalty of perjury under the laws of California that I'm a patient advocate or ombudsman as designated by the State Department of Aging and that I'm serving as a witness as required by subdivision (f) of Section 2432 of the Civil Code.

Signature: _____

CONVENTIONAL POWER OF ATTORNEY

Recording requested by and when recorded mail to

_____

_____

_____

Power of Attorney

I, _____, of _____
appoint _____ of _____,
as my attorney in fact to act in my place for the purposes of [specify particular
powers granted]._____

_____

_____

except that [he/she] shall not have the power of [specify powers reserved]. ____

_____

_____

I further grant to my attorney in fact full authority to act in any manner both
proper and necessary to exercise the foregoing powers, including

_____,

and ratify every act that [he/she] may lawfully perform in exercising those
powers.

[Add if power of attorney is extended for limited time:]

This power of attorney is granted for a period of _____ and shall
become effective on _____, 19__ , and shall terminate on _____,
19__.

Executed this ___ day of _____, 19__, at _____.

_____
(your signature)

_____
(print your name)

Notarization

State of _____

County of _____

    On this _____ day of _____ in the year 19__, before me a Notary Public, State of _____, duly commissioned and sworn, personally appeared_____ , personally known to me (or proved to me on the basis of satisfactory evidence) to be the person whose name is subscribed to in the within instrument, and acknowledged to me that _____ executed the same.

    IN WITNESS WHEREOF, I have hereunto set my hand and affixed my official seal in the _____ County of _____ on the date set forth above in this certificate.

_____

Notary Public

State of_____

My commission expires _____

REVOCABLE LIVING TRUST
(PROBATE AVOIDANCE)

The following form may be used, or adapted, for a revocable living trust used for a "probate avoidance" purpose. The goal of the trust is to transfer property outside of probate on the death of the settlor. This is a simple trust form, since there's no need for complex administrative provisions. Living trusts are covered in far more depth in Clifford, *Plan Your Estate* (Nolo Press). If substantial amounts of money are involved, you should have any trust you prepare reviewed by a knowledgeable attorney. The fees for this shouldn't be immense, and it might add to your peace of mind.

Any trust property with a document of title must have title re-registered in the trust's name.

Real Property Reminder: If real estate is transferred into (or from) a revocable living trust, there must be a deed actually transferring the property. The deed must be recorded with the County Recorder's office. A simple quitclaim deed form will suffice.

The "probate avoidance" living trust can be used for several different beneficiaries and/or different forms of property. You can place several different types of property—a house, car and boat—in one trust and one beneficiary, or you could place them in three separate trusts for one beneficiary (making it easier to revoke a trust for any one item), or you could place them in three trusts for three different beneficiaries.

This trust form is for a trust where the settlor names himself as trustee. If you wish to set up a probate-avoidance trust, but you don't want to be your own trustee, use the alternative form in Section 1(a). The trust should be typed on 8 1/2 x 11 typing paper. Do not do a trust in handwriting.

Declaration and Instrument of Trust

I. Trust Name

This trust shall be known as The [your name] Trust.

II. Trust Property

[Your name], called the "settlor," and/or "trustee," as is appropriate in the context, declares that [he/she] has set aside and holds in the [your name] Trust, all [her/his] interest in that property described in the attached schedule.

The trust property shall be used for the benefit of the trust beneficiaries, and shall be administered and distributed by the trustee in accordance with this trust instrument.

(B) Additional or after acquired property may be added to the trust by listing it on the appropriate schedule.

III. Reserved Powers of Settlor

(A) The settlor reserves unto [himself/herself] the power to amend or revoke this trust at any time during [his/her] lifetime, without the necessity of notifying any beneficiary.

(B) Until the death of the settlor, all rights to income, profits, or control of the trust property shall be retained by or distributed to the settlor.

(C) If at any time, as certified in writing by a licensed physician, the settlor has become physically or mentally incapacitated, the successor trustee shall manage this trust, and shall apply for the benefit of the settlor any amount of trust income, or trust principal, necessary in the trustee's discretion for the proper health care, support and maintenance of the settlor, in accordance with (his/her) accustomed manner of living, until the settlor, as certified by a licensed physician, is again able to manage (his/her) own affairs, or until (his/her) death.

Any income in excess or amounts applied for the benefit of the settlor shall be accumulated and added to the trust estate.

(D) After the death of the settlor, this trust becomes irrevocable and may not be altered or amended in any respect unless specifically authorized by this instrument and it may not be terminated except through distributions permitted by this instrument.

IV. Trustees

(A) The trustee of The [your name] Trust shall be [your name]. Upon the death of the trustee, or [his/her] incapacity as certified by a licensed physician, the successor trustee shall be [name], or if [name] cannot serve as successor trustee, the successor trustee shall be [name].

(B) Any trustee shall have the right to appoint, in writing, additional successor trustee(s) to serve in the order nominated if all successor trustees named in paragraph IV(A) cannot serve as trustee.

(C) As used in this instrument, the term "trustee" shall include any successor trustee.

(D) No bond shall be required of any trustee.

V. Beneficiaries

(A) Upon the death of the settlor, the specific beneficiaries of the [your name] trust shall be:

1. [Beneficiary's name] shall be given [property identified] or, if [beneficiary's name] doesn't survive the settlor, that property shall be given to [alternate beneficiary's name].

(repeat as is necessary for all items of property in the trust.)

(B) The residuary beneficiary of the trust shall be [residuary beneficiary's name], who shall be given all trust property not specifically and validly disposed of by Paragraph V(A), or if [residuary beneficiary's name] doesn't survive the settlor, the alternate residuary beneficiary shall be [alternate residuary beneficiary's name].

(C) Upon the death of the settlor, the trustee shall distribute the trust property outright to the beneficiaries named in Paragraph V(A) and V(B), unless a beneficiary is a minor at the time of distribution, and that beneficiary's property shall be retained in trust pursuant to Paragraph VI.

VI. Minor Beneficiaries

All trust property given in Paragraph V to any of the minor beneficiaries listed below in Section A, and who are minors at the settlors' death, shall be retained in trust for each such beneficiary in a separate subtrust of this [your name] trust, pursuant to the following terms, which shall apply to each subtrust:

(A) Subtrust Beneficiaries and Age Limits

Each subtrust shall end when the beneficiary of that subtrust listed below becomes 30, except as otherwise specified in this section:

Trust for	Shall end at age
_____	_____
_____	_____
_____	_____
_____	_____
_____	_____

(B) Subtrust Beneficiary Provisions

1. As long as a beneficiary specified in Paragraph VI(A) is a beneficiary of a subtrust, the trustee may distribute from time to time to or for the benefit of the beneficiary as much, or all, of the net income or principal of the subtrust, or both, as the trustee deems necessary for the beneficiary's health, support, maintenance, and education.

Education includes, but isn't limited to, college, graduate, postgraduate and vocational studies, and reasonably related living expenses.

2. In deciding whether to make a distribution to the beneficiary, the trustee may take into account the beneficiary's other income, resources, and sources of support.

3. Any subtrust income which isn't distributed to a beneficiary by the trustee shall be accumulated and added to the principal of the subtrust administered for that beneficiary.

(C) Termination of Subtrust

A subtrust shall terminate when any of the following events occur:

1. The beneficiary of that subtrust becomes the age specified in Paragraph A of this trust;

2. The beneficiary of that subtrust dies before becoming the age specified in Paragraph A of this trust;

3. The trust is exhausted through distribution allowed under these provisions.

If the trust terminates for reason (1), the remaining principal and accumulated net income of the trust shall pass to the beneficiary of that subtrust. If the trust terminates for reason (2), the remaining principal and accumulated net income of the trust shall pass to the residuary beneficiaries named in this trust, if any, otherwise to that subtrust beneficiary's heirs.

(D) Subtrust Administrative Provisions

1. The interests of subtrust beneficiaries shall not be transferable by voluntary or involuntary assignment or by operation of law and shall be free from the claims of creditors and from attachments, execution, bankruptcy or other legal process to the fullest extent permissible by law.

2. Any trustee serving as trustee of a subtrust created under this Paragraph VI shall be entitled to reasonable compensation out of the trust assets for ordinary and extraordinary services, and for all services in connection with the complete or partial termination of any subtrust.

VII. Trustee's Powers and Duties

(A) In order to carry out the provisions of The [your name] Trust, and any subtrust created pursuant to Paragraph VI, the trustee shall have all authority and powers allowed or conferred on a trustee under [your state] law and subject to the trustee's fiduciary duty to the settlor and/or the beneficiaries.

(B) The settlor's debts and death taxes shall be paid from the following trust property:

_____

_____

_____

or, if this property is insufficient to pay all the settlor's debts and death taxes, the successor trustee shall determine how such debts and death taxes shall be paid.

VIII. General Administrative Provisions

(A) The validity of The [your name] Trust and the construction of its beneficial provisions shall be governed by the laws of [your state].

(B) If any provision of this Declaration of Instrument of Trust is held to be unenforceable, the remaining provisions shall be nevertheless carried into effect.

Executed on [date]

_____

your signature

I certify that I have read the foregoing Declaration of Trust and that it correctly states the terms and conditions under which the trust estate is to be held, managed, and disposed of by the trustee. I approve the Declaration of Trust in all particulars.

Dated: _____

_____
print your name
Settlor and Initial Trustee

Notarization

State of _____

County of _____

On this _____ day of _____ in the year 19__, before me a Notary Public, State of _____, duly commissioned and sworn, personally appeared_____ , personally known to me (or proved to me on the basis of satisfactory evidence) to be the person whose name is subscribed to in the within instrument, and acknowledged to me that _____ executed the same.

IN WITNESS WHEREOF, I have hereunto set my hand and affixed my official seal in the _____ County of _____ on the date set forth above in this certificate.

_____
Notary Public

State of_____

My commission expires _____

SCHEDULE A

PROPERTY TRANSFERRED TO TRUST

[List all property transferred to this specific living trust. List the property with detail, e.g., if real estate is transferred to the trust, identify that real estate as it's identified on the property ownership deed. Be sure to staple this schedule to the trust document. Be sure to clarify exactly what property is in the trust—e.g. if tenant in common property is placed in it, state whether the other tenant's interest is also put in that trust, or whether, as is usual, only your share of the property is transferred. And if there's a formal ownership document for trust property, as for a car, house, stocks, be sure to register the trust as the legal owner of that property on a new ownership document.]

REVOCATION OF LIVING TRUST

Whereas, on [date], I created a written revocable living trust, with [name of beneficiary] as the beneficiary of the trust and [your name] as the trustee; and Whereas, pursuant to Article 3(A) of that trust, I reserved to myself the full power to revoke the trust;

Now therefore, pursuant to Article 3(A) of the trust, and the laws of the State of [your state], I hereby revoke the trust created by me in the document "Declaration and Instrument of Revocable Living Trust," and state that the trust is completely revoked and all property transferred by me to the trust shall be forthwith returned to me and legally owned by me.

Signature: _____   Date: _____

Notarization

State of _____

County of _____

On this _____ day of _____ in the year 19__, before me a Notary Public, State of _____, duly commissioned and sworn, personally appeared_____ , personally known to me (or proved to me on the basis of satisfactory evidence) to be the person whose name is subscribed to in the within instrument, and acknowledged to me that _____ executed the same.

IN WITNESS WHEREOF, I have hereunto set my hand and affixed my official seal in the _____ County of _____ on the date set forth above in this certificate.

_____

Notary Public

State of_____

My commission expires _____

JOINT TENANCY DOCUMENTS—
PERSONAL PROPERTY

The following three forms can be used for placing personal property in joint tenancy. Form 1 is for occasions in which one person gives property to another person, and both become joint tenants. Form 2 is for occasions in which one person sells property to another person, and both become joint tenants. Form 3 is for occasions in which two people buy property together, as joint tenants.

Form 1: Joint Tenancy
Ownership Document

Ownership of the personal property identified below, previously owned by [your name], is hereby transferred to [your name] and [your lover's name] as joint tenants. This joint tenancy property is described as:

[List and clearly identify the property.]

Signature: _____ Date: _____
       [your name]

Signature: _____ Date: _____
       [your lover's name]

Form 2: Joint Tenancy
Ownership Document

Ownership of the personal property identified below, previously owned by [your name], is hereby transferred to [your name] and [your lover's name] as joint tenants, for consideration paid of [purchase price] by [your lover's name] to [your name]. This joint tenancy property is described as:

[List and clearly identify the property.]

Signature: _____ Date: _____
       [your name]

Signature: _____ Date: _____
       [your lover's name]

Form 3: Joint Tenancy
Ownership Document

Ownership of the personal property identified below is held by [your name] and [your lover's name] as joint tenants.

This joint tenancy property is described as:

[List and clearly identify the property.]

This joint tenancy was purchased on _____, 19__ for a purchase price of $ _____, of which [your name] contributed $ _____ and [your lover's name] contributed $ _____. of the purchase price.

Signature: _____ Date: _____
       [your name]

Signature: _____ Date: _____
       [your lover's name]

Joint Tenancy for Real Property— Grant Deed

If you decide to hold title to real property as joint tenants with one or more other persons, the procedures for doing so are simple.

If you buy real estate in the future, you can own it as joint tenants simply by instructing the title company to list you and the other owner(s) as joint tenants on the ownership deed.

If you now own real estate property in sole ownership, you can transfer that ownership into joint tenancy yourself by creating a deed listing the new owners and reciting that they hold title as "joint tenants." (This type of transaction will either be a gift to the new owner(s),[1] or, less likely, a sale of the new owner(s) actually pay you money for the creation of the joint tenancy interest.) The new joint tenancy deed should be recorded as soon as possible with the County Recorder's Office.

Following is a sample grant deed, transferring property formerly owned by a single owner into joint tenancy.

[insert Individual Grant Deed form]

---

[1]No gift taxes will be due on transfer if the new joint tenant doesn't cash in his or her new ownership interest; however, you may want to pay gift taxes on transfer if you expect the property to increase in value.

ASSIGNMENT OF LIFE INSURANCE

The undersigned [original owner] and [new owner] hereby agree that the following insurance policy issued to [original owner] on [his/her] life is assigned to [new owner] as [his/her] sole property that [original owner] releases and waives all rights to or incidents of ownership in the policy, including:

a) the right to change or name beneficiaries under the policy;

b) the right to borrow against the policy, or pledge any cash reserve it has, or cash it in;

c) the right to surrender, convert or cancel the policy;

d) the right to select a payment option.

e) the right to make payments on the policy.

The policy is described as [identify policy by numbers, etc.] [Name or Company].

Dated this _____ day of _____, 19 __.

Dated: _____   Signature:_____
                                      (Original Owner)

Dated: _____   Signature:_____
                                      (New Owner)

AIDS Referral List

AIDS Action Council
729 8th Street, SE, Suite 200
Washington, DC 20003
202-547-3101

AIDS Hotline
80 5th Avenue #1601
New York, NY 10011
800-221-7044

**American Foundation For AIDS
Research**
9601 Wilshire Blvd.
Los Angeles, CA 90210
213-273-5547

or

40 West 57th Street
New York, NY 10019
212-333-3118

**Bay Area Lawyers for Individual
Freedom (BALIF)
AIDS Legal Referral Panel**
1663 Mission Street, #400
San Francisco, CA 94103
415-864-8186

**Gay Rights National Lobby
AIDS Project**
P.O. Box 1892
Washington, DC 20013
202-546-1801

National AIDS Hotline
P.O. Box 1274
New York, NY 10113
800-342-7514

**National Gay Rights Advocates
AIDS Civil Rights Project**
540 Castro Street
San Francisco, CA 94114
415-863-3624

San Francisco AIDS Foundation
333 Valencia Street, 4th Floor
San Francisco, CA 94110
415-864-4376
800-367-2437

INDEX

A

Acknowledgement of parenthood, sample, 7:8
Adjustable rate mortgage (ARM), 5:6-7
Adoption, 7:18-24; of adults, 7:24; age limits, 7:23, 7:24; and birth certificate, 7:24; and citizenship, 10:5-6; and consent of child, 7:24; by co-parent, 7:39; legal aspects, 7:23-24; methods, 7:20-23; of Native American children, 7:24; and residence, 7:23-24; and surname, 7:24
Adults, adoption of, 7:24
Age, legal, to make a will, 9:5
Age, limit to adopt, 7:23, 7:24
Agency adoption, 7:20-21
Aid to Families with Dependent Children (AFDC), 10:6-8
AIDS: and funeral parlors, 8:30; and insurance, 4:23; and power of attorney, 8:3; and social security disability, 4:23; and wills, 9:6
Alimony, 2:7; 6:9-10; and fault, 6:8, 6:9
Alternate beneficiary, in will, 9:16
Alternative Family Services Agency, 7:28
American Arbitration Association, 11:12
Anti-discrimination ordinances, 4:2
Arbitration, 3:24-25; 11:12-14
Artificial insemination, 7:9-16; agreements, 7:14-16; and welfare, 10:8
Assets, estimating, 9:21-23
Attorney certificate and durable power of attorney for health care, 8:23
Attorney in fact, 8:4-5; 8:14; definition, 8:2
Attorneys. *See* Lawyers
Auto insurance, 4:19, 4:22
Automobile. *See* Car

B

Baby M. case, 7:17-18
Bank accounts, 4:15
Biological parents' agreements, 7:6-8
Birth certificate: and adoption, 7:24; and artificial insemination, 7:13-14
"Black market" adoptions, 7:22
Body disposition, after death, 8:27-30
Bond, and executor of will, 9:16-17
Bondsman's fee, 9:16
Burial, 8:27-30
Burial arrangements, in will, 9:17

C

California Directive to Physicians, 8:25-26
California Durable Power of Attorney for Health Care form, 8:14-23
Car insurance, 4:19, 4:22
Car, buying together, 4:18-19
Case workers, and child custody cases, 6:15-16
Catholic Church, and artificial insemination, 7:9-10
Charge accounts, 4:16, 11:4
Child custody, 6:12-24; contested, 6:15-24; definition, 6:13
Child support, 6:26-31; if visitation denied, 6:28-29; modifications, 6:29-31

Child visitation, 6:24-26; definition, 6:13; modifications, 6:29-31
Children, 6:1-31; having, 7:4-18; and wills, 9:14-15
Citizenship, obtaining, 10:5-6
Closing, of real estate transaction, 5:5; costs 5:12
Closure, and relationship, 11:2
Co-parenting arrangements, 7:36-42; agreement, sample, 7:37-38
Codicil, to will, 9:19-20
Cohabitation, 6:10; laws, 2:8
Commission, of real estate agent, 5:4
Common law states, 3:4
Community property states, 3:4
Consent of child, and adoption, 7:24
Conservatorship, 8:4; definition, 8:2
Contract, between teenager and adult caretaker, 7:39-42
Contract, between unmarried persons, need for, 2:1-9
Contract, home ownership, 5:15-34; for equal ownership, 5:16-18; for owners not on
   premises, 5:26-32; for unequal shares, 5:18-25; for unequal shares with labor/materials
   contribution, 5:21-25
Contract, implied, 2:5, 2:6
Contract, living together, 3:1-27; additions, 3:8; binding nature of, 3:2-3; definition, 2:3-4,
   3:2; deletions, 3:8; and estate planning, 9:2; importance of, 2:1-9, 3:1-2, 11:3-4; and law,
   2:4-7; and mediation/arbitration clause, 3:25; models, 3:4-6; modifications, 3:8-9, 3:27;
   notarizing, 3:9; and personal conduct provisions, 3:5; and property, 3:6-8; and sexuality,
   2:5n, 2:7-9; signing, 3:9
Contract, living together, samples, 3:8-23; and "cooling off" clause, 3:26-27; and credit
   purchases, 3:13-14; and educational support, 3:19-20; and household expenses/chores,
   3:22-23; and housework, 3:21-22; and installment purchases, 3:13-14; and joint projects,
   3:14-17; and jointly-acquired items, 3:12-14; short-form, 3:9-11; and "time off," 3:17-19
Contract, moving in together, sample, 4:10
Contract, oral, 2:5, 2:6-7
Contract, renting together, sample, 4:9
Contract, written, 2:5, 2:6, 3:2
Conventional power of attorney, 8:5; definition, 8:2
Convertible adjustable rate mortgage, 5:7
Cooperative separation agreement, sample, 6:11
Court jurisdiction, in child custody disputes, 6:20-22
Court-appointed guardianship, 7:35-36
Credit, 4:16-18, 11:4; and contracts, 3:13-14
Credit agencies, 4:16-18
Credit bureaus, 4:17-18
Credit rating, checking, 4:17-18
Cremation, 8:28, 8:29-30
Custodianship, 8:4; definition, 8:2
Custody, of child. *See* Child custody

D

Death, of mate, 9:3-4
Death taxes, 9:10, 9:27-33
Debts, 4:14; estimating, 9:21-23; and will, 9:16
Deed of trust, definition, 5:10
Directive to Physicians, 8:25-26
Disability insurance, 4:23
Discrimination, 4:2-4; in funeral business, 8:30; in homebuying, 5:3-4, 5:10; in obtaining
   credit, 4:16-17
Disinheritance, 9:7-8, 9:14; clause in will, 9:17
Divorce, 6:1-31; grounds for, 6:4-6; and property, 6:8-9
Domestic partnerships, 4:11-14; laws, 4:13

Domicile, definition, 9:32
Donation, of body organs, 8:28, 8:29
Donation, of body to medical school, 8:28, 8:29
Donor, for artificial insemination, choosing, 7:11-13
Down payment, 5:10; 5:20-21
Durable power of attorney, 8:5; definition, 8:2; for finances, 8:6-8; for medical decisions, 8:9-23; recording, 8:5
Dykes, Jim, 11:2

E

Embalming, 8:28, 8:29
Emotional document, detailing personal conduct, 3:5-6
Equal Credit Opportunity Act, 4:17
Equity, definition, 11:6n
Escrow, 5:12
Estate planning, 8:27, 9:1-34; financial, 9:21-34
Eviction, 4:3-4
Executor, of estate, 9:8, 9:16-17
Expert witnesses, in child custody disputes, 6:22-24
Fair Credit Reporting Act, 4:18

F

Fault: and alimony, 6:8, 6:9; and distribution of marital property, 6:7, 6:9, 6:10
Federal estate taxes, 9:22, 9:28-30, 9:32-33. *See also* Death taxes
Fifteen-year mortgages, 5:7
Fixed-rate mortgage, 5:6-7
Foreign adoptions, 7:22-23
Formal guardianship, 7:35-36
Fornication laws, 2:8
Foster parenting, 7:20, 7:24-30
Funeral arrangements, 8:28-30; in will, 9:17
Funeral society cooperative, 8:28, 8:29

G

Gay kids, in gay foster homes, 7:26-30
Gay Olympics, 1:1-2, 12:5
Gay Rights Advocates, 12:3-4
Generation-skipping transfer tax, 9:32-33
Gentrification, 5:2
Gifts and gift taxes, 3:6n, 9:34; and wills, 9:15-16
Government benefits, and domestic partners, 4:13-14
Graham, Linda, 7:27-28
Group ownership, of home, 5:26-32
Guardian of child, named in will, 9:14
Guardianship, 7:30-36, 8:4; contested, 7:30-31; court appointed, 7:35-36; definition, 8:2; formal, 7:35-36; informal (voluntary), 7:31-35

H

Handwritten wills, 9:9
Health insurance, 4:23; and domestic partners, 4:12
Hemlock Society, 8:24
Hill, Carl, 10:4, 12:3-4

Holographic wills, 9:9
Homebuying, 5:1-38; and closing costs, 5:12; and escrow, 5:12; and financing, 5:5-7, 5:9-12; and home inspections, 5:9; financial benefits, 5:8; finding a home, 5:3-5
Homeowner's personal property, 4:21-22
Homeownership: by group, 5:26-32; and moving in together, 5:32-34; and moving on, 5:35-38; and promissory note for down payment, 5:20-21; and taxes, 5:34
Homophobia, 1:1, 2:1. *See also* Discrimination
Hooker, Evelyn, 6:23
Housing discrimination, 4:2-4

I

Immigration and Naturalization Service (INS), 7:22-23, 10:4-6
Implied contract. *See* Contract, implied
Informal bank account trusts, 9:26
Informal guardianship, 7:31-35; documents, 7:33-35
Inspections, of home, 5:9
Installment purchases, 4:16-18; and contracts, 3:13-14
Insurance, 4:20-23; car, 4:19, 4:22; disability, 4:23; health, 4:12, 4:23; homeowner's personal property, 4:21-22; life, 4:21, 9:27, 9:33; rental, 4:21-22
Insurance, and simultaneous death, 9:17
Inter vivos trust, 9:25

J

Joint bank accounts, 4:15
Joint charge accounts, 4:16, 11:4
Joint credit card accounts, 4:16, 11:4
Joint custody, of child, 6:13
Joint ownership, of car, 4:18-19
Joint tenancy: of car, 4:19; and probate, 9:26-27, 9:28; and simultaneous death, 9:17; and title to home, 5:14
Joint wills, 9:9

K

Kidnapping, 6:21-22
Knutson, Don, 12:3-4

L

Landlord-tenant relationship, 4:6-7
Lawyers, 3:9, 3:17, 7:3-4, 12:1-4; and child custody disputes, 6:18; and guardianship, 7:36; and real estate transactions, 5:5
Leases, 4:2, 4:3, 4:4
Legal home, 9:32
Legal referrals, 12:6
Legal research, 12:4-6
Lesbian Rights Project, 6:15
Life insurance, 4:21; and probate, 9:27, 9:33
Life support systems, 8:24-26
Limited partnerships, 5:31-32
Living trusts, 9:25, 9:27
Living will, 8:24-26
Living-together contract. *See* Contract, living together
Louisiana, and wills, 9:8

M

Marriage, to circumvent INS regulations, 10:5-6
Marvin v. Marvin, 2:4-7
Mediation, 3:24-25, 11:12-13
Medical authorization form (guardianship), 7:35
Medical emergencies, 8:1-30
Meretricious sexual services, definition, 2:5
Minor's trusts, 9:15
Mortgage, 5:6-7; definition, 5:10
Motor vehicle. *See* Car
Moving in together, 4:5-11, 5:32-34; contract, sample, 4:10

N

National Gay and Lesbian Task Force, 6:23, 12:5
Native American children, and adoption, 7:24
No-fault divorce, 6:4-6

O

Olympics, 1:1-2, 12:5
Oral contract. *See* Contract, oral
Oral modifications to written contract, 3:27

P

Palimony, 2:7. *See also Marvin v. Marvin*
Parental Kidnapping Prevention Act, 6:21
Parental rights, 7:2
Parenthood, 7:1-42; statement, 7:8
Partners (newsletter), 12:5
Partnerships, 5:31-32. *See also* Group ownership
Pay-on-death account, 9:26
Permissible authority of attorney in fact statements, 8:14
Personal representative. *See* Executor, of estate
Politicization, 12:3-4; of child custody disputes, 6:20
Power of attorney, 4:15, 8:1-30; definition, 8:2, 8:4-5; for finances, 8:4-8; for medical decisions, 8:9-23
Pretermitted heirs, 9:8
Principal, 8:4-5; definition, 8:2
Private adoptions, 7:21-22
Private organizations, and domestic partners, 4:12
Probate, 9:21; avoidance, 9:24-27; definition, 9:2, 9:24; fees, 9:21, 9:24
Property: and divorce, 6:7, 6:8-10, estimating value of, 9:21-23

R

Real estate agent's commission, 5:4
Realtors, 5:4-5
Rental agreements, 4:3
Rental housing, 4:2-11; and moving in together, 4:5-11; and moving on, 4:7
Rental insurance, 4:21-22
Renting together, 4:5; contract, sample, 4:9

Residence, and adoption, 7:23-24
Residuary beneficiary, in will, 9:16
"Residue," in will, 9:16
Revocable living trusts, 9:25
Right of survivorship, 5:14, 5:15, 9:26, 9:27
Ritual of separation, 11:2
Roommates, legal relationship, 4:8-11
Ryan, Gannon F., 7:9-10

S

Safety deposit box, and will, 9:18
Saperstein, Sue, 7:27, 7:29
Self-deliverance, 8:24
Self-proving affidavits, 9:18
Separation agreement, 11:5-10
Separation, and divorce, 6:5-6
Sex laws, in U.S., 2:7-9
Sexual acts, mentioned in contract, 2:5n, 2:7-9
Signature, to will, 9:18
Simultaneous death, 9:17
Social security disability (SSD), 4:23
Sodomy laws, 2:7-8
"Sound mind" concept, and wills, 9:5-6
Splitting up, 11:1-14; emotional aspects, 11:1-2, financial aspects, 11:3-14
Springing durable power of attorney, 8:5, 8:8, 8:9-23; definition, 8:2
State death taxes, 9:32-33
Stepparent adoptions, 7:23
Successor executor, 9:16
Suicide, 8:24
Support agreements, 11:11-12
Support change agreement, samples, 6:30-31
Support groups, during custody disputes, 6:17-18
Support, of child. *See* Child support
Surname, and adoption, 7:24
Surrogate motherhood, 7:17-18
Survivorship period, in will, 9:15

T

Taxes: and homeownership, 5:34. *See also* specific types of taxes
Temporary guardianship agreement, 7:34
Tenants in common: and probate avoidance, 9:27, and title to home, 5:14-15
Thirty-year mortgages, 5:7
Title: to car, 4:18-19; to home, 5:12-15
Totten trust, 9:26
Truck. *See* Car
Trusts, 9:32-33. *See also* specific types of trusts

U

Uniform Anatomical Gift Act, 8:29
Uniform Child Custody Jurisdiction Act, 6:21-22
Uniform Simultaneous Death Act, 9:17

V

Visas, 10:5
Visitation. *See* Child visitation
Voluntary guardianship, 7:31-35; documents, 7:33-35

W

Watkins, Perry, 12:3
Welfare, 10:6-8
Wills on Wheels, 9:6
Wills, 9:4-21; challenged, 9:6; clauses, 9:10-18; and competency, 9:5-6; complex, 9:10-11; contested, 9:17; copies, 9:10, 9:18; handwritten, 9:9; holographic, 9:9; joint, 9:9; in Louisiana, 9:8; modifications to, 9:10, 9:19-20; and moving, 9:9; revocation of, 9:14, 9:21; storing, 9:18; technical requirements, 9:8-9
Witnesses, expert, in child custody disputes, 6:22-24
Witnesses, to will, 9:8-9, 9:18, 9:19
Written contract. *See* Contract, written

Z

Zoning ordinances, and unrelated people living together, 5:3-4

SOFTWARE

willmaker
Nolo Press/Legisoft
Recent statistics say chances are better than 2 to 1 that you haven't written a will, even though you know you should. WillMaker makes the job easy, leading you step by step in a fill-in-the-blank format. Once you've gone through the program, you print out the will and sign it in front of witnesses. Because writing a will is only one step in the estate planning process, WillMaker comes with a 200-page manual providing an overview of probate avoidance and tax planning techniques.
National 3rd Ed.

Apple, IBM, Macintosh	$50.05
Commodore	$39.95

california incorporator
Attorney Mancuso and Legisoft, Inc.
About half of the small California corporations formed today are done without the services of a lawyer. This easy-to-use software program lets you do the paperwork with minimum effort. Just answer the questions on the screen, and California Incorporator will print out the 35-40 pages of documents you need to make your California corporation legal.

California Edition (IBM)	$129.00

for the record
By attorney Warner & Pladsen. A book/software package that helps to keep track of personal and financial records; create documents to give to family members in case of emergency; leave an accurate record for heirs, and allows easy access to all important records with the ability to print out any section
National Edition

Macintosh	$49.95

ESTATE PLANNING & PROBATE

nolo's simple will book & nolo's simple willbook with tape
Attorney Denis Clifford
We feel it's important to remind people that if they don't make arrangements before they die, the state will give their property to certain close family members. If there are nieces, nephews, godchildren, friends or stepchildren you want to leave something to, you need a will. If you want a particular person to receive a particular object ,you should have a will. It's easy to write a legally valid will using this book, and once you've done it yourself you'll know how to update it whenever necessary.

National 1st Ed.	$14.95
wi/30-min audio cassette	$19.95

plan your estate: wills, probate avoidance, trusts & taxes
Attorney Denis Clifford
A will is only one part of an estate plan. The first concern is avoiding probate so that your heirs won't receive a greatly diminished inheritance years later. This book shows you how to create a "living trust" and gives you the information you need to make sure whatever you have saved goes to your heirs, not to lawyers and the government.

California 6th Ed.	$15.95

the power of attorney book
Attorney Denis Clifford
The Power of Attorney Book concerns something you've heard about but probably would rather ignore: Who will take care of your affairs, make your financial and medical decisions, if you can't? With this book you can appoint someone you trust to carry out your wishes.

National 2ndEd.	$17.95

how to probate an estate
Julia Nissley
When a close relative dies, amidst the grieving there are financial and legal details to be dealt with. The natural response is to rely on an attorney, but that response can be costly. With How to Probate an Estate, you can have the satisfaction of doing the work yourself and saving those fees.

California 3rd Ed.	$24.95

the california non-profit corporation handbook
Attorney Anthony Mancuso
Used by arts groups, educators, social service agencies, medical programs, environmentalists and many others, this book explains all the legal formalities involved in forming and operating a non-profit corporation. Included are all the forms for the Articles, Bylaws and Minutes you will need. Also included are complete instructions for obtaining federal 501(c)(3) exemptions and benefits. The tax information in this section applies wherever your corporation is formed.
California 4th Ed. $24.95

how to form your own corporation
Attorney Anthony Mancuso
More and more business people are incorporating to qualify for tax benefits, limited liability status, the benefit of employee status and the financial flexibility. These books contain the forms, instructions and tax information you need to incorporate a small business.
California 7th Ed. $29.95
Texas 4th Ed. $24.95
New York 2nd. Ed. $24.95
Florida 1st Ed. $19.95

1988 calcorp update package
Attorney Anthony Mancuso
This update package contains all the forms and instructions you need to modify your corporation's Articles of Incorporation so you can take advantage of new California laws. $25.00

the california professional corporation handbook
Attorney Anthony Mancuso
Health care professionals, marriage, family and child counsellors, lawyers, accountants and members of certain other professions must fulfill special requirements when forming a corporation in California. This edition contains up-to-date tax information plus all the forms and instructions necessary to form a California professional corporation. An appendix explains the special rules that apply to each profession.
California 3rd Ed. $29.95

marketing without advertising
Michael Phillips & Salli Rasberry
There are good ideas on every page. You'll find here the nitty gritty steps you need to–and can–take to generate sales for your business, no matter what business it is.— Milton Moskowitz, syndicated columnist and author of The 100 Best Companies to Work For in America
Every small business person knows that the best marketing plan encourages customer loyalty and personal recommendation. Phillips and Rasberry outline practical steps for building and expanding a small business without spending a lot of money.
National 1st Ed. $14.00

the partnership book
Attorneys Clifford & Warner
Lots of people dream of going into business with a friend. The best way to keep that dream from turning into a nightmare is to have a solid partnership agreement. This book shows how to write an agreement that covers evaluation of partner assets, disputes, buy-outs and the death of a partner.
National 3rd Ed. $18.95

nolo's small business start-up
Mike McKeever
…outlines the kinds of credit available, describing the requirements and pros and cons of each source, and finally shows how to prepare cashflow forecasts, capital spending plans, and other vital ideas. An attractive guide for would-be entrepreneurs.—ALA Booklist
Should you start a business? Should you raise money to expand your already running business? If the answers are yes, this book will show you how to write an effective business plan and loan package.
National 3rd Ed. $17.95

the independent paralegal's handbook: how to provide legal services without going to jail
Attorney Ralph Warner
Warner's practical guide highlights the historical background of self-help law, and then gives a great deal of nuts-and-bolts advice on establishing and maintaining a paralegal office …Highly recommended…—Library Journal
A large percentage of routine legal work in this country is performed by typists, secretaries, researchers and various other law office helpers generally labeled paralegals. For those who would like to take these services out of the law office and offer them at a reasonable fee in an independent business, attorney Ralph Warner provides both legal and business guidelines.
National 1st Ed. $12.95

getting started as an independent paralegal (two audio tapes)
Attorney Ralph Warner
This set of tapes, approximately three hours in all, is a carefully edited version of Nolo Press founder Ralph Warner's Saturday Morning Law School class. It is designed for people who wish to go into business helping consumers prepare their own paperwork in uncontested actions such as bankruptcy, divorce, small business incorporations, landlord-tenant actions, probate, etc. Also covered are how to set up, run, and market your business, as well as a detailed discussion of Unauthorized Practice of Law. The tapes are designed to be used in conjunction with The Independent Paralegal's Handbook.
National 1st Ed. $24.95

collect your court judgment

Scott, Elias & Goldoftas

After you win a judgment in small claims, municipal or superior court, you still have to collect your money. Here are step-by-step instructions on hwo to collect your judgment from the debtor's bank accounts, wages, business receipts, real estate or other assets.

California 1st Ed. $24.95

chapter 13: the federal plan to repay your debts

Attorney Janice Kosel

For those who want to repay their debts and think they can, but are hounded by creditors, Chapter 13 may be the answer. Under the protection of the court you may work out a personal budget and take up to three years to repay a percentage of your debt and have the rest wiped clean.

National 3rd Ed. $17.95

make your own contract

Attorney Stephen Elias

If you've ever sold a car, lent money to a relative or friend, or put money down on a prospective purchase, you should have used a contract. Perhaps everything went without a hitch. If it didn't, though, you probably experienced a lot of grief and frustration.

Here are clearly written legal form contracts to: buy and sell property, borrow and lend money, store and lend personal property, make deposits on goods for later purchase, release others from personal liability, or pay a contractor to do home repairs.

National 1st Ed. $12.95

social security, medicare & pensions: a sourcebook for older americans

Attorney Joseph L. Matthews & Dorothy Matthews Berman

Social security, medicare and medicaid programs follow a host of complicated rules. Those over 55, or those caring for someone over 55, will find this comprehensive guidebook invaluable for understanding and utilizing their rightful benefits. A special chapter deals with age discrimination in employment and what to do about it.

National 4th Ed. $15.95

everybody's guide to small claims court

Attorney Ralph Warner

So, the dry cleaner ruined your good flannel suit. Your roof leaks every time it rains, and the contractor who supposedly fixed it won't call you back. The bicycle shop hasn't paid for the tire pumps you sold it six months ago. This book will help you decide if you have a case, show you how to file and serve papers, tell you what to bring to court, and how to collect a judgment.

California 7th Ed. $14.95
National 3rd Ed. $14.95

billpayers' rights

Attorneys Warner & Elias

Lots of people find themselves overwhelmed by debt. The law, however, offers a number of legal protections for consumers and Billpayers' Rights shows people how to use them.

Areas covered include: how to handle bill collectors, deal with student loans, check your credit rating and decide if you should file for bankruptcy.

California 8th Ed. $14.95

29 reasons not to go to law school

Ralph Warner & Toni Ihara

Lawyers, law students, their spouses and consorts will love this little book with its zingy comments and Thurber-esque cartoons, humorously zapping the life of the law.—Peninsula Times Tribune

Filled with humor and piercing observations, this book can save you three years, $70,000 and your sanity.

3rd Ed. $9.95

murder on the air

Ralph Warner & Toni Ihara

Here is a sure winner for any friend who's spent more than a week in the city of Berkeley…a catchy little mystery situated in the environs and the cultural mores of the People's Republic.—The Bay Guardian

Flat out fun...—San Francisco Chronicle $5.95

poetic justice

Ed. by Jonathan & Andrew Roth

A unique compilation of humorous quotes about lawyers and the legal system, from Socrates to Woody Allen.

$8.95

dog law

Attorney Mary Randolph

There are 50 million dogs in the United States—and, it seems, at least that many rules and regulations for their owners to abide by. *Dog Law* covers topics that everyone who owns a dog, or lives near one, needs to know about dispute about a dog injury or nuisance.

National 1st Ed. $12.95

the criminal records book

Attorney Warren Siegel

We've all done something illegal. If you were one of those who got caught, your juvenile or criminal court record can complicate your life years later. The good news is that in many cases your record can either be completely expunged or lessened in severity.

The Criminal Records Book takes you step by step through the procedures to: seal criminal records, dismiss convictions, destroy marijuana records, reduce felony convictions.

California 2nd Ed. $14.95

draft, registration and the law

Attorney R. Charles Johnson

This clearly written guidebook explains the present draft law and how registration (required of all male citizens within thirty days of their eighteenth birthday) works. Every available option is presented along with a description of how a draft would work if there were a call tomorrow.

National 2nd Ed. $9.95

fight your ticket

Attorney David Brown

At a trade show in San Francisco recently, a traffic court judge (who must remain nameless) told our associate publisher that he keeps this book by his bench for easy reference.

If you think that ticket was unfair, here's the book showing you what to do to fight it.

California 3rd Ed. $16.95

how to become a united states citizen

Sally A. Abel

This bilingual (English/Spanish) book presents the forms, applications and instructions for naturalization. This step-by-step guide will provide information and answers for legally admitted aliens who wish to become citizens.

National 3rd Ed. $12.95

how to change your name

Attorneys Loeb & Brown

Wish that you had gone back to your maiden name after the divorce? Tired of spelling over the phone V-e-n-k-a-t-a-r-a-m-a-n S-u-b-r-a-m-a-n-i-a-m?

This book explains how to change your name legally and provides all the necessary court forms with detailed instructions on how to fill them out.

California 4th Ed. $14.95

legal research: how to find and understand the law

Attorney Stephen Elias

Legal Research could also be called Volume-Two-for-all-Nolo-Press-Self-Help-Law-Books. A valuable tool for paralegals, law students and legal secretaries, this book provides access to legal information. Using this book, the legal self-helper can find and research a case, read statutes, and make Freedom of Information Act requests.

National 2nd Ed. $14.95

family law dictionary

Attorneys Leonard and Elias

Written in plain English (as opposed to legalese), the Family Law Dictionary has been compiled to help the lay person doing research in the area of family law (i.e., marriage, divorce, adoption, etc.). Using cross referencs and examples as well as definitions, this book is unique as a reference tool.

National 1st Edition $13.95

intellectual property law dictionary

Attorney Stephen Elias

This book uses simple language free of legal jargon to define and explain the intricacies of items associated with trade secrets, copyrights, trademarks and unfair competition, patents and patent procedures, and contracts and warranties.—IEEE Spectrum

If you're dealing with any multi-media product, a new business product or trade secret, you need this book.

National 1st Ed. $17.95

the people's law review:
an access catalog to law without lawyers

Edited by Attorney Ralph Warner

Articles, interviews and a resource list introduce the entire range of do-it-yourself law from estate planning to tenants' rights. The People's Law Review also provides a wealth of background information on the history of law, some considerations on its future, and alternative ways of solving legal problems.

National 1st Ed. $8.95

how to do your own divorce

Attorney Charles E. Sherman
This is the book that launched Nolo Press and advanced the self-help law movement. During the past 17 years, over 400,000 copies have been sold, saving consumers at least $50 million in legal fees (assuming 100,000 have each saved $500—certainly a conservative estimate).

California 14th Ed.	$14.95
Texas 2nd Ed.	$12.95

(Texas Ed. by Sherman & Simons)

california marriage & divorce law

Attorneys Warner, Ihara & Elias
Most people marry only with the idea they are in love—that's not enough. This book should be a text in every California high school and college.—Phyllis Eliasberg, Consumer Reporter, CBS News
For a generation, this practical handbook has been the best resource for the Californian who wants to understand marriage and divorce laws. Even if you hire a lawyer to help you with a divorce, it's essential that you learn your basic legal rights and responsibilities.
California 9th Ed. $15.95

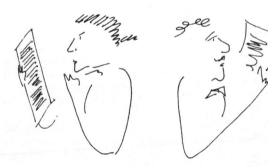

practical divorce solutions

Attorney Charles Ed Sherman
Written by the author of *How to Do Your Own Divorce* (with over 500,000 copies in print), this book provides a valuable guide both to the emotional process involved in divorce as well as the legal and financial decisions that have to be made.
Getting the "legal divorce," says Sherman, is "a ceremony you have to go through." The real divorce involves the many emotional and practical aspects of your life that are inevitably altered. To ensure the best possible outcome you must educate yourself. The worst thing you can do, he counsels, is to run directly to a lawyer and get involved in an uncontrolled battle.
California 1st Ed. $12.95

how to adopt your stepchild in california

Frank Zagone & Mary Randolph
For many families that include stepchildren, adoption is a satisfying way to guarantee the family a solid legal footing.This book provides sample forms and complete step-by-step instructions for completing a simple uncontested adoption by a stepparent.
California 3rd Ed. $19.95

how to modify and collect child support in california

Attorneys Matthews, Siegel & Willis
California has established landmark new standards in setting and collecting child support. Payments must now be based on both objective need standards and the parents' combined income.
Using this book, custodial parents can determine if they are entitled to higher child support payments and can implement the procedures to obtain that support.
California 2nd Ed. $17.95

a legal guide for lesbian and gay couples

Attorneys Curry & Clifford
The edge of the law… will be much less fearful for those who have this book. Full of clear language and concern for realistic legal expectations, this guide well serves and supports the spirit of the law.—Los Angeles Times
In addition to its clear presentation of "living together" contracts, A Legal Guide contains crucial information on the special problems facing lesbians and gay men with children, civil rights legislation, and medical/legal issues.
National 4th Ed. $17.95

the living together kit

Attorneys Ihara & Warner
Few unmarried couples understand the laws that may affect them. Here are useful tips on living together agreements, paternity agreements, estate planning, and buying real estate.
National 5th Ed. $17.95

your family records

Carol Pladsen & Attorney Denis Clifford
…a cleverly designed and convenient workbook that provides a repository for legal, financial and tax data as well as family history. —Los Angeles Times
Most American families keep terrible records. Typically, the checkbook is on a shelf in the kitchen, insurance policies are nowhere to be found, and jewelry and cash are hidden in a coffee can in the garage. Your Family Records is a sensible, straightforward guide that will help you organize your records before you face a crisis.
National 2nd Ed. $14.95

for sale by owner
George Devine
In 1986 about 600,000 homes were sold in California at a median price of $130,000. Most sellers worked with a broker and paid the 6% commission. For the median home that meant $7,800. Obviously, that's money that could be saved if you sell your own house. This book provides the background information and legal technicalities you will need to do the job yourself and with confidence.
California 1st Ed. $24.95

homestead your house
Attorneys Warner, Sherman & Ihara
Under California homestead laws, up to $60,000 of the equity in your home may be safe from creditors. But to get the maximum legal protection you should file a Declaration of Homestead before a judgment lien is recorded against you. This book includes complete instructions and tear-out forms.
California 6th Ed. $8.95

the landlord's law book:
vol. 1, rights & responsibilities
Attorneys Brown & Warner
Every landlord should know the basics of landlord-tenant law. Everything from the amount you can charge for a security deposit to terminating a tenancy, to your legal responsibility for the illegal acts of your manager is closely regulated by the law. In short, the era when a landlord could substitute common sense for a detailed knowledge of the law is gone forever. This volume covers: deposits, leases and rental agreements, inspections (tenants' privacy rights), habitability (rent withholding), ending a tenancy, liability, and rent control.
California 2nd Ed. $24.95

the landlord's law book: vol. 2, evictions
Attorney David Brown
Even the most scrupulous landlord may sometimes need to evict a tenant. In the past it has been necessary to hire a lawyer and pay a high fee. Using this book you can handle most evictions yourself safely and economically.
California 1st Ed. $24.95

tenants' rights
Attorneys Moskowitz & Warner
Your "security building" doesn't have a working lock on the front door. Is your landlord liable? How can you get him to fix it? Under what circumstances can you withhold rent? When is an apartment not "habitable?" This book explains the best way to handle your relationship with your landlord and your legal rights when you find yourself in disagreement.
California 9th Ed. $14.95

the deeds book:
how to transfer title to california real estate
Attorney Mary Randolph
If you own real estate, you'll almost surely need to sign a new deed at one time or another. The Deeds Book shows you how to choose the right kind of deed, how to complete the tear-out forms, and how to record them in the county recorder's public records. It also alerts you to real property disclosure requirements and California community property rules, as well as tax and estate planning aspects of your transfer.
California 1st Ed. $15.95

how to copyright software
Attorney M.J. Salone
Copyrighting is the best protection for any software. This book explains how to get a copyright and what a copyright can protect.
National 2nd Ed. $24.95

the inventor's notebook
Fred Grissom & Attorney David Pressman
The best protection for your patent is adequate records. The Inventor's Notebook provides forms, instructions, references to relevant areas of patent law, a bibliography of legal and non-legal aids, and more. It helps you document the activities that are normally part of successful independent inventing.
National 1st Ed. $19.95

legal care for your software
Attorneys Daniel Remer & Stephen Elias
If you write programs you intend to sell, or work for a software house that pays you for programming, you should buy this book. If you are a freelance programmer doing software development, you should buy this book.— Interface
This step-by-step guide for computer software writers covers copyright laws, trade secret protection, contracts, license agreements, trademarks, patents and more.
National 3rd Ed. $29.95

patent it yourself
Attorney David Pressman
You've invented something, or you're working on it, or you're planning to start...Patent It Yourself offers help in evaluating patentability, marketability and the protective documentation you should have. If you file your own patent application using this book, you can save from $1500 to $3500.
National 2nd Ed. $29.95

SELF-HELP LAW BOOKS & SOFTWARE

ORDER FORM

Quantity	Title	Unit Price	Total

Prices subject to change

Subtotal _____

Tax (CA only): San Mateo, San Diego, LA, & Bart Counties 6 1/2%
Santa Clara & Alameda 7%
All others 6%

Tax _____

Postage & Handling

No. of Books	Charge
1	$2.50
2-3	$3.50
4-5	$4.00

Over 5 add 6% of total before tax

Postage & Handling _____

Total _____

Please allow 1-2 weeks for delivery.
Delivery is by UPS; no P.O. boxes, please.

Name_____

Address _____

_____

☐ VISA   ☐ Mastercard

_____ Exp._____

Signature _____

Phone (   )_____

ORDERS: Credit card information or a check may be sent to:

Nolo Press
950 Parker St.
Berkeley CA 94710

Use your credit card and our **800 lines** for faster service:

ORDERS ONLY
(M-F 9-5 Pacific Time)**:**

US:	**1-800-992-6656**
Outside (415) area **CA:**	**1-800-445-6656**
Inside (415) area **CA:**	**(415) 549-1976**

For general information call: **(415) 549-1976**

☐ Please send me a catalogue

H A L T

A law reform organization worthy of your support

HALT (Help Abolish Legal Tyranny)—An Organization of Americans for Legal Reform —is a nonprofit public interest group whose activities are primarily funded by its 200,000 individual members. Like Nolo Press, HALT advocates a number of changes in the legal system to make it possible for the average American to reasonably and affordably manage his or her legal life. To name but a few of their admirable activities, HALT lobbies to increase disciplinary sanctions against dishonest and incompetent lawyers, reduce probate fees and simplify procedures, increase the role of non-lawyer (independent paralegal) legal service providers, and expand small claims court. To keep its members abreast of major legal reform developments, HALT also publishes a quarterly magazine, holds law reform conferences, and publishes excellent position papers on legal reform issues.

Nolo Press supports HALT and its members and urges all interested citizens to join for a $15 annual membership fee. For more information write to:

H A L T

1319 F Street, NW
Suite 300
Washington, D.C. 20004
(202)347-9600

One Year Free!

Nolo Press wants you to have top quality and up-to-date legal information. The **Nolo News**, our "Access to Law" quarterly newspaper, contains an update section which will keep you abreast of any changes in the law relevant to **A Legal Guide for Lesbian and Gay Couples**. You'll find interesting articles on a number of legal topics, book reviews and our ever-popular lawyer joke column.

Send in the registration card below and receive FREE a one-year subscription to the **Nolo News** (normally $9.00).

Your subscription will begin with the first quarterly issue published after we receive your card.

NOLO PRESS
A Legal Guide for Lesbian and Gay Couples Registration Card

We would like to hear from you. Please let us know if the book met your needs. Fill out and return this card for a FREE one-year subscription to the *Nolo News*. In addition, we'll notify you when we publish a new edition of **A Legal Guide for Lesbian and Gay Couples.** (This offer is good in the U.S.only)

Name _____

Address_____

City _____ State _____ Zip_____

Your occupation_____

Briefly, for what purpose did you use this book?

_____

_____

_____

Did you find the information in the book helpful?

 (extremely helpful) 1   2   3   4   5 (not at all)

Where did you hear about the book?

Have you used other Nolo books?____Yes, ____No

Where did you buy the book?_____

Suggestions for improvement:_____

_____

_____

_____

_____

_____

_____

_____

_____

_____

_____

_____

_____

▲

[Nolo books are]..."written in plain language, free of legal mumbo jumbo, and spiced with witty personal observations."

—ASSOCIATED PRESS

▲

"Well-produced and slickly written, the [Nolo] books are designed to take the mystery out of seemingly involved procedures, carefully avoiding legalese and leading the reader step-by-step through such everyday legal problems as filling out forms, making up contracts, and even how to behave in court."

—SAN FRANCISCO EXAMINER

▲

"...Nolo publications...guide people simply through the how, when, where and why of law."

—WASHINGTON POST

▲

"Increasingly, people who are not lawyers are performing tasks usually regarded as legal work... And consumers, using books like Nolo's, do routine legal work themselves."

—NEW YORK TIMES

▲

"...All of [Nolo's] books are easy-to-understand, are updated regularly, provide pull-out forms...and are often quite moving in their sense of compassion for the struggles of the lay reader."

—SAN FRANCISCO CHRONICLE

Affix
25¢
Stamp

NOLO PRESS
950 Parker St.
Berkeley, CA 94710

One Year Free!

Nolo Press wants you to have top quality and up-to-date legal information. The ***Nolo News***, our "Access to Law" quarterly newspaper, contains an update section which will keep you abreast of any changes in the law relevant to **A Legal Guide for Lesbian and Gay Couples**. You'll find interesting articles on a number of legal topics, book reviews and our ever-popular lawyer joke column.

Send in the registration card below and receive FREE a one-year subscription to the ***Nolo News*** (normally $9.00).

Your subscription will begin with the first quarterly issue published after we receive your card.

NOLO PRESS
A Legal Guide for Lesbian and Gay Couples Registration Card

We would like to hear from you. Please let us know if the book met your needs. Fill out and return this card for a FREE one-year subscription to the *Nolo News*. In addition, we'll notify you when we publish a new edition of **A Legal Guide for Lesbian and Gay Couples.** (This offer is good in the U.S.only)

Name _____   Suggestions for improvement: _____

Address_____   _____

City _____ State _____ Zip_____   _____

Your occupation_____   _____

Briefly, for what purpose did you use this book?   _____

_____   _____

_____   _____

_____   _____

Did you find the information in the book helpful?   _____

(extremely helpful) 1 2 3 4 5 (not at all)   _____

Where did you hear about the book?   _____

Have you used other Nolo books?____Yes, ____No   _____

Where did you buy the book?_____

▲

[Nolo books are]...“written in plain language, free of legal mumbo jumbo, and spiced with witty personal observations.”

—ASSOCIATED PRESS

▲

“Well-produced and slickly written, the [Nolo] books are designed to take the mystery out of seemingly involved procedures, carefully avoiding legalese and leading the reader step-by-step through such everyday legal problems as filling out forms, making up contracts, and even how to behave in court.”

—SAN FRANCISCO EXAMINER

▲

“...Nolo publications...guide people simply through the how, when, where and why of law.“

—WASHINGTON POST

▲

“Increasingly, people who are not lawyers are performing tasks usually regarded as legal work... And consumers, using books like Nolo's, do routine legal work themselves.”

—NEW YORK TIMES

▲

“...All of [Nolo's] books are easy-to-understand, are updated regularly, provide pull-out forms...and are often quite moving in their sense of compassion for the struggles of the lay reader.”

—SAN FRANCISCO CHRONICLE

- -

Affix
25¢
Stamp

NOLO PRESS
950 Parker St.
Berkeley, CA 94710